Ancient Greek

CULTURAL HISTORY OF LITERATURE

Andrew J. Webber, *The European Avant-Garde*
Tim Whitmarsh, *Ancient Greek Literature*

Ancient Greek Literature

TIM WHITMARSH

polity

First published in 2004 by Polity Press

Polity Press
65 Bridge Street
Cambridge CB2 1UR, UK

Polity Press
350 Main Street
Malden, MA 02148, USA

A catalogue record for this book is available from the British Library.

Library of Congress Cataloging-in-Publication Data
Whitmarsh, Tim.
   Ancient Greek literature / Tim Whitmarsh.
      p. cm. – (Cultural history of literature series)
   Includes bibliographical references (p.) and index.
   ISBN 0-7456-2791-9 (alk. paper) –
   ISBN 0-7456-2792-7 (pbk. : alk. paper)
      1. Greek literature–History and criticism.
   2. Greece–Civilization–To 146 B.C.   I. Title.   II. Series.
   PA3052.W48 2004
   880.9′001–dc22
                                          2003020332

Typeset in 10.5 on 12pt Sabon
by Graphicraft Limited, Hong Kong
Printed and bound in Great Britain by TJ International, Padstow, Cornwall

For further information on Polity, visit our website: www.polity.co.uk

Contents

Preface

Greek literature *matters*. Still.

This book is designed to show two things. Firstly, that Greek literature was already debating issues that are central to the way we understand the world today; that gender, culture, sexuality, class, democracy and (not least) literature raised profound questions for the ancients, too. My second point is related: that many analogous debates in the modern world are still engaging with the ideas and analytical categories of the Greeks. Not always consciously, to be sure; but the debates are all the more sophisticated and penetrating when they understand both the richness and depth of the legacy of the past, and also its profound (and often disturbing) 'otherness'.

The material within the book is organized in a way that readers of conventional literary histories may find unfamiliar.[1] It is not a chronological survey, although there are chapters that focus primarily upon historical periods. It does not divide its material by genre, although (again) there are chapters that are dominated by particular literary forms. Nor does it aim at anything like total coverage of the hundreds of authors who survive from antiquity, although of course the canonical figures are all treated. My strategy instead has been to pursue the central issues and themes that cluster around literary texts. The book has three sections: *Concepts*, which deals with the intellectual problems (for the Greeks, but also for us) that cluster around the concept of Greek literature; *Contexts*, which discusses the institutional frameworks within which Greek texts were produced and experienced; and *Conflicts*, which treats the central cultural-historical themes of the texts, principally cultural identity, gender, sexuality and class.

The central argument of the book is that 'Greek literature' is not a simple, self-evident category; rather, its contents, values and social role shift over time and across cultures. Hence the importance placed here on the 'contexts' of literary production. Each of the chapters in this section deals with a culturally central institution in which a particular, ideologically driven vision of 'the literary' is created and disseminated. My final chapters in this section discuss how the idea of literature emerges through a set of cultural institutions, including historical records, libraries and collective memories, that I call (together) 'the archive': it is the archive that, I argue in conclusion, creates and embeds the sense (which we still partially share today) of Greek literature as a particularly coherent and privileged (aesthetically and culturally) body of texts.

This book also has a rather less elevated, but no less important aim. For those who are unfamiliar with it, the corpus of Greek literary texts is a wonderful collection: by turns witty, poignant, coruscating, inspirational. If any readers are provoked to read further, then over half of the job will have been done. Almost all the texts cited here are available in translation. For Homer's *Iliad* and *Odyssey*, the favourite for many readers is Richmond Lattimore's version (Chicago, 1951–65); also recommended are the complete Greek tragedies, edited by Lattimore and David Grene (4 volumes, Chicago, 1953–9). The wide-ranging and authoritative *World's Classics* series (Oxford University Press) is particularly recommended for other texts; where these are unavailable, the *Loeb Classical Library* series (Harvard University Press) – with facing Greek text and literal translation – is a safe fall-back. All translations in *this* book, however, are mine.

A word about my notes, which are almost always entirely bibliographical; that is, they serve to point the reader towards further discussions of the ideas in the main text. I have cited only works in English, and have focused primarily upon recent works, and upon readily available and accessible books rather than specialist articles. Normally, one would expect to use notes to acknowledge debts, but for a book with this scope that would prove unwieldy and impractical. But I do happily acknowledge, here, that my debts are many; and particularly that friends, colleagues, teachers and students in Exeter, Cambridge and beyond have contributed immeasurably to this project. Particular thanks indeed to Paul Cartledge, Tim Duff, Simon Goldhill, Jon Hesk, Richard Hunter, David Konstan, Rebecca Langlands, Miriam Leonard, Lynette Mitchell, Helen Morales and John Wilkins for incalculable help with part or all of the manuscript, and to Julie Lewis for ideas and amazing support. I am also very grateful to the two anonymous referees for giving such exquisite attention to the manuscript.

This book is for Sol, the son.

Part I
Concepts

1

Greek Literature and Cultural History

What is Literature?

It is difficult to imagine a world without literature; but that is, in a sense, what we have to do. The concept of 'literature' is relatively recent, with its roots primarily in the late eighteenth century: like 'culture' and 'taste', it marks divisions between the habits of elite and masses (and, perhaps more urgently, between the traditional elite and the emerging bourgeoisie, rich from the profits of the industrial revolution), between male and female, between European and non-European.[1] 'Literature' is a political concept. Viewed in this light, a 'cultural history of ancient Greek literature' carries with it real risks: not just the intellectual risk of anachronism (a charge that could be levelled in varying degrees at all historical projects), but more urgently the 'imperialist' risk of treating our own categories of analysis (with all their flaws) as universal. Does the concept of 'literature' have any useful purchase on ancient culture? Are we condemned to misread ancient texts if we view them as 'literature', according to our own conceptions?

The English word 'literature' is, in fact, ancient in origin: it derives from the Latin *litteratura*, first found in the works of the rhetorical theorist Quintilian, where it refers to the process of education through reading undergone by the trainee orator.[2] But there are great differences between *litteratura* and literature. Firstly, *litteratura* serves, in Quintilian's view, a functional role. In the modern world, literature is thought of as entertainment or edification; Quintilian's *litteratura*, on the other hand, primarily serves the career development of the young orator. Reading the classics is, for him, a form of moral and practical training.

Secondly, Quintilian's trainee orator reads *litteratura* not to enhance, please or inform the private individual, but to speak to the community. Though the exclusively oral culture of the earliest period of Greek society gradually receded, and written texts (papyrus 'books', but also inscriptions on stone) assumed a steadily more central role in Greek society (particularly from the fifth century BCE onwards),[3] that society remained fundamentally committed to the notion of oral expression in public space.[4] Even when books were read, they may well have been read in public. It is no longer thought that all ancients read aloud as a matter of course,[5] but comparative evidence from even recent societies suggests that, in situations where literacy is limited, books may be read aloud to groups.[6] In cases like these, the written text is mediated through oral expression. There certainly were solitary readers in the ancient world, but we need to remain alert to the full range of possibilities for reading practice.

Texts in Societies

In the modern West, the reading of literature is a sophisticated pastime undertaken by the cultivated in evenings, on weekends, on holiday; in bed, on the sofa, on trains or in a deck-chair. In the rigorous economy of bourgeois capitalism, literature is irrevocably consigned to the world of *leisure*, which is to say *not-work*. Leisure practice is the central marker of personal politics in the twenty-first century: you are not just what you eat, but also what you drink, exercise yourself on, watch, inhale, snort, dance with, go to bed with and – most of all – read. Which is to say, reading 'literature' in the modern West is an act of cultural self-positioning, a calculating use of leisure time defined against the practice of more vulgar activities.

The ancient world, on the other hand, came slowly and imperfectly to the concept of 'leisure'. There were no weekends; there was only hunger, weariness and the failure of light to mark the end of the day. Song, dance and recitation were not squeezed into the marginal spaces of 'time off'; they were fully integrated into the functional rhythms of the *polis* or city-state. In all periods of ancient Greece, citizen populaces gathered on festival days to experience performances patronized and funded by the state itself, or by rich individuals within it. Book-reading, when it became a regular activity (precision is impossible, but let us say the fourth century BCE) certainly carried with it a strong element of elitist separation from the community; by the Roman imperial period, elite Greeks certainly liked to be seen with books.

But in general (there are of course exceptions) Greek culture in antiquity was a uniformly public-orientated world; even book-reading was an activity (largely) to be shared with others, in the warm glow of daylight.

Ancient texts were rarely composed for private reflection: they were worldly, not 'aesthetic'. Engagement, not contemplation, was their mode of operation. Of course, again, there were exceptions. Philosophers, in particular, were (then as now) stereotypically conceived of as other-worldly. The comic poet Aristophanes, in the fifth century BCE, portrayed the philosopher Socrates as suspended in a basket, communing with the ether (in his comedy *The Clouds*); the philosopher and orator Dio Chrysostom (first century CE) predicts mass astonishment at his solitary wandering and introversion (*Oration* 80.1). But the point is that this is eccentric behaviour, whether calculated by philosophers themselves (to mark their exceptional status) or stigmatized and mocked by the community, or both. Like all stereotypes, these are normative: these instances construct and legitimize a view of human activity (including intellectual creativity) as fundamentally socialized, by marking and mocking deviances from expectations. A human, wrote one famous ancient thinker, is a political animal, an animal of the *polis* (Aristotle, *Politics* 1253a). This assumption was, and remained, current for the entire duration of what we call ancient Greece.

The modern concept of 'literature', and the institutional apparatus it supports, impose crude limitations upon our understanding of ancient Greek poetry and prose. The issue, let me be clear, is not simply semantic. I am happy, for want of a better term, to use the term 'literature' in what follows (given, of course, the caveats above). The central point, rather, is that we should question all our modern ideas about what makes for 'literature' when we approach the ancient world. The excitement of reading these works composed two millennia ago certainly derives in part from the thrill of recognition, the perception that issues aired so long ago still retain their force and urgency; but also from the arresting shock of confronting a culture founded on wholly unfamiliar ideas.

Literature and Cultural History

I have begun by querying the idea of 'literature'. It is no less crucial to be clear about 'cultural history'. Since the 1980s there has been a proliferation of works in this genre, focusing on a huge range of topics and societies. The reasons for this cultural-historical turn are many and complex, and it is by no means clear that every practitioner espouses the same agenda.[7] I shall confine myself to drawing out four primary characteristics that I see as being centrally relevant to this project.

Firstly, cultural history focuses upon the role of texts and other media not simply as 'reflections' of history, but as active participants in the struggle to define and popularize certain perceptions of the current state of that society; upon, that is to say, the role of *representation* in the dissemination of ideas. 'Reality' is to be understood not as a concrete, static 'structure' that lies behind representation in literature and other media, but as a collection of ways of perceiving the world. Texts, then, are not second-order 'evidence' for society; they are primary building-blocks of that society, as it is experienced and understood by its members.

Secondly, and consequently, texts have a profound material value and ideological significance within societies. The romantic view of literature as springing unmediated from the author's inspired soul ('literature is written by geniuses', wrote E. M. Forster, in an ironical moment[8]) is particularly unhelpful, because it focuses upon the origins (i.e. the thought processes that led the author to write what he or she did), not their *effects* within society. In the words of the French critic Roland Barthes, we need to make the shift from work (the product of the author) to text (the challenge to readers).[9] 'Works' derive their significance from the great minds that produced them; 'texts', on the other hand, *matter* – that is, they have a material presence – in the societies that receive them.

Thirdly, the cultural meaning of a text is not single and self-evident. Whether we are thinking of the performance of a play or a poem, or the circulation, sale and reading of books, or of any other form of literary production, the text exists to provoke, to be debated over. As the late Don Fowler once wrote, 'our primal scene should be not the solitary figure in the dark of the cinema but the group of friends arguing afterwards in the pub'.[10] This does not mean, as is sometimes claimed, that individual texts have a potentially infinite range of meanings. Clearly, some texts have provocation built into their design more than others: we might contrast a playfully open-ended drinking poem (see chapter 4), for example, with a defence speech in a law court (chapter 6) which aims to shut down debate once and for all. But even a 'closed' form like forensic oratory will employ tendentiousness, presupposition and silence, and here we need to locate the weak spots that the prosecution (in this example) might be expected to exploit.

Fourthly, cultural history seeks to challenge dominant perspectives in society, precisely through this emphasis upon the dialogue and debate surrounding texts in their social context. Other forms of history have traditionally focused (albeit often critically) upon social 'structures' and 'ideologies'. Cultural history, on the other hand, emphasizes that the apparent solidity and totality of 'structure' and 'ideology' are an effect of dominant discourse; or, to put it another way, it is dominant groups who *want* us to think of their power as stable and unproblematic. When historians consider power simply as a one-way relationship between the powerful and the weak, they downplay the role of the many voices that struggle against dominance. In this respect, the works of the French philosopher and historian Michel Foucault have been highly influential. As Foucault himself puts it (in his characteristically oracular style), 'power is not something that is acquired, seized or shared, something that one holds on to or allows to slip away; power is exercised from innumerable points, in the interplay of non-egalitarian and mobile relations'.[11] In plainer terms, power is not simply a property held by the dominant, but also a set of relationships between unequal partners.

This book, then, seeks to explore how Greek literary texts signified in their various social contexts, and to show how those texts can be seen as battlegrounds for power relationships between dominant and other groups. This explains the structure of the book. After Part I, where I introduce the theoretical issues and concepts, Part II focuses upon social contexts for the production of literature, rather than (as traditional literary histories do) on literary genres. Part III, meanwhile, offers a series of synoptic overviews, ranging across a number of contexts, teasing out issues of central cultural-historical importance: cultural identity, gender, sexuality and class. The emphasis throughout, that is to say, is upon texts as sites for social dispute.

This project, however, raises some evident problems. How, in practical terms, can we hope to trace the range of responses to an ancient text? Many, in some cases all, of the contemporary reactions have vanished without trace; those that survive are exiguous, decontextualized, and the products of very limited groups of individuals (fame for the FAME: freeborn, adult, male elite). How do we restore the urgency and vitality of 'real' culture to the limited, fragmentary and often deracinated remains that survive?

This book aims to meet these challenges by deploying one of the skills most traditionally associated with classical study: close reading. A careful focus upon the texture of literary texts, sited in their historical and cultural context, will (I hope) reveal the assertions, silences, accommodations and fudges at their heart. Such problematic passages – the cracks and fissures, as it were, under the smooth surface – offer us our best chance of discerning the preoccupations of a range of interest groups. Now this is, clearly, not the same thing as having verbatim reports from a full spectrum of social groups, but we shall never have that level of information for the ancient world – and even if we did, it is questionable whether a cultural history of literature would be the best forum for its analysis.

Any history of Greek literature will, of necessity, be dominated by the voices of the freeborn, adult, male elite. What I hope will single out this particular one will be the emphasis upon that small group's dialogue (often, albeit, unspoken) with a much wider spectrum of society.

The Problem of 'Greek Literature'

Questions still remain, though. No historical study can include everything. Which authors count as 'literary'? And behind this lies Michel Foucault's question: 'what is an author?'[12] Why is it that we use this title of some individuals who have etched marks upon a page (or spoken or sung), and not others? It is not the simple fact of publication (however we define that) and wide dissemination: after all, safety advice leaflets, for example, are published and reach a large readership, but we would not usually count these as the works of 'authors'. Nor is it simply a question of a writer of high quality, since (even if we accept the existence of objective criteria for defining quality) a brilliant writer of works that no one had read would not usually qualify. Rather, 'authors' are invented by external social processes: they are acknowledged and sanctioned as such by institutions (magazines, the radio, television, prize committees). A cultural history of literature must not limit itself to exploring authors: it must also question what social processes have contributed to our understanding of the concept of authorship.

Equally elusive is the notion of a 'text'. What kind of materials count as texts? The decisive factor is the use that society makes of the artefact in question: the text is conventionally understood as a particularly privileged form of writing (or speaking, or singing), one that is to be appreciated, admired and – especially – studied. It is the educational system, with its syllabuses and 'set texts', that primarily determines the status of the text. This does not mean that literary texts cannot be said to have 'quality': an artfully constructed or brilliantly inspired work stands a better chance of cultural elevation than one that is neither. But the fact that patterns of taste shift radically across even short periods should caution us against an over-confidence in determining exactly what counts as 'quality'. 'Textuality' (what makes a text a text) no more resides within a text than 'authoriality' does within the author.

Which brings us to the question of 'the canon'. Canons are bodies of texts that are promoted as worthy, and in particular worthy of study by students at school and university. In recent years, there have been vigorous debates (especially on North American campuses) about the traditional under-representation of women and ethnic and religious minorities in the established canon of humanities authors. If we accept – as indeed I have argued above – that it is principally the establishment, rather than necessarily any intrinsic quality, that determines what makes a text, then three conclusions may follow. Firstly, the canon is based upon relative not absolute principles; secondly, strategies of inclusion and exclusion are likely to be (in part or wholly) motivated by political and/or ideological considerations; thirdly, it is open to educational establishments to modify the canon at will to reflect diversifying demography and to answer the demands of minorities. Which is to say that canons are sites for political conflict just as much as texts are, according to my previous section.

The response from defenders of the established canon has been to attack the supposed cultural impoverishment brought about by such 'relativism', citing the intrinsic superiority of Shakespeare and Dante over any 'minority' texts.[13] Harold Bloom, in the most sophisticated (but also most mystifying) formulation of this position, places canon-formation at the heart of the act of literary writing: 'good' writers are such because they engage powerfully, critically and creatively with literary tradition.[14] There is certainly much to be said for Bloom's defence of close reading and humane criticism against mechanical cultural theory. His ideal reader of literary texts, however, who 'does not read for easy pleasure or to expiate social guilt, but to enlarge a solitary existence', comes across as an absurdly romantic figure.[15] *Why* should reading be a 'solitary' act? *Why* is socially engaged reading opposed to ethical or aesthetic 'enlargement'? *Why* is it to be thought of as 'easy'? *Why* is it said to be motivated by crude 'guilt'? There is a series of unexamined assumptions underlying Bloom's position here, assumptions that too hastily associate cultural-historical criticism with shrill cant and strident philistinism.

However one reacts to these debates, one thing is certain: there can be no conception of 'literature' without a canon. Canons are not just collections of texts; they are narratives, invested with purpose and direction; and also (like texts themselves, as we concluded in the previous section) sites for conflict and debate. Next, we shall consider an example of a canon, and attempt to unpack the significance of its various choices.

Reading the Canon

At the end of Bloom's book comes an extended list of books, his recommended reading list. The canon is structured chronologically, with Greek literature coming near the beginning (though eight Near-Eastern and Sanskrit texts precede it).[16] This is, in general, a judiciously chosen and informed canon; these are, broadly, the authors around whom the book you are reading will focus. But it is far from innocent, for all that. I do not mean simply *that* it contains omissions (canons are by definition exclusive); the point is that it matters *which* texts are excluded, how the list is ordered, and how hierarchies between texts are created.

There are two features of Bloom's canon I wish to emphasize. Firstly, he recommends translations for some of the texts, a choice that he explains as follows: 'I suggest translations wherever I have derived particular pleasure and insight from those now readily available.'[17] Now, there are translations suggested for all the poetic texts (bar Callimachus, a relatively late poet) but for none of the prose texts (bar Plutarch, for whom the preference is for the version of Dryden – himself, of course, a poet). What are we to make of this distinction? Does it not matter how prose is translated? Is prose intrinsically less likely to offer 'particular pleasure and insight'?

Secondly, the section on 'Greek literature' is divided into two groupings by period, 'the ancient Greeks' (encompassing the period roughly from the eighth to the fourth centuries BCE) and 'the Hellenistic Greeks' (fourth century BCE to the second century CE). 'Hellenistic' is a rather vague term, employed here to cover post-classical antiquity as a whole.[18] The division between 'ancient' and 'Hellenistic' suggests a firm break, and might be taken to imply a substantial difference between the two. That this difference is one of literary quality is suggested by the number of texts in each category that make it into the canon: 47 from the 'ancient' period, 9 from the 'Hellenistic'. This imbalance is all the more striking for that, in fact, many more texts from the later period survive.

Bloom's canon makes no explicit evaluative statement about Greek literature, but it does hint at (and by merely *hinting* at, disguise and naturalize) a preference for poetry over prose, and for earlier over later texts. The schematic division between 'ancient' and 'Hellenistic', moreover, passes up the opportunity to challenge a deeply engrained idea that Greek literary history follows a clear narrative pattern of rise and fall. Homer is the origin, and the literature of 'classical' Athens (particularly tragedy) the pinnacle; the story of later literature is one of sad decline into prosaic banality. In this respect, as we shall see in the following section, Bloom's canon demonstrates close affinities with the nineteenth-century, romantic canon, itself a palpably political construct.

The Limits of Literature

Any narrative history has to involve choices, not only about inclusions and exclusions, but also about the kind of story that it will tell.[19] Periodization – the zoning of a body of texts into historical 'periods' – is a crucial part of that process.[20] Bloom's distinction between 'ancient' and 'Hellenistic' Greeks is a case in point. How might we explain the idea that at a certain historical point the Greeks stopped being the one and started being the other? This question can be answered in two different ways. Firstly, we could argue that the massive historical shifts that took place at the end of the fourth century, as a result of the conquests of Alexander the Great (see chapter 8), represented the single biggest upheaval in Greek culture: this decisive phase, then, marked the beginning of the 'Hellenistic' period.

Whatever the merits and demerits of that proposition as a historical argument, though, the division between 'ancient' and 'Hellenistic' also has ideological significance within the modern world. This is the second of my two answers to the question: periodization is not simply inherent in history itself, it is a strategy that *we adopt* to allow us to make sense of history. And 'making sense' is not an innocent practice: this involves squaring historical data with modern perceptions of how societies work.

The idea that the most perfect expression of Greek culture could be found in one particular city-state, Athens, in one particular period, the fifth century BCE, has its roots in the nineteenth and early twentieth centuries (although it was significantly foreshadowed in the ancient world itself: see chapter 9). It was in the nineteenth century that the term 'classical' came to be used of fifth-century Athens, and the term 'Hellenistic' of the Greek world in general after the conquests of

Alexander (who died in 323 BCE).[21] The period before the 'classical' period was known as the 'archaic' period (roughly eighth–sixth centuries BCE), as though its role were simply to foreshadow and build up to the 'classical' pinnacle.

With this periodizing distinction came a strong sense of a distinction in quality between the vigour of the early period and the decadence of the later. Nineteenth-century classicists (under the influence of the eighteenth-century Italian intellectual Vico) often construe human history as a series of cycles that can be broken down into different phases. Using the Greek myth of the five ages of man, they sometimes speak of 'golden ages' of Greece and Rome in their supposedly 'classical' periods.

Also influential were the literary and artistic ideals of romanticism, which privileged 'originals' and decried 'imitations'. On this understanding, 'classical' literature was seen as spontaneous and emotive, 'post-classical' as calculating and (the worst insult, in the aftermath of the industrial revolution) 'mechanical'. All post-classical literature was perceived to be derivative. Sometimes, where a later Greek text was clearly nothing like any surviving earlier text, scholars invented lost 'sources'.[22] This happened, for example, to Lucian, the author of satirical dialogues (second century CE): in 1906, Rudolf Helm published a book in which he claimed that Lucian cribbed his ideas from Menippus (third century BCE), an author whose works, conveniently, survive only minimally.

This view of post-classical literature persisted well into the twentieth century. The entry under 'Alexandrian poetry' in the second (now supplanted and infinitely improved) edition of the *Oxford Classical Dictionary* (1970) makes the following claim:

> All Alexandrian poets were hampered by the weight and the splendour of classical Greek literature. Unable to create original poetic forms, they mixed and mingled elements from the old and clearly defined types of poetry. Scholarly and highly polished verse became the main criterion of great art. This often led to an artificial and fastidious style.[23]

Subsequent years, however, have seen a sudden and swift reappraisal of the post-classical world. The kind of attitude embodied in the quotation above lingers in places, but few contemporary academics would react to it with anything more than embarrassment. This shift in attitudes is related to aesthetic and cultural changes in society at large. Romanticism has had its day: the cult of 'the original' has been radically challenged by postmodernism, with its celebration of pop iconography and mass production. Historians (literary, social, cultural) are often suspicious of any grand historical narratives (like the nineteenth-century 'cycles'), preferring to read history as a procession of fragmentary, discrete episodes. In this climate, the firm distinction between 'classical' (or 'ancient', in Bloom's terminology) and 'post-classical' Greece looks decidedly uncongenial.

Neither the romantic view of periodization nor the postmodern fragmentation of history represents an absolutely true picture of Greek culture (although we might well have views as to which is the more helpful). Each is a response to intellectual and cultural trends in contemporary society. As I stated at the beginning of this section, it is impossible to approach any historical project without a sense of periodization, and dishonest to deny that one is doing so. Periodization provides the 'narrative' framework for the story that is being told. But we need to remain aware that this narrative is provisional, and likely to be displaced. Though there are certainly 'false' versions of literary (as in any other form of) history, and no doubt 'truer' ones, there are no absolute truths.

Questions of Politics

If questions of periodization were *simply* a matter of doing justice to all the phases of Greek culture, the issues would be important, but perhaps narrowly specialist. But nineteenth-century classicism is also, and arguably more importantly, a *political* issue. The 'golden age' of Greece was often presented as an example (albeit a complex one) to contemporary citizens. In Friedrich Nietzsche's *Birth of Tragedy*, for example, the tragic poet is held to have inspired the fifth-century Athenians in a way that only Wagner could in the present. Wagner, Nietzsche claims, might awaken 'the German spirit . . . in all the morning freshness that follows a tremendous sleep'.[24] Nietzsche might well have been a 'mere' academic, but these words, read with hindsight, have a much wider, more chilling resonance. Many nineteenth- and early twentieth-century Germans believed that the 'original' Greeks (supposedly the Dorians) had invaded the land from the North, from Germany itself (more on this in chapter 2). Hitler himself exploited this connection, both in the 1936 Olympics and in his sponsorship of the Hellenizing architecture of Albert Speer. The perceived connection between the races of Greece and Germany in part served to legitimize the 'purification' of the German people.

Not all 'classicisms' have been right-wing: the Greek world has
served all variety of causes. In nineteenth-century Britain, for example,
liberals looked to Athens for its democracy, others to the austerity of
Sparta; idealist Christians pointed to the supposed proto-monotheism
of Aeschylus and Plato, materialists to the supposed invention of
scientific secularism in the historian Thucydides; conservative moral-
ists applauded the Athenian emphasis upon self-control, while Oscar
Wilde cited Plato at his trial to support his case, and John Addington
Symonds used Greek evidence to support his call for the decriminaliza-
tion of gay sex.[25] Reformists, meanwhile, sought to democratize Greek
learning, bringing it to the masses (at working men's clubs and public
lectures, but also in new publications like the Everyman library).[26]
At the same time, the humanist values imbibed by the young were
held to stand them in good stead as civilized rulers over the colonial
'natives' (it is telling that candidates for the civil service were examined for their skills in interpreting Greek).

But despite this proliferation of perspectives, it has been, until relatively recently, principally upon classical Athens that commentators
have focused (though also, of course, on Homer: see chapter 3). How
might we explain this in political terms? One immediate answer is
obvious. Athens of the classical period was an imperial power: in
uniting commitment to culture, internal democracy and (at least until
404 BCE) political supremacy over others, Athens provided a congenial model for Western Europe's view of itself as dominant, whether
politically, culturally or morally. The later periods, however, saw
Greeks under the domination of other peoples, first Macedonians
and then Romans. (The issues are in fact more complex, but I reserve
full discussion for chapters 8 and 9.) For this reason, traditional
classicism has homed in on democratic Athens as the pinnacle of
Greek achievement.

The literature of Greece under Roman rule (from approximately
31 BCE: see chapter 9), in particular, has often brought out the worst
form of unguarded colonial prejudice in commentators. In 1965, one
commentator inveighed in the strongest terms against the 'museum
of fossils' that was produced in the second century CE. Warming to
his theme, he drew a direct analogy between political submission and
intellectual weakness:

> Real art, real literature as well, cannot thrive unless in freedom.
> It is the achievement of independent, responsible minds . . . The Greek
> literature of the second century is the work of a powerless community

... It is a neglected one in a neglected century, and, generally speaking, it deserves this neglect.[27]

In the light of post-colonialism (both as an intellectual approach and as a reality in world politics), however, the priorities might be inverted. It is precisely *because* Greece was dominated by an imperial power that its literature, 'the work of a powerless community', commands interest.[28] Texts do not have to be produced by the politically dominant in order to represent 'real literature'.

One of the primary values of a cultural-historical approach to literature, as we have seen, is that it seeks to give full weight to marginal or repressed voices. It is, in fact, highly debatable whether the Greek texts that have survived from the Roman period are the work of powerless people: most (if not all) of their authors, as we shall see in chapter 9, were members of the super-rich and politically well-connected elite. But later Greek literature also offers perspectives that earlier periods do not. In part, this is a matter of the volume of literature available. There is, notably, much more female-authored material (particularly in the form of letters surviving on papyri) and more diverse evidence for women's lives in the later periods (see chapter 11).[29]

It is impossible to say for sure whether classical Athens appealed to nineteenth- and twentieth-century scholars specifically because it seems to have imposed such a radically oppressive regime upon its women, although given what we know about Victorian conceptions of gender roles it seems likely. When we come to questions of race, the ground is more certain. Classical Athenians propounded myths of their own uncorrupted ethnic purity, claiming descent from Erichthonius, the first Athenian, who was born by 'autochthony' from the soil of Attica (see chapter 10). Later Greek literary history, on the other hand, is characterized by cultural mixture: with Greek now spoken in much of the known world east of Italy, the question of who was and who was not Greek became more complex and involved (see, again, chapter 10). There are a number of disturbing nineteenth- and early twentieth-century attacks upon barbarians (as they were seen) who were held to have polluted the stock of Greek literature. These centred particularly on the figure of Lucian, a Syrian who learned his Greek at school in the second century CE. Lucian was widely reviled in nineteenth-century England and Germany, on the grounds of infiltrating the pure Hellenic tradition: a 'disgusting Semite', in the words of one eminent German historian.[30]

History in Practice

Felicitously, the French for 'history', *histoire*, also means 'story'. Any literary history will tell a story, and stories always have direction, purpose, (ideological) *point*. An account of Greek literature in particular will have to confront its own relationship to present-day ideologies, to address its own founding conception of periodization and 'the canon'.

In this book, I have avoided any grand narratives about rises and falls, ebbs and flows. This is, in one sense, an anti-narrative book, in the postmodern tradition: a work of fragments, a series of discrete visits to independent sites of literary production. Yet, as I have already admitted, no literary history – even an anti-narrative history – can do without its narratives, and I want to conclude this chapter by flagging up some choices that have been taken.

At some levels, this book is rather traditional. Chronologically, it ranges from the Homeric poems (the earliest parts of which are probably from the eighth century BCE, through until the third century CE (although there are brief references to later authors). The choice of an ending point will always be to some extent arbitrary. This book ends in the third century because I have chosen not to include, except in passing, any Christian material (the Roman emperor Constantine Christianized the empire, including Greece, in the early fourth century). It would have been impossible to do justice to Christian literature in a book of this length; for the same reason, there is only minimal reference to the Jewish Greek authors Philo and Josephus. These are the kind of hard choices one confronts in a book like this. Is 'Greek literature' by definition pagan? Does Christian and Jewish material 'belong' in a cultural history of Greek literature? Complex, politically loaded questions, these, and there are no easy answers.

This book, moreover, focuses primarily upon the kinds of text that make their way into Bloom's canon. There are no detours into marginal texts, such as the magic spells and letters fortuitously recovered in the papyrus dumps of Egypt. There is little on religious unorthodoxy: no Pythagoreans, no devotees of Mithras and Isis. Nor is there much on technical writing, such as philosophy and medicine, that a larger and more catholic project might have encompassed. Readers will see the risks immediately: despite what was said earlier about the modernity of the idea of 'literature', this book focuses precisely upon genres that are conventionally thought of as literary: what we might call the 'expressive' genres of poetry, rhetoric, historiography and fiction.

But I return to my central point: history simply cannot be written without boundaries, without inclusions and exclusions. What is vital is to be fully aware of these boundaries and their implications. Where this book differs from conventional histories of Greek literature is in its repeated *questioning* of the notion of the canon. It attempts to expose the cultural, ideological and political labour that goes into canon-formation, as well as the underlying conflicts. 'Greek literature', as I hope this chapter has made clear, is anything but a self-evident category: the 'story' that underlies its 'history' is never innocent.

2

The Problem of Tradition

Literary Traditions

In the last chapter, we saw that the writing of literary history is closely bound up with the politics of the author of that history. We cannot simply 'describe' the literature of ancient Greece; we need to make a series of editorial decisions (what counts as literature, what does not?), and we need to explore the question of what historical narratives the account will present.

How can we conceptualize anything like an ancient framework for categorizing and experiencing texts? The commonplace metaphor of 'reconstructing' ancient thought is not helpful: it implies that ancient thought was as unitary and inflexible as a stone building, and that the modern critic (who becomes a kind of architect or engineer) can comprehend it (and describe it) in its totality. The model that we want to help us understand Greek literature, on the other hand, must accommodate not only the variety of Greek thought (across time, across cultural-political zones, across social classes, across the gender barrier . . .) but also the non-neutrality of the critic's own position. Our model must be capable of acknowledging that modern scholarship is not simply the 'subject' looking dispassionately at 'objects' in the ancient world, but also necessarily the object of its own analytical gaze. In order to think about Greek texts, we also need to think about how *we* think about Greek texts.

The central concept I intend to use in this chapter is that of a 'tradition' of literature. The Latin word *traditio* has two core meanings. In the sense that will be recognized by English-speakers, it means a handing-down (literally a process of 'giving' that crosses boundaries) of heirlooms or knowledge through generations. But the primary meaning of the Latin term is an 'exchange', or 'trade' between one person or group and another, particularly in mercantile contexts. A literary tradition, as I conceive of it, has as much to do with the latter sense as the former: it rests upon the two-way trafficking of ideas between communities. When authors – any authors, including modern critics – invoke traditions, they are not simply drawing attention to something that already exists, but creating ('constructing', to use a modish term) a certain kind of relationship between one culture and another.

Inventing Traditions

Traditions are often thought of as fixed and inflexible, but it will be clear from what I have said above that my view is that they are more of a fluid process. In a book published in 1983 (and now a standard text for cultural historians), Eric Hobsbawm and Terence Ranger coined the phrase 'the invention of tradition'.[1] This seemingly paradoxical phrase embodies the argument that traditions are subject to constant re-creation in accordance with the requirements of the present. 'Invented' traditions are not necessarily fake: although some may have been created out of nothing embarrassingly recently (the Victorians, in particular, were great ones for concocting spurious rituals), others certainly have deep roots. The crucial point is that the notion of 'authenticity' is unhelpful: if a tradition is being appealed to, the question to ask is not 'what authentic traces of the past are being preserved here?', but 'what agenda in the present does this vision of the past serve?' What goes for the social traditions also goes for literary ones: any invocation of a continuity of values must be provisional, strategic and, to an extent, arbitrary. When we explore literary traditions, we are looking not to map the common values shared by temporally, spatially and socioculturally disparate groups, but to investigate how these disparate groups appeal to the notion of common values.

The work of the cultural theorist Stuart Hall adds another layer of theoretical sophistication. For Hall, traditions are not given or fixed, but imagined and invoked in order to substantiate one particular vision of shared identity. His interest is primarily in cultural identity, which he sees as fundamentally 'constructed' by social institutions, such as traditions. Identity is, for him, not an essential quality that exists within us, but something imposed from without by the state and other bodies.[2] Traditions are, in his words, 'powerful attempts to reconstruct purified identities . . . in the face of hybridity and diversity'.[3] The contrary dynamic to 'tradition', in Hall's view, is 'translation', which celebrates cultural fusion across received boundaries.

Traditions, however, are not simply illusionary devices designed to con the gullible: they are an indispensable feature of all communication within a society. In a self-styled forward-looking society like the contemporary West, where rapid economic growth is predicated on constant technological innovation, the word 'traditional' is most often used in a haughty, patronizing manner. 'Traditional societies' are, in common parlance, only found in the developing world, or in provincial backwaters. But the West is as traditional as any developing society, in that it lays great rhetorical emphasis upon history, upon the (supposedly) continuous inheritance of democratic values, upon the canon of literary and artistic culture. That the West is a culture of innovation does not make it non-traditional, since tradition is (as we have seen) always open to change. And, conversely, 'traditional' cultures are not ossified: the impression of homogeneity across time and space is constructed partly by members of that culture themselves (and they construct it actively and deliberately); and then redoubled by the narrow perspective of western observers, who presume that theirs is the only culture that can accommodate inventiveness.

The Greek Literary Tradition

The creation of the Greek literary tradition began in antiquity itself. At this point, I want to emphasize two crucial aspects of the Greek tradition: the invention of Homer as the founding father of the tradition, and the creation of what I call the 'archive', a set of institutions devoted to preserving and manipulating Greek culture's sense of its literary traditions.

I begin with Homer. For the Greeks (and, indeed, for western culture in general), literature has always begun with Homer, the (perhaps mythical) creator of the epic poems the *Iliad* and the *Odyssey* (probably between the eighth and sixth centuries BCE: see chapter 3). In Plato's dialogue the *Ion* (from the early fourth century BCE, though the dramatic date is the late fifth), the singer of the title maintains the absolute authority of Homer in every field (*Ion*, 536e). Some 800 years later, a brilliant poet – Nonnus – from Panopolis in Egypt, also credited with a paraphrase of the gospel of St John, invokes him as 'father Homer'.[4] Even at this distance, and despite his composing in the radically different context of the Christian Roman empire, Nonnus still presents Homer as the father of his poetic tradition.

But the Homeric tradition was far from stable and uniform.[5] The first phase of displacement of Homeric authority came in the sixth and fifth centuries BCE. This period saw what historians of science would call a 'paradigm shift' in scientific thought, driven by Ionian cosmologists such as Anaximander and Anaximenes, who sought to understand the structure of the universe in terms of physical elements rather than theological creation myths. In addition, the invention of the new prose genres of history and forensic oratory demanded from narrative new thresholds of plausibility.[6]

Already by the beginning of what we call the 'classical' period, then, the Homeric texts could be perceived as belonging to an obsolete thought-world. For many readers of epic, the problem was primarily the gods.[7] In addition to the shift in scientific understanding alluded to above, more and more commentators began to voice concerns over the ethics of the epic divinities. Xenophanes of Colophon, in the sixth century BCE, writes that 'Homer and Hesiod have attributed to the gods everything that is shameful and culpable among humans: stealing, adultery and deceiving each other' (fragment 11). It is principally (if not exclusively) the perceived immorality of the Homeric gods that leads Plato's Socrates to his first argument for the expulsion of the poets from his ideal city (*Republic* 377e–83b).

Proposing the expulsion of Homeric poetry is a deliberately extremist confrontation with the originator of the tradition. Other interpreters came up with alternative solutions, more defensive but no less radical. Theagenes of Rhegium, in the late sixth century, produced the first allegorical interpretation of Homer. The gods, for Theagenes and others, symbolized the elements, and their battles the disharmony of the elements. Despite a supercilious press from philosophers like Plato and Plutarch,[8] allegorical interpretations persisted throughout antiquity, becoming ever more elaborate and complex.

Allegory offered a flexible technique whereby interpreters could map their own cultural and ideological agenda onto the prestigious originator of the Greek literary tradition.[9] Heraclitus, the author of a collection of *Homeric Questions* (first century CE), reads the texts of Homer in such a way as to reflect the philosophical ideas of his day; the Christian Clement of Alexandria (second century CE) reads them as dimly foreshadowing Christianity; the Neoplatonist Porphyry of Tyre (third century CE) interprets the account of the cave of the nymphs (in book 13 of the *Odyssey*) as allegorical of the structure of the universe.[10] In each case, allegory is used to reinvent the Greek tradition in the light of new paradigms of thought, demonstrating at once the continuing power and the adaptability of the Homeric tradition.

The magnetic power of the originator of the Greek literary tradition is one theme of this book. Another theme, equally important, is the invention and development of what I call 'the archive' (see Part II, especially chapters 7–9). From the fifth century onwards, Greek identity was increasingly bound up with the study of literature, which it came to see as a defined body of texts (even if strict questions of definition remained open). To this end, institutions like schools, libraries and performance halls were created to disseminate awareness of literature. During this period, also, there developed canons of great works from the past. These canons shifted and realigned over time, in response to social and political pressures. This book, then, not only provides a cultural history of Greek texts; it also explores the various ways the Greeks themselves narrated their own literary history, and the role of the archive in maintaining and disseminating those narratives.

Original Sins

While Homer was always conceived of as the originator of the Greek literary tradition, nobody could agree who he was, or what he represented. Invented biographies appeared early on, often modelled on features within the poem.[11] The Homeric Hymns offer a good example. These poems purport to be the works of Homer; and the early (sixth century?) *Hymn to Apollo* claims to have been composed by 'a blind man from rocky Chios' (172). That Homer was blind is clearly an inference from book 8 of the *Odyssey*, where we meet a blind bard, Demodocus.

The claim that he came from Chios, on the other hand, is at first sight more difficult to rationalize. But this assertion needs to be seen in the light of multiple claims for Homer's birthplace, which was famously controversial. In third-century Alexandria, there was a temple to Homer (the Homereion), containing a visual representation of the mystery: Homer seated in the middle, with all the claimant cities surrounding him.[12]

For this reason, it is too crude to speak of Homer's 'influence' on Greek literature, as though we were thinking of a unidirectional force flowing from origin to later Greece. The later tradition also 'influenced' Homer: individuals and cities moulded and reconceived him, in accordance with their own agendas and sociocultural imperatives.

Nor is it only ancient writers who construct Homer as an origin; as we saw in chapter 1, modern canons invest considerably in the primacy of the Greeks, which inevitably means the primacy of Homer. In particular, Europe and (by extension) that extraordinarily vague phenomenon we call 'the West' are often claimed to derive from him. Harold Bloom, the author of *The Western Canon* (1995), wrote in 1975 that 'everyone who now reads and writes in the West, of whatever racial background, sex or ideological camp, is still a son or daughter of Homer'.[13] Hanson and Heath's *Who Killed Homer?* (1998), more recently, takes contemporary academics (particularly in the USA) to task for their voluntary disconnection from the Homeric roots of the western tradition, for 'killing' the father in an act of blindness and jealousy.

But there are problems with any simple identification of Homer as the originator of the western tradition. Let us consider the words of one knowledgeable and respected critic: 'The *Iliad* . . . is the beginning of European literature, although, as we shall see, it is set in what is now Asia, and it draws upon a long tradition of eastern writing.'[14] How do these two claims, that the *Iliad* springs from eastern culture but initiates European, square? The claim that older texts from further east lie behind the Homeric poems is undeniable. Parallels between these and Hittite, Akkadian and Babylonian epics point to a common core of themes and imagery across a broad geographical spread and extending much earlier than our earliest Greek texts.[15] The phenomenon is comparable in other fields. The Greek alphabet, an invention of the eighth century BCE (and so roughly contemporary with the Homeric poems) was based on that of the Phoenicians, a Semitic people. And other artistic media from the eighth century BCE onwards – notably statuary, architecture and vase-painting – were, probably, energized in a comparable fashion by influence from a variety of eastern sources (including Egypt).[16]

So the claim that the *Iliad* 'draws upon a long tradition of eastern writing' is accurate. What is questionable (leaving aside the odd distinction between eastern *writing* and European *literature*: what is at stake in the choice of different terms?) is the relationship between Homer and 'Europe'. The Greek world of the eighth and seventh centuries BCE was not in any significant sense part of 'Europe'; it is more constructive (as the previous paragraph implies) to site it at the north-western corner of a vigorous and dynamic complex of east-Mediterranean and Levantine cultures. It is true that the *Iliad*'s narrative describes a war set in (to borrow Griffin's careful phrasing) 'what is now Asia'; but the Homeric poems (in contrast with later Greek works) manifest little sense that Troy was ethnically, culturally or geographically divided from the mainland.[17] The Trojans are the same kind of people as their foes from Greece.

Imagining Europe

The *Iliad* was not the first work of 'European' literature. What Griffin means, presumably, is that it *became* such; that later generations (starting in antiquity) read the poem as theirs. This process can already be seen in democratic Athens (fifth–fourth centuries BCE). After Athens and Sparta had combined to repel the mighty army of Persia, the *Iliad* was reinterpreted as a poem about Greeks and barbarians (a term that now carried rich resonances of Persia).[18] The fourth-century orator Isocrates, for example, refers to the prestige that accrued to Homer 'as a result of his praise of those who fought against the barbarian' (*Panegyric* 159). A hard geographical dividing line between West and East was now imagined: the Hellespont (the modern Dardanelles), which the Persian King Xerxes 'yoked' to build a chain bridge 'between Europe and Asia' (Herodotus 7.33). The *Iliad* was now – or was to be read as – a poem about Greek and barbarian, about Europe and Asia.

Greece, and particularly the city-state of Athens, reconceived its literary tradition in the light of its own military and imperial priorities. But if it was now that Homer became a 'European' text, this was only the beginning of a new set of problems. The concept of Europe has been subject to constant revision, as contemporary debates over the membership of the European Community clearly show. (Can a Muslim country be European? Are former Soviet-bloc countries European? Does the UK have strong ties with Europe or the USA?) Europe is not a single, stable entity, but an imaginary site for intense ideological and political debate.

If we are to take a 'constructionist' reading of Europe and its literary tradition – that is to say, if we are to interpret Europe as a continuously reinvented idea – then we can agree with Griffin to the extent that Homer has repeatedly been appropriated as a founder.[19] But even this is not enough to justify the claim that the *Iliad* 'is the beginning of European literature', because that claim excludes the small but significant group of appropriations of Homer effected by non-Europeans, indeed victims of European imperialism. Derek

Walcott's *Omeros* (1990), most notably, sets his Homerizing narrative on the island of St Lucia, probing the tension between European-colonial and Afro-Caribbean colonized identities.[20] Rather than rejecting Homer as a symbol of European values, Walcott invents an alternative tradition, in which the Homeric world becomes a universal cultural inheritance.

Grey Athena

One of the best-known recent accounts of the origins of Greek culture is Martin Bernal's *Black Athena*.[21] This highly influential, and controversial, book argues that classicists have conspired to deny the Afro-Asiatic roots of Greek civilization, falsely promoting instead (what Bernal calls) the 'Aryan' view of the Greeks as an essentially European people. According to the Aryan view, formatively proposed by the nineteenth-century German historian Karl Otfried Müller, the crucial moment in Greek civilization was the so-called Dorian invasion from northern Europe.[22] 'For 18th- and 19th-century Romantics and racists', argues Bernal, 'it was simply intolerable for Greece, which was seen not merely as the epitome of Europe but also as pure childhood, to have been the result of the mixture of native Europeans and colonizing Africans and Semites.'[23]

This is not the place to explore Bernal's claims that racist imperatives have determined the way in which the narrative of Greek (and hence European) history has been constructed. On this point, Bernal is (in my view) broadly right, though his account arguably lacks the subtlety and nuance that informs, for example, Edward Said's account of the emergence of 'orientalism' as an academic and popular field in the West.[24] My central point, though, is that any narrative of origins – including, crucially, Bernal's own – must be partial and ideological. There can be no 'truth' about the origins of cultures or civilizations, inordinately messy phenomena as they are. The weakest part of Bernal's argument is the claim, over the course of a lengthy and variegated discussion in volume 2 of the work, that bronze-age Greece (roughly the fourth–second millennia BCE) was 'civilized' thanks to Egyptian and Levantine trade and conquest. It is not just that many of his conclusions are hypothetical (shaky conclusions extrapolated from legends, thin data and unwieldy cultural comparisons), a criticism that might be levelled at much work from this period; it is more that, like the racists he opposes, Bernal manifests an over-confidence in the individuality, distinctiveness and cohesion of cultural groupings. It is simply not clear that there was, as Bernal argues, a distinctive concept of 'Greece' by the middle of the second millennium BCE.

Black Athena is most successful when it critiques others' over-investment in the narrative history of Greece, and least successful when it practises its own. The concept of 'Greece' is irredeemably diffuse; it cannot be grasped in terms appropriate to a biological organism. It was not 'sown' at any one specific time; we cannot identify its 'roots'. Any narrative of origins and roots – that is to say, any 'tradition' – betrays as much about the ideological agenda of its proponent as about historical reality. Rather than questing for the 'true' roots of Greek culture, it is preferable to consider the variety of ways in which individual thinkers and institutions have *constructed* Greece in terms of its origins.

The Textual Tradition

As we have seen above, the Greek literary tradition is not a single entity with an existence independent of its interpretation. It is, rather, an invented, and continuously reinvented, narrative; and thus also a political allegory, a map of the (perceived) order of things. Matters become still more complicated when we consider the ways in which texts themselves have quite literally changed since antiquity. No 'literary' (as conventionally understood) text survives from the ancient world in manuscript form; only a few survive inscribed on stone, and even these are often fragmentary. When we consider any ancient literature, we are invariably confronted at some point by questions of 'transmission', of the traditions of copying that pass them down from antiquity to the present day.[25]

Most Greek texts have been transmitted through the ages thanks to the laborious process of manual reproduction, first by scribes in the ancient world (our limited information suggests that most were literate slaves), then by monks in the Middle Ages.[26] The decisive period lay between late antiquity and the early medieval period, when political, religious and stylistic choices – and in some cases pure hazard – determined the texts that would survive. Such choices were made, of course, on the basis of a 'canon', which was in turn constructed on ideological grounds. Texts were much more likely to be preserved if they were deemed to have educational value: if they could serve as a model for stylistic emulation, or if they were repositories for appropriate moral apophthegms (although the survival of large numbers of astonishingly graphic works by Aristophanes and Lucian, for example, suggests a commendable degree of tolerance of obscenity, scatology and sexual representation).

For most complete Greek texts that we have, we still possess in their entirety at least some, and sometimes many, of the medieval manuscripts on which the earliest printed copies were based. This means that scholars can check our editions against an earlier textual tradition, and sometimes (with the help of aids such as microscopy, or simply a better understanding of palaeography and/or the Greek language) come up with improved readings. But editorial decisions are rarely straightforward. What is to be done when different manuscripts offer different readings? Or the manuscript readings conflict with other sources (e.g. quotations in other authors)? Or the reading does not make any sense? What authorizes an editor to decide the correct reading?

There are, certainly, cases where ancient texts are preserved directly. A number of poems survive inscribed on stone. This is in general terms the least problematic form of textual transmission, but complications of course ensue when the inscription is damaged or broken. Ancient papyri (pages made of matted, pulped rushes) also survive in some conditions, usually either carbonized in the eruption of Mount Vesuvius (79 CE) or preserved in the benign soil of Egypt. The stock of texts has increased hugely over the last century, thanks to papyrus finds: there are certain authors, of whom the most famous examples are probably the lyric poet Sappho and the dramatist Menander, whose works were largely lost until recent times. But although papyri are genuine ancient texts, they need great care. They are rarely undamaged, and often severely mutilated. What is more, most of our papyri are relatively late in date, from the period of the Roman empire, and are (in some cases) themselves the results of centuries of copying. The processes of corruption and interpolation began at an early stage; scholars can sometimes, paradoxically, find papyrus texts less satisfactory than the manuscript tradition.

The quest for the 'original' text, then, is a complex process. Producing an edition of a text transmitted by the manuscript tradition (like most of our Greek texts) requires elaborate heuristic models, central among which is the 'stemma'.[27] Stemmata are hypothetical family trees that seek to account for the development of existing manuscripts from an ideal original (or 'archetype'). By identifying deviant readings, omissions or interpolations shared between manuscripts, scholars posit the existence of a 'family' descended from a single progenitor (or 'hyparchetype'), which may or may not be an extant manuscript. The editor then proceeds to discount certain manuscripts which derive from a faulty branch of the stemma, and by gradually working backwards in this way seeks to arrive as close as possible (which may not be very close) to a notional authorial text.

This process is fraught with potential problems. Textual critics speak of the problem of 'contamination': an individual copyist may have had access to two or more manuscripts from different branches of the stemma, and thus 'contaminated' the direct genealogy. Once we admit this kind of problem, then the elegant simplicity of the genealogical model becomes compromised. But a larger problem may lie with the method itself. The controlling metaphor for stemmatic criticism is genealogical: the family of manuscripts is conceived of as a patriarchal dynasty. 'Contamination' is, arguably, a highly judgemental term, implying an adulterous pollution of the bloodline. The theory of stemmatics invokes normative morality, as though exhorting the textual family to legitimate reproduction. The study of the history of manuscripts is certainly indispensable to the study of Greek texts, and those patient figures who increase the stock of knowledge perform an invaluable task – but it is nonetheless grounded in ideology for all that.

Stemmatics, however, is only one aspect of the practice of textual criticism, which has, historically, turned upon the critic's ability to spot and emend deficient or uncharacteristic Greek. This branch of criticism often invokes a raft of 'laws' about metre and grammar, affiliating itself to the hidden authority of science or the state. But, crucially, it is not simply a question of applying rules: the best critics have always acknowledged that mechanistic approaches can never escape their own self-justifying, circular logic.[28] Many of the 'geniuses' of classical scholarship – Scaliger, Bentley, Porson, Wilamowitz, Housman – owe their reputations to their ability to come up with imaginative, learned and (most of all) unforeseen emendations to received textual readings. Each of these was undeniably a brilliant Hellenist, and there have been many others too. But textual criticism is not an ideologically neutral activity. It is rooted in the particular idiosyncrasies of classics as a university discipline, with its mythology of cut-and-thrust machismo. Particular emendations may or may not make for a more 'authentic' text (it is rarely, if ever, that we are able to judge this matter with any confidence); but the institutional *practice* of emendation springs (in part at least) from the seductive desire to join the mythical pantheon of famous intellects.

Readers of Greek literature often distinguish between reading 'in the original' and 'in translation'. But there is no such thing as 'original' ancient Greek: every text is (to a degree that it is never possible to determine with absolute certainty) a compendium of different readings from across the ages. Greek texts that we read always embody invented traditions.

Thou art Translated

Most readers nowadays, however, access Greek texts through translation. In recent years, translation theory has challenged the strict distinction between 'original' and 'translation'.[29] Many modern approaches to this topic propose that there is no such thing as 'accuracy' in translation, since all translation is appropriation; and that the boundaries between translation, interpretation and creative reworking are hazy indeed. Translations, that is to say, are texts in their own rights.

Is there such a thing as 'accuracy' in translation? A difficult question. On the one hand, texts can certainly be *inaccurate*; based, for example, on a misconstrual of the original. But such errors are relatively rare in professional scholarship. More commonly, we might find the same text rendered with a different emphasis, tone or style. Let us take, by way of illustration, three different versions by contemporary translators of the beginning of a well-known poem by Sappho (further discussed in chapter 12):

> To me it seems
> that man has the fortune of the gods,
> whoever sits beside you, and close,
> who listens to you sweetly speaking
> and laughing temptingly;
> my heart flutters in my breast,
> whenever I look quickly, for a moment. (Diane Rayor)[30]

> To me he seems like a god
> as he sits facing you and
> hears you near as you speak
> softly and laugh
> in a sweet echo that jolts
> the heart in my ribs. (Willis Barnstone)

> He looks to me to be in heaven,
> that man who sits across from you
> and listens to your soft speaking,
> your laughing lovely: that, I vow,
> makes the heart leap in my breast. (Martin West)

Three modern translations (of a poem first translated, to our knowledge, by the Roman poet Catullus in the first century BCE), resting on three very different interpretations of the poem. Let us take the first phrase. The Greek means something like 'that man seems to me to be like the gods'. In what way 'like the gods'? Rayor thinks that Sappho is alluding to his good fortune in being close to the girl ('has the fortune of the gods'), while West thinks the man is godlike because he is delirious with happiness ('in heaven'). The urge to disambiguate in translation is strong. Of the three, only Barnstone's version ('he seems like a god') retains the uncertainty of the Greek.

Is Barnstone's the more 'literal', then? Hardly. The phrase 'he seems like a god' is unconventional English, and it is hard to imagine what it might mean in the vernacular. Perhaps it connotes vigorous masculinity (as 'he looks like a god' might). It certainly would not usually suggest extreme fortune (as Rayor's translation suggests), or happiness (as in West's), both possible meanings of the Greek phrase. Paradoxically, in seeking to retain the ambiguity, Barnstone ends up with a narrower range of possible meanings.

There are a number of other issues raised here. Rayor makes the man an indeterminate figure (*'whoever* sits beside you'), whereas Barnstone and West think Sappho is imagining a particular scene with a specific, real individual. Rayor has the figures seated beside each other, Barnstone and West opposite (which in fact better fits the Greek). Rayor links the narrator's palpitations to the following line ('whenever I look quickly'); Barnstone and West link them to the scene previously described. Barnstone's description of the palpitations is harsh ('jolts'), and uses the austere language of physiology ('the heart in my ribs'); Rayor ('my heart flutters in my breast') and West ('makes the heart leap in my breast') describe gentler actions, and employ the more feminine term 'breast'. Finally, of the three, West's is the most linguistically ambitious, introducing archaism ('I vow') and a bold combination of striking alliteration with chiastic hyperbaton ('your soft speaking, your laughing lovely').

Ultimately, what we have here are three different poems, each with a distinct claim to be an accurate rendering of Sappho's Greek. Rayor's is a 'realist' poem, narrating the jealousy of a love-struck narrator pursuing a serial flirt; Barnstone's emphasizes the violently physical impact of love on the body; West's is more abstract, both in its lyrical phrasing and its reference to the other-worldly distraction of the male lover. Although one might argue about individual points, none of these translations has a particular claim to greater 'accuracy'. Each represents a different *interpretation* of Sappho's poem, accentuating, developing or isolating aspects of the Greek.

Translations offer yet another means of rewriting and representing the original text so as to allow it to signify in the modern world. Once again, we see that the Greek texts that we read are not simply inert relics of a distant past, but flexible and responsive to the demands of contemporary society. Through translation, the Greek literary tradition is continuously reinvented, in the manner we identified earlier. We may like to speak of some translations as 'truer to' the original or 'more authentic', but in practice this is likely to mean little more than that the translation chimes with *our own ideas about* what the original stands for.

In fact, even to distinguish between the 'original' and the 'translation' in this way may be too crude. From a philosophical perspective, Jacques Derrida has argued influentially against the received privileging of the 'originary' meaning of a text or speech-act over its 'dissemination' through later interpretation. For Derrida, meaning is not dictated to us by the authoritarian figure of the originator; it derives, rather, from a process of *supplementation*, from the play of possible interpretations among listeners or readers.[31] In classical literary studies, this kind of approach has been most influential via so-called 'reception theory', which argues that the meaning of texts is not deformed or obscured by subsequent traditions (which are to be purged by scientific historicism), but *produced* by them. Charles Martindale, one of the key proponents of this view, writes:

> Texts ... have a capacity for reingrafting themselves within new contexts, and thus remaining readable ... Every reading of a work becomes a fresh 'instantiation' with its own character ... The process of *re*contextualization was already in motion with the text's first receivers, so that there was never an obviously fixed original context. Rather, each work becomes an intervention within an intertextual field, which however much it tries to stake out a position, never wholly succeeds in doing so, and whose meanings are constantly realized anew at the point of reception.[32]

Martindale's model deliberately problematizes any interpretative venture. If we cannot access the original text, we must analyse its reception in later tradition; but then the receiving text becomes another original, so that too must be inaccessible except via its own receptions. We are left with an infinite regress of interpretative possibilities.

There are evident risks in adopting such an extreme form of scepticism: taken to its logical conclusion, this argument rules out the possibility of saying anything meaningful about the ancient world – or, indeed, about any historical period. The position I adopt in this book is more pragmatic. While I accept that any statement one might make about Greek literature will be motivated by modern questions (and hence modern ideologies), this does not mean that reading ancient texts is *simply* an exercise in self-projection on our part. On the contrary, a critical reading of ancient texts will expose surprising facets, facets that are alien to our experience as modern subjects. Now of course these instances of otherness in ancient texts are, at one level, themselves products of modernity's desire to construct antiquity as exotic. At another level, however, modern readers of Greek literature usually find the activity strikingly unpredictable, exciting and instructive; and this is because ancient texts speak through their own voices as well as those of later traditions. To read Greek literature is to enter into a creative *dialogue* with the past.

Part II
Contexts

3

Festival

Epic Poetry and Public Festival

Greeks always claimed that their literary tradition began with the poets Homer and Hesiod. The influence of these two figures was thought to extend well beyond literature. In the fifth century BCE, the historian Herodotus writes that Homer and Hesiod 'constructed the Greeks' account of divine coming-to-be (*theogonie*), giving the gods their cult-names and apportioning them their honours and arts, and indicating their forms' (2.53). For Herodotus, at least, Homer and Hesiod were the very founders of Greek culture as a whole.

The genre that we call 'epic' (from the Greek *epos*, 'word' or 'utterance') comprises substantial narrative texts composed in an embellished form of the Ionic dialect of Greek, and in hexameter verse (that is, in lines of six metrical 'feet'). The only epic poems that survive complete from this period are the *Iliad* and *Odyssey* attributed to Homer and the *Theogony* and *Works and Days* of Hesiod, composed over a period (the extent of which is debated) between the eighth and the sixth centuries BCE, but using narrative material and linguistic forms that derive from substantially older, Indo-European forms.[1]

In the predominantly oral culture of early Greece, epic was most likely to be encountered through the medium of song. There is some evidence (particularly in Homer's *Odyssey*) that in the earliest periods a 'singer' (*aoidos*) would sing of heroic deeds at aristocratic banquets, but for most Greeks the primary access to epic poetry would have been through performance at public festivals.[2] At these gatherings, a rhapsode (or 'stitcher of song') would perform from an established repertoire of epic poetry, centring particularly on that of Homer and

Hesiod (at least by the fifth century, the source of our earliest evidence for rhapsody).[3]

Through public performance, early epic poetry played a fundamental role in the establishment of Greek identity. These poems presented a core set of religious, ethical, military and political values that all Greeks were expected to subscribe to.[4] There is no explicit favouritism of any one city (although we shall have to qualify this in chapter 10). Linguistically, the poems borrow from a range of Greek dialects. Greece was not politically united: each *polis* (or city-state) was self-governing. Epic poetry was 'panhellenic', in that it appealed to values that could be shared by all the states of Greece alike.[5] Like the Olympic games (traditionally held to have begun in 776 BCE), panhellenic poetic festivals were open to all Greek states.

This panhellenic context, however, does not rule out more local meanings. For a start, as we shall see in chapter 10, these canonical poems do privilege certain groups (notably the Thessalians, the original *Hellenes* or 'Greeks'). Any process of unification requires the creation of a hierarchy. What is more, different meanings can be lent to the same sequence by subtle accentuating devices. Poetic narratives could be selected and edited according to the requirements of the situation. In Homer's *Odyssey*, for example, the disguised Odysseus requests from the bard Demodocus a story that redounds to his credit (8.499–520).[6] Patrons were key producers and controllers of meaning in local contexts (as with later 'praise poets' like Pindar).[7]

There was, moreover, an immense variety of festivals, from the small and local to the large and panhellenic. We can glimpse this in the so-called Homeric Hymns, the earliest of which probably served as preambles to epic performances (they later developed into an independent genre).[8] These poems served to link the epic performance in question to a precise context, the specific cult of a particular divinity. The *Hymn to Apollo*, notably, makes explicit reference to the performance context:

Your heart, Phoebus, takes particular pleasure in Delos,
where the Ionians with their trailing robes gather
with their children and their reverent wives;
they give you pleasure by invoking you with boxing,
    dancing and song,
whenever they hold the contest. (146–50)

As this quotation shows, local festivals could incorporate a range of events, including athletics as well as dancing and song. The songs themselves included choral performances (in a variety of metres), as well as solo recitals of epic or elegy (the latter often on local historical themes) by bards.[9] But it was the epic performer who was the centre of attraction. One of Plato's earliest dialogues, the *Ion*, describes the glamour that still, even in the late classical period (it is set in the late fifth century, though written in the early fourth) accrued to rhapsodes like Ion. Not only is he dressed in spectacular clothing (530b), but also his performance is expected to make a powerful emotional impact upon the audience (535b–e). The rhapsodic performance conveyed fundamental truths to its Greek audience. Homer, according to Ion (at least before Socrates challenges him), teaches everything (536e). (It is this culturally central role, of course, that Plato seeks to displace onto philosophy.)

Invented Origins

Early Greek epic was a central medium for the dissemination of the core values of Greek identity. The poems themselves only dimly acknowledge the existence of a body or people called *Hellenes* (the Greek word for 'Greeks'): in the *Iliad*, for example, the host that attacks Troy is said to consist of 'Achaeans', 'Argives' or 'Danaans'.[10] But one can see easily how panhellenic values might have been detected in the *Iliad* (with its account of a united military front against the Trojans) and the *Odyssey* (especially in relation to Odysseus' travels among strange, exotic peoples).

Epic poetry provided, moreover, a set of ready-made cultural origins for Greeks, narrating a sequence of divine and heroic acts that were held to have formed the world as it was understood. In this sense, epic poetry represented what we have called (in the previous chapter) an 'invented tradition', a culturally privileged narrative linking present to past.

Epic presents a strong consciousness of the relationship between past and present.[11] Human history is characterized as decline from the heroic past: 'Aeneas picked up a stone with his hand, a mighty thing, such as two men such as men are today could not lift' (*Iliad* 20.285–7). In Hesiod's *Works and Days*, we find an account of the 'five ages' of humanity: golden, silver, bronze, heroic and iron (109–201). Although the pattern is not one of consistent decline – the heroes are 'more just and better' than the men of iron (158) – the primary purpose of the myth is to express humanity's descent from its former state of godlike happiness to the suffering and immorality of the present. The relationship between past and present is complex: the two are linked in terms of cultural continuity, and severed in terms of quality.

In a world before historical records, epic provided a collective memory for the people. The surviving heroic epics we have, the *Iliad* and *Odyssey* of Homer, form part of a larger mythic compendium the ancients called the 'epic cycle'. This is now lost, except for a few fragments and some summaries preserved in the *Chrestomathia* of Proclus, written in the fifth century CE. The cycle included poems on the battles between the gods and the Titans (the *Titanomachy*), king Oedipus and the later history of the city of Thebes (*Oedipus*, the *Thebaid*, the *Epigoni* or *Next Generation*), the events leading up to the Trojan war (including Helen's abduction by Paris, in the *Cypria* or *Events Inspired by Aphrodite*), events at Troy after the death of Hector (the *Aethiopis*, the *Little Iliad* and the *Sack of Troy*), the returns of various heroes from Troy (the *Nostoi* or *Returns*), and events in the wake of the *Odyssey* (the *Telegony*). Although many of these poems are attributed to different authors, it is clear that a grand-scale editorial process (whether deliberate and decisive, or gradual and organic) has conspired to construct a genealogy of heroic affairs beginning with the earliest memories of the past. Proclus – as mediated through an even later source, the ninth-century Byzantine bishop and bibliophile, Photius – tells us that the epic cycle 'begins with the mythological union of Heaven and Earth'.[12] The survival of the Homeric and Hesiod poems, and probably even their composition, was determined by a larger project to map the entirety (or at any rate all that was deemed memorable – a different thing, necessarily) of human time.

Some early Greek epic is 'genealogical', which is to say it constructs family trees for gods and heroes (see further chapter 10). Genealogical poetry is pretty boring to modern taste, but it serves a crucial role in a preliterate culture. Like the lists of 'begats' in the Pentateuch, these genealogies serve as records of the stages that unite peoples to their pasts, the links in the chain of identity. It was Hesiod who was thought of as antiquity's foremost genealogist, and two texts are of particular importance.[13] The first is the *Catalogue of Women*, a genealogy of the human race listed according to mothers (see further chapter 10). The second Hesiodic text, and the most impressive narrative of origins in all of Greek literature, is the *Theogony*, or 'poem of the coming to be of the gods'. This complex poem begins with a 115-line address to the Muses, in which the poet prays for inspiration. The conclusion to that section runs as follows:

Tell me how first the gods and earth came about,
and the rivers and the boundless sea with its raging swell,
the glittering stars, and the broad heaven above;
how they [i.e. the gods] distributed wealth and divided their honours,
and also how they first came to inhabit Olympus with its many vales.
Tell me these things, Muses who dwell upon Olympus,
from the beginning, say which of them came first to be. (108–15)

'First . . . first . . . from the beginning . . . first'. The *Theogony* is (as Herodotus recognized) the poem that most conspicuously deploys the rhetoric of origins to authorize the theological and political structure of the world as it presently exists. These concepts will be discussed in greater detail below.

The Homeric Tradition

Epic poetry, then, embodied the cultural tradition of the Greeks. There is, however, another sense in which early epic poems can be said to be 'traditional', and this relates to their authorship, and particularly to that of the Homeric poems. Nothing is known of Homer; since antiquity, much fun has been had supplying him with biographies.[14] Over the last two hundred years, however, the so-called 'Homeric question' has taken a different turn. Most classicists credit a German scholar, Frederick Wolf, with the first idea that the Homeric poems were created not by one man (as had been assumed until then), but by successions of singers over a lengthy period.[15] Writing in 1795, Wolf was heavily influenced by romanticism and its celebration of folk traditions.

In the twentieth century, Albert Lord and Milman Parry, using comparative data from Serbian singers (*guzlars*), reinforced the analyst perspective by pointing to the high incidence of 'formulaic' language, an indication of the improvisational vitality of the poem (although of course it did cease to be improvised when it was written down, probably in the sixth century).[16] If the comparativist perspective is anything to go by, every performance of Homer and Hesiod (at least until the poems were solidified by writing) would have been different – even when the performers in question were claiming it was the same song. What Parry and Lord also show is that a poem authored by a tradition over time need not be an incompetent 'patchwork' (as earlier scholars had claimed); on the contrary, what may have begun as a loose aggregation of disparate tales may have been gradually refined into the ambitious but elegant and architecturally complex narratives that we read today.[17]

This hypothesis, though generally accepted, is not without its opponents. Some still maintain that Homer was a single author; others argue that the texts were written down at an early date. But if we do accept it, tentatively, then a very interesting possibility emerges: these are texts that can integrate their own reception built into them. There is no 'original' Homeric or Hesiodic text, only the revisionist labour of generations, even centuries of tradition. These poems are created by process, not by the 'event' of authorial creation. As a result, they cannot be considered in any straightforward sense as the 'origins' of Greek literature; they exist, rather, already after the event, as records of traditions in action.

The Poetry of Power

Whether or not we reject the idea of single authorship, the Homeric and Hesiodic poems certainly represent the ideological tensions of a society in transition. The political landscape over the time of composition was still (as it was for the earlier Mycenaean world that forms the subject of the heroic poems), dominated by the *basileus* or *anax* (most easily translated as 'king', but the medieval baron is perhaps a better analogy for these local dynasts).[18] The innovation that was emerging, however, was the focus upon community life, upon the social and religious obligations within the *polis* or city.[19] From the eighth century onwards, Greek society saw a progressive expansion in the ideology of the *polis*, culminating in the phenomenon we recognize as citizenship, best known from the Athenian democracy in the fifth and fourth centuries (but also identifiable elsewhere, and already in the sixth century).[20]

The Homeric and Hesiodic representations of the role of the king, on which more will be said below, reflect the uncertainties of contemporary society. In the military sphere, on the other hand, the epics describe a model of individual combat between aristocrats that was (in contemporary society) being gradually eroded and supplanted by the model of the *phalanx* (literally 'spider'): a unit of men fighting together in common defence of the fatherland. Arguably, the texts exploit the (in historical terms) increasingly problematical status of the paradigm of the lone warrior-aristocrat in whom all power is invested. And so the force of Greek epic can be said to emerge precisely from the deep chasm slowly yawning between the tectonic plates of past and present.

Let us return to Hesiod's *Theogony*, and to the passage cited above from the end of the address to the Muses. The concept of *order* is crucial for Hesiod, in a double sense. Chronological sequence is of course a fundamental form of order; but this narrative order also serves to undergird the cosmic, political and poetical order. The poem tells of the dividing and structuring of the universe into its proper zones, and makes that structure contingent primarily upon the accession and permanent rule of Zeus, the divine *basileus* or king, and – notably – his suppression of all opposition.

Power has no concrete existence; it needs to be invoked and displayed. The conquest of adversaries is a primary forum for such manifestation. Zeus' two most serious opponents are the Titans (617–733) and a many-headed monster called Typhoeus (820–80). These beings, plausibly, represent allegories for, respectively, jealous aristocrats and the insurrectionary mob.[21] The Titans share with Zeus descent from Ouranos (the personification of heaven), and are hence rival claimants for the throne; Hesiod derives their name from the verb *titainein*, to 'strive for' usurpation (209). Typhoeus is characterized by vocal multiplicity: he has one hundred heads, and his language is 'multiform' (830), in that he speaks with a different voice from each head (sometimes divine, sometimes bestial). Each symbolizes, in a more or less allegorized form, an element in society that threatens the rule of the mortal king.

Poetic Order and Political Order

With the assaults on heaven of these creatures comes the fear of elemental confusion. Let us consider Hesiod's description of the disorder caused by the Titans. I also print the Greek, transliterated, for reasons that will become clear:

> The limitless sea resounded horribly,
> the earth roared mightily, broad heaven groaned
> as it reeled, and tall Olympus was shaken from its roots
> at the charge of the immortals . . .
>
> *deinon de periakhe pontos apeiron*
> *ge de meg' esmaragesen, epestene d' ouranos eurus*
> *seiomenos, pedothen de tinasseto makros Olumpos*
> *ripe hup' athanaton . . .* (678–81)

Not only do these lines represent the threat posed by the Titans to the stability of cosmic order, but also the raucous alliteration challenges the smooth, mellifluous harmony of poetic order. In the hymn to the Muses that prefaces the *Theogony*, Hesiod alludes to the sweet song that they inspire (10, 22, 39–40, 43–5, 65, 67), causing 'forgetfulness of cares' (55). The alliterative passage just cited flouts the aesthetic code promulgated by the Muses, as though the dissonance of the poetic form mirrored the chaos of the cosmos – and, indeed, that of the political order, for the survival of the cosmos is clearly predicated upon the sovereignty of Zeus. These three axes – poetical, cosmic, political – are mutually interdependent. Here, then, we can see clearly how a narrative of origins conveys a powerful vision of social order.

But Hesiod's conception of the relationship between his song and sovereign kingship is more complex. A famous passage towards the end of the prefatory hymn to the Muses expands this relationship in suggestive ways:

> She (Calliope) is the most conspicuous of the Muses,
> For she attends upon worshipful kings.
> Whomsoever of divinely-nourished kings the daughters
> of great Zeus honour and watch over as he is born,
> on his tongue they pour sweet dew,
> and from his lips flow honeyed words. All the people
> look to him as he settles disputes with
> true judgements; and he, speaking surely,
> would soon make a wise end to even a great strife.
> That is why kings are intelligent, because when the people
> are being torn apart in the assembly, they set matters right
> with ease, persuading them with gentle words.
> And when he passes through a gathering, they greet him like a god
> with honeyed reverence, and he is conspicuous among the assembled.
> Such is the holy gift of the Muses to men.
> For it is thanks to the Muses and far-shooting Apollo
> that there are bards and cithara-players on the earth,
> and thanks to Zeus that there are kings. He is blessed whom
>   the Muses
> love: sweet flows the voice from his mouth. (79–97)

It is immediately notable how strongly Hesiod emphasizes the role of the voice in this passage. The 'beautiful' song of the Muses is now given a socially beneficial function: sweet speakers calm disputes and maintain order in the assembly. But this passage poses its challenges, not least in its interweaving of the voices of the singer and of the king. The narrator begins by discussing the Muses, and then transfers smoothly to kings and the sweetness of their voices. That section is capped by the line 'Such is the holy gift of the Muses to men'. Hesiod then hits his audience with a surprise. 'For' in the next line suggests that that sentence will explain the previous one, but in fact (though we have to wait an extra line to discover this) the subject is now not kings but singers: a sharp distinction is drawn between singers, who derive their power from Apollo and the Muses, and kings who derive theirs from Zeus. So to whom do the last lines ('He is blessed whom the Muses love: sweet flows the voice from his mouth') refer: to kings or singers? The audience is left in a quandary: is social order dependent upon political control, or upon the palliative powers of song? Or, to put it more forcefully, who pulls the strings, the king or the poet?

Readings such as this, foregrounding the ambiguities and tensions of poetry, are sometimes accused of anachronistically retrojecting an inappropriately postmodern playfulness. But ambiguity is, in this case, an eloquent expression of a precise historical situation. The *Theogony* was composed, as we have seen, at a time of considerable tension in what we now call Greece, as new paradigms gradually emerged to destabilize older ones. This aetiological-genealogical text is, undeniably, a poem that promotes the *basileus* or king as the necessary stay of social and cosmic stability. But it also interrogates this position, questioning whether the power of the *basileus* is inherent in the order of things, or fundamentally dependent upon poetry's ability to manufacture ideologies and disseminate them to the people. When the Muses first address Hesiod, they famously tell him that 'we know how to tell many lies like the truth, and, when we want to, we know how to tell the truth' (27–8). A complex and difficult sentence, this, and it has inspired many different interpretations:[22] is Hesiod claiming that his poetry tells the truth, while other poetry lies? Or that all poetry, his included, contains an element of fiction? But the best conclusion to draw, perhaps, is that its ambiguity is precisely the point: the audience can never be certain whether the *Theogony* is a true representation of the crucial role played by kings in upholding order, or a knowingly fictitious glamorization of an imperfect political system.

Epic reflects upon (reconstructs and re-enacts) distant origins. But although the temporal distance invoked is wondrously large, the myth of the origin plays a crucial role in the here and now. Epic uses its status as a collective cultural memory bank to anchor the political system of the present; and, arguably, simultaneously to dramatize its tensions and crises.

Ennobling Heroes

As much as the *Theogony*, heroic epic also explores the role of the
basileus or king. In the world represented by the *Iliad*, these figures
hold an exclusive and largely unquestioned monopoly in the political
arena; they are also the most physically beautiful and (in general) the
guardians of ethical values. If their pre-eminence as a class goes unquestioned, however, the relative statuses of the individuals involved
certainly does not. The *Iliad* stages a series of competitions between
aristocrats, in which political confrontation and verbal jousting become as much a means of the individual's worth against and over
that of another as does military combat.

The poem as a whole commemorates one unique individual,
Achilles, who is named 'the best of the Achaeans'.[23] He is announced
as the subject in the very first line, and even when absent from the
action (as he is for much of the poem), he is conspicuous by his
absence. In a famous passage in the ninth book, Achilles refers to the
choice his mother has outlined for him: a long life in obscurity, or
a short life with 'imperishable fame (*kleos*)' (9.412–15). This is a
moment of profound self-consciousness, on the part of both Achilles
and the poet, for the fame referred to is perpetuated through poetry
itself. As well as a subtle meditation upon human mortality (the body
may die but fame is 'imperishable'),[24] Achilles' account of his choice
also illuminates the intimate relationship between the ideology of
aristocratic power and the fame-giving mechanisms that perpetuate
it. Heroic epic is a poetry of power.

Power Struggles

But the *Iliad* is also a poem about a crisis in power, the celebrated
quarrel between Achilles – whose status as supposed 'best of the
Achaeans' is premised upon his excellence in military valour – and
Agamemnon, the leader of the host, 'the best' in a different, political
sense. Agamemnon, it is said, 'boasts of being by far the best of the
Achaeans' (*Iliad* 1.91; 2.82) – the emphasis that it is *his own* assertion is highly significant.[25] The opening books of the poem describe
the battle between the two for status in the eyes of the people. Status,
in the *Iliad*, rests upon public recognition: honour (what the Greeks
called *time*) is not the abstract quality it would later become, but a
materially quantifiable phenomenon.[26] Honour is acquired by public

acknowledgement of valour (the award of a choice cut of meat at a banquet, or a significant share of the spoils), and shame by a public put-down. The quarrel between Agamemnon and Achilles that leads to the latter's withdrawal springs from precisely this complex of values: Agamemnon is required to return a girl he has taken as spoils of war (Chryseis' father is a priest of Apollo, and Apollo has brought a plague on the Achaeans); to compensate for this loss of face, he appropriates Achilles' slave, Briseis,

> ... that you may learn well
> how much greater I am than you, and another man may shrink back
> from likening himself to me and contending against me. (1.185–7)

Agamemnon's problem, however, is that he is *not* 'greater' than Achilles. He may have the superior station, but he is also the lesser fighter. In response to the insult, Achilles rages: although Athena intervenes to prevent him from killing the king there and then, he assaults him verbally with a coruscating denunciation of this 'wine sack, with a dog's eyes, with a deer's heart' (1.225), before dashing the sceptre (symbol of kingship, and also of the right to speak in public) upon the ground (1.245–6). As so often in the *Iliad*, language is the vehicle of aggressive assertion.[27] Achilles' response is (as befits such an exceptional figure) extreme: not only does he withdraw from battle, but he even prays to his mother, the goddess Thetis, for the destruction of the Achaeans, a desire for vengeance that continues well beyond Agamemnon's later attempts to make reparation.[28] But extreme though it may be, Achilles' behaviour pursues the logic of the competitive ethos of Iliadic society – to the very limits.

The 'lesson' Agamemnon seeks to teach Achilles falls flat, because the king's symbolic power is not in this case married to physical power: in the efficient economy of Homeric politics, kingship needs to be underwritten by brute strength. According to the *Theogony* (see earlier in this chapter), 'Force' (*Kratos*) and 'Violence' (*Bia*) are seated on either side of Zeus (the embodiment, of course, of kingship) on Olympus (388). In the *Iliad*, however, it is only Zeus who successfully unites physical and political power: the ordered assembly of the gods that concludes the first book of the poem, an episode in which Zeus quells the dissent of certain gods by threatening them with injury, offers a strong contrast to the rankling unease that ensues in the wake of the mortal confrontation between Agamemnon and Achilles. In the mortal sphere, political and physical pre-eminence are – disturbingly – embodied in different figures.

The *Iliad* may be the poetry of power, but it also questions whether one man can claim all the necessary qualities of the ideal king. In this respect, it dramatizes the problems that lie at the heart of kingship as a model of political order. For the festival audience, this poem must have *both* dramatized the glamour and charisma of the powerful dynasts who overshadowed their lives *and* underlined the need for newer, more consensual and broad-based models of community.

Fighting for Status

Political capital is also exchanged on the battlefield: Homeric warfare is a competition for status.[29] Unlike later Greeks, whose martial ideology was based around the notion of self-sacrifice for the city, Iliadic aristocrats win, and die, for the sake of their own glorious reputations, in the eyes of both their peers and posterity.[30] When the Trojan Andromache begs her husband Hector to stay within the city walls to protect her and her family, he responds (while acknowledging the force of her argument) by alluding to the 'shame' (*aidos*) he would feel before the city folk if he were to skulk (6.442–3). 'Nor', he continues, 'does my heart bid me to do that, since I have always learned to be noble [*esthlos*] and fight with the first Trojans, seeking to gain great fame [*kleos*] for father and myself' (6.444–6). The Greek word *esthlos*, like the English 'noble', describes pre-eminence in both social and ethical terms: as an aristocrat, Hector has to behave like one. This means fighting with 'the first Trojans', another pregnant phrase, which alludes simultaneously to the social elite and to the front-rank fighters.

In analysing the competitive culture of the modern Mediterranean, anthropologists have introduced the concept of the 'zero-sum game'.[31] According to this principle, status is acquired through competition, one's own 'face' being enhanced by detracting from that of another (hence the aggregate is zero). Iliadic society operates according to a similar competitive principle. The desire to obtain 'fame' and 'honour', and to avoid 'shame', is a primary motivation for action for all warriors, not just Hector. These concepts are not abstract: each of them is directly linked to one's status in the eyes of others.

The Body Beautiful

Homeric warfare is also an opportunity for the display of the aristocratic body.[32] The plain of Troy above all maximizes visibility, providing a space for the display of the elite: aristocratic warriors see, and are seen by, other warriors. This theatrical quality of the plain is emphasized in a powerful scene in book 3, where King Priam and other Trojan elders look down over the battlements at the impressive sight of the Greek nobles, three of whom (Agamemnon, Odysseus and Ajax; Achilles has withdrawn) are named and described by Helen (3.161–242). The dominant figures in the narrative are the most physically conspicuous figures, as though the audible space of the poem were an analogue of the visible space of the plain.

The central figure of the poem, Achilles, announces his willingness to rejoin the fray with a spectacular visual display. As yet unarmed (Hector has stripped his original armour from his friend, Patroclus), he displays himself naked on the top of the defensive ditch, where the goddess Athena crowns his head with a burning golden cloud (18.203–6), and the beam reaches up into the ether (18.214). The brilliance of Achilles' naked body borrows the qualities of armour, manufactured to terrify; and, indeed, when his new armour does arrive (built to order by the divine smith Hephaestus), even his own troops cannot bear to look upon it without terror (19.14–15). The fearsome physique of the warrior is the result of a fusion of nature and culture, of the innate qualities of the individual enhanced by the intelligence of the artisan. The young noble is even handsome in death: when Hector falls at the hands of Achilles, the Achaeans gather around to marvel at his 'body and enviable beauty' (22.370).[33]

This aestheticization of the male aristocratic body in such cases is not simply born of 'homosexual' desire: even if we recognize that such scenes do influence later models of pederastic (older man/younger boy) relations,[34] we must still acknowledge firstly that there is no mention of male–male sexuality in Homer or Hesiod, and secondly – more importantly – that it is only a Freudian world-view that sees the desire for sex as the final answer to the question of human motivation. In Lacan's revision of Freud, we find a (for our purposes) more useful model of sexuality, which stresses the *symbolic* functions of desire. If we follow this model, then the Homeric emphasis upon male beauty becomes a means of impressing sociocultural dynamics onto the body. The human form becomes phallic, symbolic of the power to dominate; and if there is desire on the part of the onlookers, it is a desire (born of a sense of lack) to usurp that power for themselves. The Achaeans' wonder at Hector's body is an admission of his superior power. It is paradoxical, but not meaningless, that it is

the inert, vanquished cadaver of Hector that manifests this insuper-
able power: the heroic corpse, stripped of the active vigorous life,
becomes a passive spectacle, 'a pure object of vision'.[35] In death, the
body fully enters the realm of the symbolic.

In other contexts, however, a deeper and more complex response
to visuality is explored. When the Achaean forces are hard-pressed,
following Achilles' withdrawal, his friend Patroclus arranges to borrow his armour, a deal specifically designed to fool the Trojans and
Achaeans alike into thinking that Achilles has reappeared on the
battlefield (16.41–3). Armour can disguise the warrior within, as well
as enhancing his innate qualities.

In the scene in book 3 alluded to above, in which Helen and the
Trojan elders observe from the wall, the figure of Odysseus represents a different kind of bodily spectacle. His body is more diminut-
ive, 'lesser by a head than Agamemnon' (3.193), though he is broader
of shoulders; and his armour (usually, as we have seen, an integral
part of heroic physique) lies on the ground while he prowls around
'like a ram' (3.196). This last simile may deliberately evoke the story
in the *Odyssey* of his escape from the Cyclops' cave, disguised under
a ram (*Odyssey* 9.432). The Cyclops made the error of underestimat-
ing Odysseus by his paltry appearance, as he came to realize;[36] and
the apparent allusion to this episode in the Iliadic scene seems to
warn Priam (and us) against assuming too close a fit between appearance and essence. Indeed, another Trojan noble, Antenor, tells a
cautionary tale about the visit of (Agamemnon's brother) Menelaus
and Odysseus to Troy before the war: Menelaus seemed the more
impressive to look at, but Odysseus was by far the better speaker
(*Iliad* 3.204–24). In both the *Odyssey* and the *Iliad*, Odysseus represents a different paradigm of heroism, one who excels in artful cunning rather than open force: it is by the trick of the wooden horse
that he captures Troy, by dissimulation that he escapes from the
Cyclops, and by disguise that he manages to return to and re-enter
his house, kill off the suitors and reclaim his wife.[37]

In cases like this, Homeric narrative explores the *problems* inherent in a competitive, face-to-face, aristocratic society. If the worth of
the person is to be viewed in terms of that person's standing in the
eyes of others, how do we deal with the cheat, the fake, the person
who strategically mismatches exterior and interior? In other words,
the Homeric poems not only construct an idealized, aestheticized
vision of the beautiful, noble hero, but also allow for a certain social
pragmatism, a manipulation of the ideals.

Alternative Epics

The *Iliad* and the *Theogony*, with their narratives of power, violence and physical glamour, explore the identity of the *basileis*, the kings or aristocrats who dominated the political landscape of early archaic Greece. But epic poetry is not just about these figures. In the Homeric *Odyssey* and the Hesiodic *Works and Days*, notably, we find an extended range of social representation. The *Odyssey* tells of Odysseus' long return home from the Trojan war to his household on the island of Ithaca.[38] It is also, symbolically, a return from the idealized glory of Iliadic warfare to the homely, peaceful life of a civilized community. The second part of the *Odyssey* presents the former warrior of the *Iliad* now mixing among herdsmen and slaves, disguised as a beggar. This poem carefully reminds its audience that civilization depends upon loyal workers as well as idealized aristocrats. The *Odyssey* also gives unprecedented prominence to women and the household.[39] This poem serves as a corrective supplement to the *Iliad*, expanding that poem's narrow focus on a limited demographic group.

It is, however, the poem that we call the *Works and Days* (attributed to Hesiod) that offers the most engaging sub-elite perspective. In this poem, the narrator identifies himself as a farmer who has been conned by his brother, Perses, who has connived to receive a disproportionate amount of inherited land. The narrator particularly attacks the 'bribe-devouring rulers' (38–9), who have (presumably) failed to prevent the injustice. In this poem, the *basileis* are distant and dangerous powers, certainly not the patrons of the poet.

The early parts of the poem consist of a series of myths designed to illustrate the need for honest, hard work, for the poor at least. Two tales are particularly important: the myths of Prometheus (47–105) and of the five ages of man (which we have briefly met already, 109–201). Both illustrate humanity's fall: once men lived in abundance with the gods, now they must toil.

Let us focus briefly on the story of the Titan Prometheus (also told in the *Theogony*, lines 507–616), which links together a complex of themes. Firstly, Prometheus tricks Zeus at a banquet into accepting bones wrapped in fat as his share (this episode only appears in the *Theogony*'s version). This element in the myth provides an 'aetiology' (explanation of origins) for the Greek practice of animal sacrifice, whereby the inedible parts of a meal were burnt for the gods to enjoy. Sacrifice is humanity's way of marking its submission to the gods (and indeed superiority over the beasts). In return, Zeus withholds fire from mortals, but Prometheus steals it in a fennel stalk. Fire is the primary means of technology and civilized cooking: humans without fire are no better than beasts. In response to this trick, Zeus creates Pandora, the first woman, the origin of all human woes: 'previously, the races of men on earth lived apart from sufferings, heavy labour and grievous illnesses' (90–2). With the advent of women come reproduction and mortality, and the need for surplus agricultural production. Hesiod conceives of women as consumers rather than producers, posing a real risk to the delicate equipoise of the agrarian economy ('do not let a woman poking into your barn deceive your mind by showing off her arse and whispering deceptive words', 373–4).[40]

This lapsarian narrative may remind some readers of the story of Adam and Eve in Genesis, and indeed certain strong similarities may well indicate a common source in Middle Eastern folk narrative: in both cases, it is the advent of woman and sexuality that effects the divorce between gods and men, between paradise and suffering. There are, however, important differences. In Hesiod, there is an emphasis unparalleled in the Pentateuch upon the economic implications. As well as narrating the chronological shift from the plentiful past to the desperate present, Hesiod is also marking the social chasm between rich and poor. It is, implicitly, the *basileis* (aristocrats) who live close to the gods, and the workers who are consigned to their lives of subsistence labour.

This poetry, then, is specifically directed towards the people. The target market becomes clearer still in the later parts of the poem, which consist of practical advice: an agricultural calendar, the 'days' of the poem's title, detailing the seasons for woodcutting, ploughing, pruning and so forth (381–617); instructions for sea travel (618–94); general ethical advice (695–764); and the days of the month (765–828). If the *Iliad* maps out exploits of the founding fathers of aristocratic dynasties, the *Works and Days* memorializes the wisdom of the fields and the seas. Festival poetry addresses a broad demographic range.

The Homeric and Hesiodic epics were composed (probably) over a long period of time, a period that saw radical changes in the structure and organization of Greek society. Performed at public festivals across the Greek world, these poems stage the tensions and complexities that arose when the vast tectonic plates of pre-archaic and archaic society slid apart, when Greek politics gradually began to interrogate the concepts both of limited franchise and of peasant labour.

Festive poetry is centrally about building and perpetuating traditions, about constructing, exploring and challenging the relationship between the contemporary world and the mythical past. Poetic festivals were always, intrinsically, engaged in the process of highlighting the gap between the charismatic, idealized leaders of the past and the tense, fissile status of political hierarchies in the increasingly community-focused present. These festivals provided a forum for competing voices to be heard, for the central debates of a rapidly developing society to be aired.

4

Symposium

Food and drink were central to ancient Greek culture. Consumption of solids and liquids is, of course, physiologically necessary for human beings; but solids and liquids are not quite the same thing as food and drink, which require artfulness, cultivation, a stylistics of living. Foodstuffs and drinks are central indices of cultural and class identity; you are what – and, crucially, *how* – you eat and drink.[1]

In the archaic period, meals were focal points for the organization of social relationships. The dividing (*daiesthai*) of meat at the Homeric banquet (*dais*) indicated status: banquets were the place for making, challenging and patching up relationships between prickly heroes.[2] It is at such a *dais* that Odysseus and Achilles are said to have fallen out (*Odyssey* 8.76), and at another such that Agamemnon and Achilles are said to have made up (*Iliad* 19.179). What is more, eating was a religious event, requiring due sacrifice to the gods.[3] It had to be done *properly*. When Odysseus' crewmen, contrary to Odysseus' (and, ultimately, Circe's) advice, eat the cattle of Helios, their transgression is redoubled by their failure to follow correct protocols. They tear leaves off trees, 'since they did not have white barley on their ships with the fine thwarts' (*Odyssey* 12.357); they offer a libation of water, since 'they did not have any wine to pour on the sacred burnings' (362). This is their last action before they are vengefully destroyed in a storm.

Drinking Cultures

My focus in this chapter, however, is upon not the meal itself, but its epilogue, the symposium, a phenomenon not found in any developed form in Homer or Hesiod.[4] There was a time when scholars spoke of a 'lyric age' (see p. 56) succeeding the 'epic age', but it now seems that the earliest sympotic poems may have been broadly contemporary with early epic (though, as we have seen, it is unclear exactly how and when those poems were composed), products of the archaic period (seventh–sixth centuries BCE).[5] It is on this early sympotic material that this chapter will focus, glancing at later periods.

During the archaic period, symposia became a central, definitive part of Greek culture. These were not just drinking parties, but fundamental institutions for education, social definition, testing boundaries of acceptability and instituting cultural norms. There were conventions governing the transition from meal to symposium, marking the distinctive importance of this new phase. The tables were removed and the floor swept; guests were sometimes garlanded and anointed; libations (or drink offerings) were poured, the first of which went to Zeus. A *symposiarch* or 'master of the symposium' was appointed to supervise the mixing of the wine. The symposium represented not just drinking, but *civilized* drinking – which was one of the central markers that distinguished Greeks from barbarians, respectful comrades from overweening tyrants and men from women.

At one level, clearly, the symposium offered release from the normal regulations of society. Heavy drinking was permitted: even the sophisticated intellectuals who gathered with Socrates at the symposium described by Plato (fourth century BCE) admit to having overdone the drinking the night before (*Symposium* 176a). Sexually explicit images and performances were also part of the fun. The only women present were flute players or courtesans,[6] whose remit could include, but was not limited to, sexual gratification. Symposia were probably held in the *andron* or men's quarters (it is likely that Greek houses were specifically designed to prevent the women of the family from meeting the guests).[7] In addition, erotic performers could be brought in. Xenophon's *Symposium* (also fourth century) concludes with an erotic revue portraying the relationship between Ariadne and Dionysus (9.2–7). As Xenophon presents it, this exquisite performance progressively blurs the boundary between simulated and real intimacy: 'you could see them imitating people kissing and embracing one another . . . not playing but really kissing each other with their mouths . . . they looked like people who had not been taught to imitate, but were actually being permitted to do what they had long desired to do.' This artfully managed confusion between representation and reality is, apparently, what turns the onlookers on. The scene is narrated through the eyes of the onlookers, whose reactions are described in detail: 'they kept clapping and crying "more" . . . they all looked on aflutter . . . the unmarried swore to marry, while the married jumped on their horses and rode off to their wives, so as to enjoy them.' Symposia were also, certainly, sites of sexual courtship between men and boys, though these relationships are often depicted on pots and represented within poems (see below, on Theognis) as demure and civilized, in contrast with the wild eroticism of the *hetaera* scenes (admittedly, exceptions can easily be found).[8]

The central point, however, is that sympotic pleasure always operates within carefully defined – if rarely articulated – *limits*. A marker of civilized values (and these are precisely what the symposium tests for) is an awareness of just how far you can go. For all that Xenophon's revue teases the viewers, the symposium itself, crucially, does not offer the symposiasts sexual contact; they are only ever onlookers, separated off from the real thing. For that they have to go back to their wives (those who are married, that is). Now Xenophon's symposium, for sure, may have been an exception. There are a vast number of erotic pots surviving from this period showing symposiasts engaging in (often vigorous) sex.[9] Some poems also suggest sexual activities on the part of symposiasts (see below). But how do we interpret this evidence? Does it mean that sex was always on offer at symposia, part of the package of pleasure, as some have suggested?[10] Or are the poems and pictures fantasies, stimulating images that (like Xenophon's revue) tempt the symposiasts with the vision of what *might* be?

Politics of Friendship

It is impossible to recover the social reality of symposia, which was no doubt as richly diverse as that of any modern house, club or dinner party. Certainly, there were wild symposia. In one of Demosthenes' speeches, *Against Conon*, the speaker has been beaten up by some drunken upper-class yobs, members of gangs with names like the 'Erections' and the 'Beggars', always fighting over *hetaerae* (54.14). But the crucial point here is the moral outrage that Demosthenes is cultivating in his audience, which invokes the standard norms of behaviour, norms that the 'Erections' and 'Beggars' flouted (or so Demosthenes wants us to believe). Drinking and sex were expected to be conducted within civilized limits; and while the symposium, as we have seen, promised a form of liberation from the regular conventions of society, the symposiast remained subject to moral codes. It is a curiously mixed message at one level: how can one simultaneously be liberated and constrained? But this ambiguity made for a highly effective tool of social disciplining, for it allowed the question of civilized limits to remain urgent and alive. As we shall see in the following section, symposia were highly visual environments, where behaviour was carefully scrutinized; the elusive line between pleasurable indulgence and boorish excess could manifest itself very suddenly to others.

Similarly problematic was the line between playful abuse and offence. The symposium, writes Plutarch (second century CE) in his *Sympotic Questions*, is characterized by 'quantities of free speech' (707e). An earlier passage in that text preserves a story about Ptolemy Philadelphus, the third-century BCE ruler of Alexandria (see also chapter 8). A certain Timagenes, it is said, spoke of Ptolemy's wife (and sister) Arsinoe, deliberately mispronouncing a line of Euripides: *tende Mousan*, 'this muse', became *tend' emousan*, 'this vomiting woman' (*Sympotic Questions* 634e; see also Athenaeus, *Sophists at Supper* 616c). Risqué jokes at others' expense seem to be, for Plutarch, part of the *pleasure* of conviviality. For in Plutarch's view, commensality was the primary route to friendship among the cultivated classes: 'the table makes friends' (*Sympotic Questions* 612d).

But it was also possible for joking to go too far, for symposia to dissolve into enmity. The same author's *Life of Alexander*, a biography of the Macedonian general Alexander the Great, tells of two manifestations of (what is explicitly labelled) 'free speech' at symposia. Both of them end in death for former friends of the general.[11] In the first, the drunken Clitus celebrates the blessings of those who have died before seeing the present state of affairs (51). Like the soldier cited above, Clitus is wittily adapting a literary precedent (namely *Odyssey* 5.306–12, where Odysseus, clinging to his wind-battered raft, pronounces blessed those who died at Troy); but Alexander is in no mood for forgiveness, and strikes him dead. In the second example, Callisthenes is challenged to provide a rhetorical denunciation of the Macedonians, a task that he undertakes with rather too much vim (53). Callisthenes, according to Aristotle, was (Plutarch reports) 'a capable speaker, but he lacked sense' (54). He is killed in due course – at another symposium, where he refuses to bow down to the king (54). Symposia could make bitter enemies as well as close friends.

As with drinking and sex, so with language. Sympotic culture demanded provocation, play, a glimpse of the limits of acceptability. The best jokes are those with bite. The stakes are higher, and the pleasures keener, when one stands close to the edge; but the closer you stand to the edge, the greater the risk of a fall.

The Literature of the Symposium

The symposium was also, crucially, a context for the performance of literature. What is particularly interesting about Plutarch's presentation of Clitus and Callisthenes is that both doomed symposiasts deliver material that conforms to the sympotic expectations: witty, exuberant and piquant variations on traditional forms. While most symposia undoubtedly passed more peaceably, Plutarch's anecdotes show how tense and energized this literature of relaxation could be.

Plutarch's anecdotes are also evidence for the variety of literary forms within a sympotic context.[12] In the period on which we are focusing, sympotic poetry can be divided broadly into 'lyric' and 'elegiac'.[13] 'Lyric' (the Greeks called it 'melic') is a rather clumsy term, covering poetry sung in a variety of metres, by choruses and by individuals, in a variety of contexts. Its best known early exponents are Alcman of Sparta (seventh century), Alcaeus and Sappho of Lesbos (sixth century), Anacreon of Teos (sixth century; see below), Bacchylides of Ceos (fifth century) and Pindar of Thebes (fifth century). We know less than we would like about the performance contexts of these poets, but insofar as we can deduce from the subject-matter, the principal sympotic poets were Alcman, Alcaeus and (especially) Anacreon. All three composed poetry on love, politics and other sympotic themes (though we also have a major fragment of one of Alcman's choral poems for performance by young girls at a festival). Of the others, Sappho composed hymns and intimate poems (see chapters 11 and 12), and though it might seem at first blush unlikely, there is evidence that they were performed at symposia.[14] Bacchylides and Pindar composed paeans (celebratory hymns) and poems in other metres, but are best known for their epinicians, songs sung for victors in festival competitions on their return.[15]

Despite this diversity, there are certain common features across the range of lyric: the poems are relatively small-scale pieces, narrated in a personal voice identified (at least at the superficial level) with that of the poet or singer(s); and they also in general present themselves as 'occasional' poetry, commemorating or dramatizing a specific, historically and geographically determined event. Lyric poetry associates the poet's voice specifically with a temporal and spatial context and an individual narrator or set of narrators. Lyric poetry is, or at least presents itself as, poetry *in action*, explicitly articulating a creative, mutually constitutive relationship with its context. Lyric expresses the new fascination with interpersonal relationships in the archaic period, a time when the city-state or *polis* was taking on an intensified role in shaping the identity of its inhabitants.

Elegiac poetry is in one sense easier to define. The elegiac couplet is a pair of metrical lines, a single hexameter followed by a single pentameter. In terms of content, however, there is again an impressive variety, covering the Spartan militarist Tyrtaeus (seventh century); the sympotic poets Semonides of Amorgos (probably seventh century; see below), Callinus of Ephesus (probably seventh century) and Anacreon of Teos (sixth century; see below); Mimnermus (sixth century) who wrote of his love for Nanno and of the city of Smyrna; the Athenian law-giver Solon (sixth century); and various composers of commemorative epitaphs, most famously Simonides of Ceos (sixth–fifth centuries). Elegy is a flexible medium, capable of accommodating both longer poems on political themes, for performance at festivals, and shorter poems for performance at symposia.[16] Like lyric, however, the sympotic elegies do consistently evoke a sense of time and place, staging their various scenes against the backdrop of the *polis* in the present. Like lyric, elegiac poetry presents an almost exclusively human world, largely dominated by material realities: love, death, class, politics, war.

Theognis: Aristocracy Reviewed

I want to turn now to consider the elegiac poet Theognis, who composed in the mid-sixth century BCE, in Megara, a prosperous town by the Corinthian isthmus.[17] The text as we have it is a series of discrete poems, mostly brief, and probably only partially the work of Theognis himself. In what follows, however, I am less interested in questions of textual purity, and more interested in the value of the corpus as evidence for a performance culture in archaic symposia.

For despite the apparent disconnectedness of the text, there is a continuous theme discernible throughout the entire text: the poet constructs the pleasures of the symposium – friendship, drinking and sexual encounters with boys – as a refuge from the corruption of Megara, whence true friendship and trustworthiness have disappeared. These reflections are often directed towards a certain Cyrnus (also called Polypaides). Cyrnus is imagined as a love-object, but also (and primarily) the recipient of moral and pragmatic instruction. Greek pederasty, or love between an older man and a boy, was conceived of as both an erotic and an educative relationship.

In addressing Cyrnus, Theognis assumes the position of the author-itative preserver of cultural traditions and established knowledge, as set against the false friends who would mislead him:

> Cyrnus, a noble man always has a firm mind,
>   and endures whether in good fortune or bad;
> but if the god gives a base man livelihood and wealth,
>   the fool cannot hold back his baseness. (319–22)

This is not simply a claim to being a teacher, it is a *performance* of teaching. Wisdom, in archaic Greek culture, was not conceived of as a simply a quality possessed of certain individuals; it needed to be striven for and acknowledged in a public, competitive environment.[18] The symposium provides Theognis (or the singer of his words) with a forum in which to assert his claim to pedagogical authority, at the expense of those 'fools' whom he characterizes by their baseness. In the archaic period, sympotic performance was a central vehicle for preserving and disseminating privileged information about the world.

In its competitive aspect, sympotic performance has something in common with the zero-sum game of Homeric warfare (discussed in chapter 3): in both cases, the subject establishes authority by defeat-ing others, while the community watches on. As with warfare, more-over, that authority is tied to aspects of wider social identity. The authoritative speaker lays claim to a higher social status: the Greek words for 'noble' and 'base' (like the English terms I have chosen to translate them) indicate not just moral, but also social pre-eminence (as is clear from the reference to the base man's wealth, which is acquired rather than inherited). Importantly, however, the member-ship of the group he attacks is left unclear. It is up to the audience to work out which members of society are the 'base', whether any of that group are present at the symposium in question. And, indeed, whether even that description applies to themselves; for the scrutiniz-ing gaze of the symposium can, and should, be turned back on its owner as well.

Decline and Fall

The passage discussed above also implicitly marks historical change. Bad men are not just a fact of life, but also a symptom of the decad-ence of contemporary society. Theognis presents Homeric characters as paradigms of constancy: Odysseus and Penelope, most explicitly

(1123–8). This, of course, implies a highly selective reading of Homer: imagining Odysseus as unwaveringly constant to his home and family involves overlooking, among other things, the year he spent in bed with Circe, described in book 10 of the *Odyssey*. For our poet, however, the Homeric texts showcase a series of examples of a heroic age characterized by established, just, proper order. The world is now inverted:

> They have deposed the pilot,
>   the noble one, who was standing guarded with expertise.
> They seize possessions by force, and order is destroyed.
>   There is no longer an equitable division of possessions,
>   in the common interest,
> but the carriers of merchandise rule, and base people
>   are above the lofty. (675–9)

The extension of the (aristocratic) privilege of political rule to the merchant classes is presented as the root cause of the decline. With this subversion of the proper hierarchy comes a corruption of moral values. Friends now betray each other (cf. 575; 812; 861). 'Trust, a great goddess, has gone', we hear; 'self-control has gone from men, the graces have left the earth' (1137–8) – a passage that clearly invokes Hesiod's account of the grim final phase of the Iron age ('Reverence and Retribution will leave mankind', *Works and Days* 199–200). The past, on the other hand, was a golden age.[19] The Theognidean conception of friendship is deeply political: the desire for a 'trustworthy friend' is a nostalgic yearning for aristocratic community of the past, unsullied by interlopers from the lower classes.[20] The symposium serves as a microcosm of the city as a whole; the drive to exclude interlopers from the sympotic community also serves to authorize the aristocracy as the true leaders of the community.[21]

Reading Deceit

For Theognis, the present is characterized not just by moral decadence, but specifically by deception. We saw in the previous chapter (see p. 48) that deceit is particularly problematic for a culture of display and self-presentation; for Theognis, likewise, 'base profiteering' is one of the evils that has 'thrown us from our many luxuries to ruin' (835–6). The word for 'profiteering', *kerdos*, implies both trade – the source of the wealth of the merchant class – and trickery. It is precisely the faculty that, according to Homer's Athena, the tricky goddess shares with Odysseus (*Odyssey* 13.297). From Theognis' perspective, the merchant classes are deceptive not simply because they are out for gain, but also because their social identity is based on an illusion: they claim to be what they are not, namely aristocrats. This artful self-presentation leads to a crisis in the sympotic community: how can we tell who is a true aristocrat and who not? How can we tell what another's intentions are? In one of his most memorable (and repeated)[22] metaphors, Theognis links the false friend with counterfeit currency:

> There is nothing more difficult than knowing a counterfeit man,
> Cyrnus, and nothing more worth the enterprise.
> The delusion of counterfeit gold and silver is bearable,
> Cyrnus, and it is easy enough for a wise man to uncover;
> but if the mind of a friend in his chest deceives,
> being false, and he has a cheating heart in his breast,
> this the god made the most counterfeit for men,
> this the most troublesome of all to ascertain. (117–24)

The inability to probe inside the mind of another is a recurrent anxiety in sympotic literature. In one of the Athenian drinking songs (or *skolia*), luckily preserved in a late source, the poet expresses a similar wish that 'it were possible to know what sort each man is by piercing his chest, and then examining his mind, and then closing him again' (Athenaeus, *Sophists at Supper* 694d–e).[23] The symposium requires an insistent scrutiny of appearances for signs of a mismatch between external display and internal identity; a constant process of verification, that is, that the symposiast is a true comrade, a bona fide member of the aristocratic community.

The monetary imagery in the passage just quoted is also significant. Firstly, the reference to gold invokes the idea of the golden age (see above), from which we have now passed; the contemporary age is, by contrast, a 'counterfeit' age. Secondly, money raises profound questions about knowledge and value. Coined money was a recent invention (very late seventh century), which had a huge impact upon Greek thought.[24] If it is coinage to which he refers (rather than bullion: there is some debate), then Theognis is making a very interesting move. As distinct from bullion, coinage opens up a gap between intrinsic worth and exchange value. The value of a coin in the marketplace, that is to say, is different from (and usually greater than) the worth of the metals that make it. Money is a system of *signs*: the coin (a 'signifier', to use the vocabulary of structuralism) stands as a substitute for bullion (the 'signified'). The introduction of money into the Megarian economy (if, to repeat, it is indeed money that we are talking of) has introduced a radical new principle of substitution, of signification, of representation, that is open to manipulation by counterfeiters. Money is bad not just because it is associated with the merchant class, but also because it introduces the possibility of a mismatch between appearance and reality, between representation and truth.

Against all the odds, there is a close parallel between Theognis' presentation of sixth-century BCE Megara and Balzac's vision of nineteenth-century CE Paris, as Christopher Prendergast inteprets it:

> The argument . . . is that material changes in the post-Revolutionary economic and social formation (the frenetic pursuit of private interests, the increasing degree of social mobility around the phenomenon of *arrivisme*, the displacement of aristocratic rule by the combined forces of 'le talent, l'argent et la puissance') engender a corresponding problem of social semiotic, an attenuation, even an obliteration of the traditional markers of class difference.[25]

And just as Balzac's obsessional concern with counterfeit currency underlines his analysis of Paris as a city of illusions, so Theognis' anxiety over the introduction of money serves to represent the new, post-epic context of the Greek city as a place of shady transactions, concealed self-interests and underhand subversions. The symposium, as we have seen, is, for Theognis, the central institution for exploring the relationship between worth and appearance, between true and false friendship.

Ordering Men

As we have seen, one of the central aims of the symposium is educative: it is where knowledge is institutionalized, culturally sanctioned and shared among the community. Theognis' addressee, Cyrnus, is constructed as a suitable target for the poet's authoritative knowledge; as, by implication, are we, the readers. The poet's task in the symposium is to *order knowledge*; to provide his listeners with a guide to the world, but also to seek to define (through shared knowledge and shared values) the identity of the aristocratic community.

This strategy of poetic self-authorization has wider implications for the sympotic community, bearing particularly upon gender relations. We discussed above the question of sex at symposia, concluding that it is risky to assume that the normative expectation of these events was of unlicensed, orgiastic sexual practice, as depictions on pots might suggest (at first sight at least). But that does not mean that the *hetaerae* present at the symposium played a negligible role. As the only women present, they assumed the role of representatives of their sex, and their sexual availability – to the male gaze, fantasy and, no doubt, sometimes touch – played a crucial role in imagining gender hierarchies within the symposium, and by extension within the city as a whole.

The role of women within Greek literature will be discussed more comprehensively in chapter 11, but gender dynamics are too central a component of the symposium to ignore in this context. One of the central functions of sympotic poetry, I suggest in what follows, is to consolidate – in a playful and slippery way, certainly – the subordinate position of women. Theognis' poetry, we saw in the previous section, attempts to marginalize and control the merchant classes, usurping aristocratic privilege; analogously, erotic poetry attempts to manage the threat posed by women to male domination within the sphere of sexuality and the household.

Ordering Through Abuse

I want to turn first of all to consider briefly a well-known poem by Semonides of Amorgos (seventh century), known to us as fragment 7.[26] This poem, written in iambics (a metre appropriate to abuse), presents a list of different types of women, each indexed to a particular animal. As one commentator has argued, it was probably composed for a symposium; in its mix of sophistication and risqué material, it stands comparison with the sexually explicit sympotic pottery we discussed earlier.[27] Yet it also has affinities with a different genre, namely catalogue poetry. The 'catalogue of ships' in book 2 of Homer's *Iliad* and Hesiod's *Catalogue of Women* (see chapter 3) perform the important functions of inscribing territorial and genealogical data into the cultural memory-bank, of mapping Greece in terms of the interrelations between its various parts. Semonides 7 borrows the prestige and power of this genre, but playfully remodels it so as to map, semi-comically, the varieties of womanhood.

The poem is structured precisely as a list:

> From the start, the god created the mind of woman
> In diverse ways. One out of a hairy sow...
> Another out of a criminal vixen...
> Another from a bitch... [and so on] (1–2, 7, 12)

Like epic catalogues, this poem derives its rhetorical force from its length (it is the longest non-epic archaic poem), from the number of its constituent elements and particularly from the insistently repetitious formulae that introduce each woman-type. Semonides presents his poem as a comprehensive, exhaustive anatomy of womankind, a powerful performance of self-arrogated authority. This authority underlines the centrally pedagogical role the poem assumes within the symposium. Not only does Semonides educate young men in the art of understanding women, but also (and more pungently) he teaches them to conceive of women as *objects of knowledge*, capable of being intellectually mastered by careful taxonomy.

This strategy of domination through knowledge is rendered all the more necessary because of the (paradoxically) weak position in which men find themselves, dependent as they are upon women. The necessity of cohabitation is 'the greatest evil' that Zeus imposed on men, the poem concludes (115). This is established folk wisdom (deriving ultimately from Hesiod, *Theogony* 603–12), a bite of comforting certainty to bind together the male audience in common sympathy; jokey perhaps, but (like all jokes about the way of the world) still culturally authoritative for that. The poem's ironic mournfulness is no less an education than its taxonomy of woman: both seek to empower the symposiast by creating an aloof, magisterial perspective upon women.

The Order of Desire

I want to turn now to Anacreon of Teos, the sixth-century writer of elegies and lyric poems. As with Theognis, we are bedevilled by questions of authorship here, only even more intensely. The anacreontic form, with its mellow reflectiveness and emphasis upon genial pleasures, was easily imitated; the corpus transmitted under his name contains poems written as late as the Byzantine period. In the following discussion, questions of precise authorship do not concern me (it is sympotic culture, not artistic individuality, that we are exploring), but I shall confine myself to those poems widely accepted to be early; these are few and fragmentary, but (as we shall see) eloquent.[28]

The eroticism presented by Anacreon's narrator is often pederastic (or boy-loving), but – I shall argue – he treats boys and women in tellingly different ways. Let us take, for example, fragment 359:

> Cleobulus is the one I love
> Cleobulus the one I'm mad for
> Cleobulus the one I gaze upon.

The threefold repetition of the boy's name at the beginning of each line (anaphora, in stylistic terms) emphasizes the grip the boy has on the narrator. The syntax and poetic form lend a mesmerizing power to this name. But the narrator is also attempting to control the boy, or his passion for him. Three is a mystic number. The magical goddess Hecate, for example, has three aspects, and she requires three invocations. The dead are called upon three times.[29] Repetition, moreover, is a feature of magic.[30] Is the poet attempting to master the boy, and his passion, through magical formulae? It might even be claimed that the invocation (if such it is) actually works. In the course of these three lines, the poet passes from maddened desire to gazing, a markedly more active, self-possessed state (although still obsessed: the rare Greek word used for 'gaze' apparently suggests a trance-like state).

Other pederastic poems also present the narrator's submission to the boy. In poem 357, a conventional prayer formula is adopted to invoke Dionysus (god of wine, hence of the symposium): the god is entreated to become the 'counsellor' (10) of Cleobulus, to persuade him to 'accept' (11) his love. In this poem, the boy is imaged as a haughty king; even the god Dionysus can only act as an intercessor. Fragment 360 addresses a 'boy with the look of a maiden' (1), chiding him that 'you do not heed me, unaware that you hold the reins to my soul' (2–4). Images of horse-riding have powerful connotations of control and mastery.

Very different, then, is the horse-riding imagery in fragment 417, which describes a female love-object:

> Thracian filly, why do you look me askance
> and persistently flee me, thinking me lacking in wisdom?
> Be sure, I could put the bit on you well,
> and holding the reins turn you around the limits of the course.
> But as it is, you graze in meadows and play, skipping lightly;
> for you lack any clever rider, experienced on horseback.

The 'Thracian filly' is probably to be imagined as a courtesan in attendance at the symposium; Thrace (roughly modern Bulgaria) supplied many a slave and courtesan to the Greek world to the south. Strikingly, however, the imagery applied to her suggests a virgin. Greek maidens – such as Homer's Nausicaa (*Odyssey* 6.109 and 228) and Apollonius' Medea (*Argonautica* 3.4) – were routinely described as 'untamed', as though marriage represented the breaking-in of a wild animal. The fantasized transition from the carefree frolicking of the filly to domestication strongly suggests the metaphorical subjugation of the girl's independent spirit that coincides with defloration. Yet as we have seen, the poem probably describes a *hetaera*. The effect of the adoption of this language so strongly suggestive of defloration is to generalize the imagery of heterosexual union as domination and conquest. The *hetaera*'s resistance to the poet's mastery is presented as bestial and uncivilized, in need of domination. Moreover, the gender hierarchy is substantiated by reference to knowledge: the poet lays claim to 'wisdom', 'cleverness' and 'experience'. It is because he *know*s – because, that is, of his poetic authority – that Anacreon vaunts his superiority over the female.

Yet the mastery is, as readers will have noticed, anything but complete. The Thracian filly *rejects* Anacreon. Similarly, in fragment 358 a girl from Lesbos (for reasons we shall discuss in chapter 12) turns her back on him. The Anacreontic *persona* is a loser, incapable of dominating the *hetaera* he desires (just as he is crushed by love for boys). Does this not undermine the gender hierarchy I have proposed? Does Anacreontic irony not turn out to ridicule the aggrandizing pretensions of the would-be macho man? From one perspective, yes. But we need to be careful: irony does not rule out power-play. As with Semonides, Anacreon's cultivated irony offers the symposiasts a culturally authoritative perspective upon women, resting upon a pleasurable paradox: women require control, but do not accept it. Irony is another means of knowing – and hence of objectifying – women.

Let us conclude this section by drawing together the primary contrasts between Anacreon's approach to pederasty and to 'heterosexual' desire. In the pederastic poems, the poet attempts to manage his own domination by the boy's charms. Eros, the god of love, is for Anacreon a violent, aggressive force. In a series of two-line fragments, plausibly dealing with the poet's relationship with boys, Eros is notably violent: he engages him in a boxing-match (396); his dice are 'maniacal and surging' (398); he hits the poet with a hammer, like a smith (413). Pederastic desire *subdues* the poet: it batters and wrecks him (albeit that this process of destruction is described in the form of witty, elegant poems that imply anything but emotional desperation). In the 'heterosexual' poems, however, it is the poet who proclaims control. Whereas the boy in 360 holds the reins to the poet's heart, in 417 the poet wants to rein in the Thracian filly.

Similarly, the manner in which Eros strikes is significantly gendered. In (what we can tentatively identify as) pederastic contexts, as we saw above, Eros strikes with a hammer or a fist. In a heterosexual context, however, the best he can muster is a ball (358) – presumably chosen because of its associations as a girls' plaything (*Odyssey* 6.100).[31] It is as though the degree of virility behind Eros' blow is dictated by the degree of virility of the love-object. Love for boys is powerful; for *hetaerae*, merely playful. Boys dominate; women are there to be dominated.

The crucial difference between boys and *hetaerae* is that the former are only temporarily in the position of love-objects; in time, they will be the masterful subjects of the symposium. Women, on the other hand, are determined by their gender always to be excluded from the privileged position of subject: they are ever objects of knowledge, objects of poetic desire, objects of song (even if the poet ironically concedes these women the power to resist and mock). Their status as objects also, of course, serves the reciprocal purpose of empowering the male symposiasts.

Sympotic Knowledge, Sympotic Identity

I have argued that the symposium is principally a forum for educating and empowering the elite, male subject, through scrutiny, testing and play. In symposia, young men learn how to position themselves against groups of 'others' – lower classes and women, principally – by becoming intellectual masters, by learning how to speak authoritatively, by cultivating the civilized values of irony and wit.

The symposium remained central to Greek literary production throughout antiquity.[32] Plato (see chapter 12) and Xenophon (discussed briefly above) both wrote texts called *The Symposium*, featuring the intellectual and ironist par excellence, Socrates. In the new circumstances of the democratic city (see chapter 5), the symposium could (though did not always) serve as an emblem of the elitism that was so inimical to democracy. In Plato's text, Pausanias (the lover of the host, Agathon) distinguishes between two forms of desire: 'vulgar' (heterosexual) and 'heavenly' (pederastic; 180d). These words, in addition to providing a pederastic manifesto (they were referred to by Oscar Wilde at his trial), clearly privilege the elite over the vulgar, a hierarchy that none of the participants at this exclusively pederastic gathering challenges.[33] This symposium, at any rate, was a highly select gathering, both intellectually and socially.

In third-century Alexandria, Callimachus used a symposium as the dramatic setting for book 2 of his *Aetia*, or 'causes' (see chapter 8). The *Aetia* is a display of prodigiously erudite learning; and, moreover, a polemical text, extolling (in a famous prologue) the poet's intellectual superiority over the uncultivated, a group he identifies as 'Telchines' (fragment 1). The symposium, with its established techniques for scrutinizing guests, is an important setting for this poem of intellectual and social distinction. Callimachus and his Ician friend, we are told, gaze on in horror at the 'Thracian-style' drinking around them, preferring themselves to drink in moderation and to converse (fragment 178.11–12, 16). The poet's more cultivated approach to the symposium is a clear marker of the superiority he claims for his poetry as a whole.

By the second century CE (see chapter 9), the symposium was firmly established as one of the definitive markers of Greek identity. We have already in this chapter briefly discussed Plutarch's mammoth *Sympotic Questions*, a collection of intellectual discussions pursued by an all-star cast. Even more massive is Athenaeus' *Sophists at Supper*, fifteen books worth of table-talk (some of which survives only in epitome) set at the house of Larensis, a wealthy Roman.[34] For Larensis, this is an opportunity to reinforce his credentials as a cultivated grandee; for the Greek sophists present, it is an opportunity to indulge not only in free food, but also in vicious bickering. Athenaeus does not exactly satirize his sophists (as, for example, the satirist Lucian does in his own *Symposium*),[35] but certainly their cantankerous bitchiness stands in strong contrast with the serenity of Platonic, Xenophontic and Plutarchan symposia. Excessive or uncivilized behaviour, at any stage of Greek antiquity, was enough to compromise the identity of the symposiast.

5

Theatre

Imperial Visions: Culture and Power in Fifth-century Athens

We turn now to fifth-century Athens, a radically different context for literary production.[1] Athens is thought of today as the first democracy, but although it offered its citizens an extraordinarily high degree of partipication in political decision-making, its wealth and success were founded upon principles that were far from democratic, in the modern sense. Athens was largely dependent upon a massive body of slaves (see also chapter 13), often working in horrific environments, such as the notorious silver mines at Laurion. In addition, women were denied any political voice and were – so, at least, our sources tell us – largely segregated from public space (chapter 11).

Athens was also engaged in foreign imperialism for much of the fifth century BCE, the head of a powerful empire (often called the 'Delian League') encompassing the Aegean islands we now call the Cyclades. Though taxation crippled the subject-states, the city policed this empire with uncompromising fierceness: when, for example, the island of Melos refused to join their struggle against the Spartans, the Athenians in 415 BCE butchered the men and enslaved the women and children. Thucydides, the late fifth-century Athenian historian, prefaces his account of this event with a dialogue between Athenian representatives and the Melian council (5.84–114), in which the Melians argue uprightly for principles of fairness and justice, while the Athenians simply assert the need for their powerful dominance to be acknowledged by all. Though an Athenian (albeit one exiled for incompetent generalship), Thucydides is far from uncritical of Athens's imperialist activities, even on occasion allowing speakers to refer to the league as a 'tyranny' (2.8.4; 2.63.2). This was a powerful accusation: tyranny was, in Athenian eyes, ideologically polarized to democracy.

Perhaps the most symbolically meaningful individual action was the relocation of the treasury of the League from Delos to the Acropolis of Athens, under the stewardship of the most famous of Athenian democratic leaders, Pericles. The new treasury was a specially built temple to Athena Parthenos ('the virgin'), begun in 447 and completed in 432. Throughout its history, this temple – better known as the Parthenon – has been subject to both praise and controversy.[2] This enormous, splendid building, with its subtle architectural *trompe l'oeil* and its magnificent statuary (designed by Phidias, the leading artist of the day), would have inspired even more awe when structurally and artistically intact, fulsomely decorated and unshielded by smog. But for the ambassadors of the Delian League, arriving at Piraeus to deliver their heavy tributes before the Athenian people, this symbol of Athenian imperial appropriation would no doubt have inspired different sentiments.

Culture and power were part of the same package in Athens.[3] The same citizens voted for massive expenditure on prestige building projects and on the suppression of unruly subjects: both expressed the dominance of the Athenian people over others, whether Greek or barbarian. In Thucydides' account of his speech for those who died in the war with Sparta, Pericles presents Athens as 'an education for Greece' (2.41.1): in his view (at least as the historian presents it), Athens was vying to become a model of Greek culture, even as it was seeking to establish political hegemony.

Theatre and State Ideology

But it was the theatre that represented (and for many still represents today) the most vibrant symbol of fifth-century Athenian culture.[4] The origins of tragedy and comedy were debated even in antiquity, and are no doubt beyond recall (Thespis, the first 'thespian', is a shadowy figure); what is certain is that Athens took the theatre (a feature of the cultural life of many Greek city-states) and made it its own, enhancing the scale and scope of the event.

Athens had three annual dramatic festivals: the Lenaia (sacred to Dionysus Lenaios), the rural Dionysia, and the Great or City Dionysia.[5] The last is the best-known of these festivals, and the best attested (and I concentrate upon this for now). Huge numbers gathered in the theatre of Dionysus on the slopes of the Acropolis, the sacred and political heart of the city. A conservative estimate for numbers would be 14,000; even that would make for one of the largest gatherings seen in the Greek world. Though some foreigners were certainly present, the question of the presence of women is still open.[6] At any rate, the vast majority would have been citizens of Athens (which is to say, adult males born of free, Athenian parents), probably seated in their 'tribes' (the institutional units into which the city was divided). From about 420 BCE, citizens were paid from public funds for attending.

The festival lasted for five or six days. There were competitions in choral performance of song in the 'dithyrambic' metre (of which very little survives today), tragedy and comedy. Tragic poets produced a 'trilogy' of three tragedies followed by a lighter 'satyr' play (see p. 83 below). State sponsorship saturated the event.[7] Expensive choruses were publicly allocated, and paid for by citizens who owned more than three talents (some 1 per cent of the population); this 'liturgy' served the democratic end of taxation, but also served as a vehicle for self-promotion and display among the elite.[8] The performances themselves, meanwhile, were framed by rituals that reminded Athenians (and the world) of the real context in which the dramatic events were to be situated: pig sacrifices by the generals, the presentation of crowns to the 'best citizens', awards to the orphans of dead war heroes, and – significantly – the parade of tribute submitted by members of the Delian League. Just as much as the Parthenon building, steepling above the audience members, the dramatic performances embodied and paraded the cultural and (simultaneously) the imperial power of democratic Athens.

But Athenian drama was not just about the public face of the city. Tragedy in particular also probed the darker spaces behind the façade, the invisible, private recesses of the house and the human mind. The dramatic action would unfurl (probably) in the circular space of the *orkhestra*, or dancing place, partially enveloped by the horseshoe of seated audience members; at the back of it, though, lay the *skene*, the set building that often represented the house.[9] In the centre of the set building stood the door, the point of transition between private and public, and the limit of the viewers' visual field. The Greek theatre exactly inverts the spatial relations of the modern theatre, which is usually imagined as representing an interior (hence the stage directions 'enter' and 'exit', which would have had the opposite significance in the ancient world). The public world represented by the tragic theatre was ever shadowed by the dark and unknowable private world behind it.

Past and Present

Athenian drama, and particularly tragedy, repeatedly looks back – albeit obliquely – to Homer, the supposed founder of the Greek poetic tradition. In folding the mythical past into the centre of the modern city, Athenian democracy asserted its status as the true guardian of Greek culture, the inheritor of the mantle of Homeric culture. But as much as it paraded continuity with the past, it also articulated difference. The French classicist Jean-Pierre Vernant famously refers to the historical 'moment' of tragedy as an equipoise between two phases:[10] fifth-century Athens was Janus-faced, simultaneously looking back to the rich legacy of the past, and forwards, to new, democratic forms of social organization unimagined by, and to an extent antithetical to, Homeric society. The world described in the Homeric poems turns, as we saw in chapter 3, around a limited group of individuals who exclusively possess special status and powers. Athenian democracy, on the other hand, self-consciously emphasizes the power of the collective to transcend the individual. The powerful creativity that characterized the fifth century derived, in large measure, from Athens's delicate oscillation between appropriation and rejection of the Homeric legacy.

As an institution, tragedy emitted a powerful signal to the other Greek cities (some of which had their own theatres, albeit smaller and less prestigious), that Athens was the primary claimant to the Homeric legacy. But there was also a sense in which the Homeric world, while culturally prestigious, represented a radically different set of values that could not be accommodated in democratic Athens. Homer had described a society of individuals vying for individual status in the eyes of their peers and resonance on the lips of descendants. Honour (*time*) and glory (*kleos*) were, as we have seen, keyed to exceptional performance, performance that (in the case of the sulking Achilles or the travelling Odysseus) disaggregates the subject from his or her community. That community does, of course, matter to Homer: the impending destruction of Troy in the *Iliad* and Odysseus' loss of his companions in the *Odyssey* are represented as calamities. It is a matter of readjustment and new emphasis, not an absolute break with the past.

With the rising importance of citizenship and collective enfranchisement in the centuries after the Homeric texts emerges the ideal of the transcendent importance of the community: the individual has status only insofar as she or he partakes of the collective. Aristotle's well-known phrase encapsulates the new ideology of the post-Homeric world: a human being, he claims, is a 'political animal', which is to say, an animal of the *polis* (or city-state); to be without a *polis* is to be greater or lesser than a human, a god or a beast (*Politics* 1253a). Athenian democracy, though far from unique in extolling the value of the collective, represented perhaps the most extreme application of the principle.

The contrast between Homeric and later, 'collectivist' models can be seen in a number of fields across, to varying degrees, the whole of Greece. In politics, as we have seen, the emergence of the concept of citizenship entailed the conceptualization of a city as a space unified by ideology as well as geography. In law, the mass jury-trial replaced (at least in Athens) the arbitrary judgement of the potentate. In warfare, the Homeric paradigm of single combat between aristocrats was supplanted by the new *phalanx* (or 'spider'), a unit of heavy-armed 'hoplite' soldiers, the efficacy of which depended upon cooperative values. Whereas Homeric poems commemorate the glory (*kleos*) of an individual, Athenian 'funeral speeches' (for those who died in war) commemorate the glory of the *city*.[11] And in the intellectual sphere, the older model of the inspired singer as the exclusive possessor of (divinely, politically and culturally) sanctioned authority, as the 'master of truth' (in Marcel Detienne's phrase),[12] was gradually replaced by a more adversarial system prizing competition and debate.[13]

Chorus and Agent

The tension between individual and community is fundamental to tragedy; it is built into its very structure. In its earliest incarnation, we are told, the genre represented interaction between a single actor and the chorus; a second actor was added by Aeschylus, a third by Sophocles. Even as the number of actors grows, however, tragedies remain centrally focused upon the dynamic of incorporation and exclusion. Chorus members are never named in tragedy: they represent the faceless anonymity of the collective, offsetting the intractable eccentricity of the named individual characters. But it is not the case that the collective is dogmatically valued over the individual. While named characters may be too hasty in action, choruses tend to be vacillatory and weak; while the former may express overstrong opinions, the latter frequently have recourse to inherited aphorisms and folk-wisdom; and while the former are often exciting and glamorous, the latter usually belong to culturally undervalued groups (women, slaves, old men, foreigners).[14]

In Aeschylus' *Agamemnon*, the first play in his Oresteian trilogy (the only trilogy that survives), the chorus consists of old men too frail to have left with Agamemnon to support the assault on Troy. They do, for sure, have a certain dramatic authority, providing responses to events and perhaps cues to the audience – a device sometimes called 'interpassivity'.[15] For example, when Clytaemnestra leads her husband into the house, intending to kill him (partly in retribution for his sacrifice of their daughter, Iphigenia; partly out of a desire to share power with her lover, Aegisthus), the chorus sings a lengthy ode beginning 'Why does this fear continually hover over my visionary heart?' (975–7). Such sentiments, expressed in reaction to the dramatic action, serve as authoritative guides to the audience. The chorus's reactions can be treated ironically too: witness its blithe optimism on the matter of Oedipus' paternity at Sophocles' *Oedipus the King*, 1086–1109, introduced with the misguided words: 'If I am a prophet, and intellectually astute, . . .'.

On some occasions, the chorus's reactions invoke the ideological norms of the Athenian democratic collective. At the end of the *Agamemnon*, the chorus responds as follows to the arrogant vaunting of Aegisthus, the new king:

> Aegisthus, I do not praise you for your insulting behaviour
>   in the midst of woes.
> You say you deliberately killed this man,
> that you alone plotted this pitiable murder.
> Your head, I think, will not escape curses justly hurled upon it
> by the people, know it well, curses that will end in your stoning.
>   (1612–16)

Not only is Aegisthus condemned, but the terms used to do so actively guide the audience towards an adverse judgement: his behaviour is 'insulting' (in the Greek, he is said to practise *hubris*), the murder of Agamemnon was 'pitiable' (insinuating that the proper response is pity) and he will be condemned by 'curses justly hurled upon it by the people'. The last sentence is phrased with unusual assertiveness for a chorus: 'I think . . . know it well.' To this extent, then, the model of interpassivity works well: the chorus supplies affective and moralistic responses to a mass audience. But the chorus does more than simply supply an unreflective audience with ready-made reactions. Earlier in the play, for example, in the scene in which Cassandra prophesies the gloomy events unfurling (in animated and metrically complex verse forms), the chorus's reaction is uncomprehending and inadequate – it is, ironically, incapable of seeing the horror that is approaching (1072–330). In this context, the audience inevitably knows and understands more than the chorus. Their response is guided not by the chorus, but by their awareness that they know more than it does.

Although tragedy often stages the clash between communities and individuals who are overpowerful or difficult to assimilate, the clash is unresolved. It does not simply extol the virtues of the community over those of the individual; rather, it plays out the tensions between a weak, manipulable mass and dynamic but intractable individuals. From this perspective, tragedy is fundamentally devoted to exploring the city of Athens and its people.[16]

Athens and the Other

Although few Athenians appear in Homer, there were certainly prestigious mythical Athenians.[17] Notably, Theseus, the hero, king and (in some versions) founder of democracy, offered opportunities. Intriguingly, though, these opportunities are largely passed over in surviving texts: only Euripides' *Suppliants* makes him a central figure (though he does also appear in Sophocles' *Oedipus at Colonus* and Euripides' *Hippolytus*), integrating democratic ideology into his royal persona: 'I turned the people to monarchy, setting them free and giving them an equal vote' (352–3). In general, Athenian dramatists prefer to explore the status and values of the city at arm's length, distancing their subject-matter from the here-and-now. Apart from Aeschylus' *Persians*, the earliest extant Greek drama, all surviving tragedies are set in the mythical past.

And tragedians generally steer clear of Athens as the setting for their plays – though again, with the qualification that we only have a tiny proportion of the total number of tragedies (Euripides' now-lost *Erechtheus*, for example, was set in Athens). So far as we can judge, in general Athens is in tragedy a space to which exiles (like Medea and Oedipus) flee, or from which others arrive (like Creousa and Xuthus in Euripides' *Ion*). Some tragedies are set in the bordering regions, such as Colonus and Eleusis; but the city itself is the setting for, among extant tragedies, only Aeschylus' *Eumenides* (where the action takes place on the Areopagus hill, and becomes a rationalization of the Athenian homicide court there).

Why this avoidance of Athenian subject-matter? One explanation would point to Herodotus' report of Phrynichus' play *The Capture of Miletus*, describing a recent disaster: 'The audience burst into tears, then fined him 1,000 drachmas for reminding them of matters close to home' (6.21.2). Case law might well have warned other poets away from topics that were similarly 'close to home'. But the whole phenomenon of tragic 'distancing' is not just a case of necessity turned to virtue. Tragedy inherently devotes itself to 'otherness', to experimentation with the unfamiliar, the 'far from home'.

To explain this phenomenon, we might look to the figure of Dionysus, the god to whom the dramatic festival was dedicated. Dionysus was a complex god, whose aspects include presidency over wine, ecstatic dancing (especially for women), mystic initiation and transvestism.[18] Like other aspects of Dionysiac cult, tragedy encourages multiple role-playing and self-detachment: the wearer of the theatrical mask is at once both the character and the actor.[19] Analogously, the theatrical show permits the city of Athens to adopt multiple roles, to look upon itself as it were from without. Like drunkenness, ecstasy and (as Judith Butler has argued)[20] transvestism, Dionysiac tragedy offers a perceptual dislocation and defamiliarization of the world as it is known. When Pentheus, in Euripides' *Bacchae*, falls under Dionysus' spell, he emerges (dressed as a woman) with the words 'I seem to see two suns, and two cities of Thebes' (918–19). The king's double vision of his city encapsulates the Dionysiac effect that we see at work in a wide range of tragedies.

Addressing Athens: Praise and Provocation

How does this process work for Athenians? Let us take an example from a well-known tragedy.[21] Euripides' *Medea* is set in Corinth, to where Jason and Medea have relocated in the aftermath of the expedition for the Golden Fleece. Medea has now been disowned by her husband, who wishes to marry Glauce, the daughter of Creon, the king of Corinth; and in the course of the play, Creon exiles her out of fear for her revenge. Corinth, then, is not only a non-Athenian place, but also a society that permits acts of arbitrary tyranny and lawlessness. Medea repeatedly charges Jason with broken oaths and betrayed trust. In one particularly resonant episode, Medea beseeches the Athenian king Aegeus, who happens to be passing through, for sanctuary, pleading her scandalous treatment. Aegeus' agreement conforms to a deeply rooted ideological projection of Athens as a city of refuge from tyrannical persecution. The children of Heracles, notably, were rescued by the Athenians from Eurystheus, as Euripides' tragedy *The Children of Heracles* relates. The orator Lysias, in his public speech in praise of those who died protecting the city, makes much capital out of this myth of sanctuary: the Athenians 'chose such great danger on their behalf, pitying the ill-treated and despising the abusers, seeking to halt the latter and thinking to succour the former' (2.14).

So the subsequent choral ode in praise of Athens seems to contrast the divinely favoured liberty of the one city with the oppressive tyranny of the other:

> Descendants of Erechtheus, blessed from ancient times,
> offspring of the blessed gods,
> from a holy place unravaged, feeding on
> the most renowned wisdom, always travelling
> in luxury through the most brilliant aether, where they say
> that once the nine Muses from Pieria
> gave birth to blonde Harmony. (824–32)

The allusion to the story of Erechtheus, the first Athenian king,[22] combined with the reference to the city's 'ancient' blessings, its resistance to foreign invasion, and its ethereal intellectual achievements, place this first stanza of the choral ode squarely within the tradition of propagandistic encomium. But the third stanza changes tack (underlining this with a change of metre):

> So how will this city of holy rivers,
> or this escort-giving
> land of friends,
> receive you, the child-killer,
> who cannot dwell in holiness with others? (846–50)

The contract to which Aegeus is party does not simply offer sanctuary to a victim; it also commits him (unaware though he is as yet) to accommodating an unholy infanticide. Medea's escape to Athens, projected at the end of the play, is a disturbing possibility. And yet it is not inappropriate. Athens, as this ode makes clear, is the city of 'wisdom', or 'cleverness' (in Greek, *sophia*; another reference at line 843, not cited above). The word *sophos* is associated repeatedly throughout the play with Medea, suggesting both her facility with drugs and her artful manipulation of Jason and Creon (303–5, 320, 385, 409, 485, 539, 675). Medea too is an offspring of the gods, a granddaughter of Helios, the sun. And just as Athens is militarily strong ('unravaged') so Medea too repeatedly constructs Jason as an 'enemy' who is not to be allowed to 'worst' her: 'let no one think me paltry and weak, nor inactive, but of a different kind, grievous to my enemies and kind to my friends' (807–9).[23]

But Medea is not the only figure in this play who worryingly reflects Athens's self-projection. Jason's speech justifying his treatment of Medea (522–75) employs a series of tricks associated with sophists in contemporary Athens. Sophists were itinerant intellectuals who taught a variety of skills, from (what we would now call) philosophy to linguistics to cosmology; but it was with the artful manipulation of language, with rhetoric, that they were particularly closely related (see chapter 6). In the *Medea*, Jason introduces his speech as an example of fine speaking: 'This situation calls, it seems, for no poor speech' (522). The chorus responds to it in like manner: 'Jason, you have ornamented your speech well' (576). And most readers agree that his arguments are specious in the extreme:[24] it was not Medea who aided him in Colchis, he claims, but Aphrodite (that is, the love she felt for him); he has given her enough benefits by bringing her from a barbarian land to Greece, where her cleverness is appreciated; she should be grateful, as his remarriage will benefit their sons; it is her jealousy that is at fault, obsessed as she is (like most women) with sex.[25] Jason's weak arguments, decked out with strong-seeming sophistry, exhale the unmistakable air of the intellectual scene of contemporary Athens.

In the *Medea*, then, there is a prima facie idealization of Athens and denigration of Corinth, with its tyranny, bad faith and destructive relationships. But this construction of Corinth as the photographic negative of Athens is problematized by a series of unsettling allusions that connect the major characters in the play with the most identifiable characteristic of contemporary Athens: its wisdom, its *sophia*.

Theban Inversions

What goes for Corinth goes even more so for Thebes, presented across a range of tragedies as a site for decaying and implosive social relations. The cycle of stories connected with the figure of Oedipus presented rich material for the presentation of Thebes as a site of sexual aberration and political tyranny: Aeschylus' *Seven Against Thebes*, Sophocles' *Oedipus the King*, *Oedipus at Colonus* and *Antigone*, Euripides' *Phoenician Women* (the trilogy opened with the now lost *Chrysippus*, which identified Laius, Oedipus' father, as the inventor of pederasty or boy-love).[26] Euripides' *Bacchae* represents the arrogant young tyrant Pentheus in a city beset by disorder, particularly in the sphere of gender (the women practise Bacchic cult on the hillsides). Thebes is the backdrop for, in Froma Zeitlin's phrase, the 'theatre of the other'.[27]

Thebes was widely reviled in the fifth century, having supported the Persians in the Persian Wars. But at the same time, the Theban paradigm in tragedy is worryingly close to that of Athens. It is not just that Theban figures betray disturbingly 'Athenian' character-istics, such as Oedipus' relentless faith in the questing power of the intellect in *Oedipus the King*: many have noted the similarities be-tween Oedipus and Pericles, the popular leader of Athens, whose rule also culminated in a plague. It is also notable that the Thebans, like the Athenians, explained their origins by reference to the myth of 'authochthony', or birth from the soil.[28] For endogamous families (families that encourage marriage within the kinship group), issues of rivalry and incest always hover – and this goes for Thebans and Athenians alike. We can only guess what it must have been like to watch Euripides' *Phoenissae*, a play centring upon the reciprocal fratricide of Polynices and Eteocles (intended co-rulers of Thebes). The play was produced some time before 408 BCE, and probably in the aftermath of the vicious recriminations following the 'Oligarchic Revolution' of 411 (which succeeded for three months in installing a council of 400 as rulers of the city). Brother fighting brother – like a mirror, Thebes showed Athens an inverse of itself that also, in a sense, graphically represented the frictions of the city itself.

Nature and Culture

The fragility of the line separating ideological opponents was not the only cautionary message for Athenian viewers. In the heart of the hyper-civilized, hyper-modern, bejewelled city, Dionysiac theatre functioned as a potent reminder of the limited extent of man's domin-ance over the wild.[29] In general, Greek 'nature' is wholly unlike the Romantic conception of innocent, pastoral spaces threatened by the incursion of machines; it is instead a violent, destructive force, to be tamed by the beneficent powers of civilization.

In several tragedies, characters or choruses extol this 'progressivist' vision of human evolution. In the *Prometheus Bound* attributed to Aeschylus (but probably the work of a poet from later in the fifth century),[30] Prometheus ceases to be the playful deceiver of Hesiodic myth, and becomes instead the inventor of the cultured arts. In this play, the theft of fire symbolizes not simply (as in Hesiod) a subversive challenge to divine authority, but also (as it would, centuries later, for Shelley) the opening up to humankind of the possibilities of technological progress. Prometheus becomes a symbol of democratic self-help, Zeus an icon of tyrannical control-freakery. In Sophocles' *Antigone* (possibly composed as early as 441), meanwhile, the chorus sings a famous 'ode to man':[31]

> There are many awesome things, and none
> more awesome than man.
> It is man who travels across
> the grey sea on its wintry back,
> traversing over
> the far-bellowing swell, and wears away
> the oldest of the gods,
> using the race of horses
> to churn the imperishable, unwearying Earth,
> as ploughs wind back and forth year on year. (332–41)

The chorus continues, praising man's acculturated dominance over all manner of nature ('he conquers with his devices . . .', 348–9), his resourcefulness and the power of his thought. Both these lines and the *Prometheus Bound* evoke the burgeoning intellectual climate of Athens, the new confidence in the power of human creativity. Sophocles' words here echo the words of the sophist Protagoras in Plato's dialogue of the same name (written in the fourth century, but dramatizing a meeting which, if it took place, would have done so in the 430s or 420s).[32] Protagoras' doctrine is built around the concept of relativism: ethical and political systems develop, historically, out of self-interest, self-protection and exigency; the concepts of justice and goodness, then, are rooted in 'culture' rather than 'nature'. The centrepiece of Protagoras' argument is a mythical parable describing the emergence of mankind from primitivism thanks to the divine gift of technology, stolen from Athena and Hephaestus (the gods of craft and manufacture) by Prometheus (320c–22d).

But if contemporary sophists were proclaiming man's dominance over nature, tragedians were dramatizing the frailty of such claims. The celebratory words of the choral ode in the *Antigone* are at best ambiguous, in the context of the play's action. Creon has just discovered that, contrary to his commands, someone has begun to bury the corpse of the traitor Polynices; the culprit, it will transpire, is Polynices' sister, Antigone. Here is the final stanza of the ode:

A clever thing is man, who has the ability
beyond all expectation to contrive devices.
Sometimes he proceeds to evil; sometimes to good,
accomplishing the laws of the land
and the sworn justice of the gods,
and he and his city are elevated. But he who dwells with wickedness,
for the sake of recklessness, is cast from his city.
May whoever does this
not share my hearth, nor think thoughts
like mine. (365–75)

The conclusion, then, strikes a more ominous note: human ingenu-
ity conjures up great power, but the power to manufacture evil as
well as good. This feeds a larger ambiguity: what does the chorus
actually mean here? That Antigone is the criminal, for transgressing
'the laws of the land' (that is, Creon's edict)? Or that Creon is, for
going against the 'sworn justice of the gods' (a female's right to
mourn her family)? The lack of any clear resolution points towards
the practical difficulties involved in applying the apparently forth-
right language of nature and culture. And even if we do decide that
we think we know to whom the chorus refers, the supposed dominance of mankind to which the chorus alludes is subverted by the later
action of the play: Antigone ends up committing suicide and Creon
finishes the play broken-hearted, his son having joined Antigone in
her suicide. Neither side can be said to 'conquer' the threat posed by
the other.[33]

Tragedy and Psychology

Tragedy also explores the psychological aspects of this interplay between nature and culture. Athenian culture expected its citizens to
act in a responsible way in their personal lives, in exchange for their
political franchise.[34] And, indeed, the 'political' myth discussed in the
previous section of the city's emergence from its primitive past into a
civilized present overlapped at the personal level with the myth of the
Athenian citizen's mastery over his natural desires.[35] As democratic
citizens were by definition not ruled by overlords, they were expected
to be rulers of themselves, masters of their own appetites and pleasures. Such self-rule is the marker of the civilized, 'free' behaviour that
Athens identified as characteristic of its citizens. (The opposite, as
we shall see in chapter 13, was 'slavish' behaviour.) Tragedy troubles

this comfortable myth, exposing the thinness of the civilized overlay that conceals violent natural forces beneath.

And indeed Greek 'nature' – or *physis* – takes in a much larger range than its modern counterpart, including (notably) the emotions that must be dominated by the civilizing force of rationality. It is instructive that the Greek word for emotion, *pathos*, means at root 'something that happens to one'. Like an illness (another meaning of *pathos*), an emotion attacks one from without, and threatens one's well-being and rational stability; it is, then, best rooted out or repressed, certainly not indulged. We are, then, far from the modern psychotherapist's conception that emotions are 'natural', and that they are best 'expressed'.

In tragedy, there is no positive means of dealing with emotion: repression and expression are equally destructive. Euripides' *Hippolytus*, for example, tells of the young man of the title, who in his devotion to Artemis (goddess of hunting, his favourite pastime, but also a virgin goddess) refuses to worship Aphrodite (which is to say, to submit to sexual feelings).[36] Angered and vengeful, Aphrodite causes Hippolytus' stepmother, Phaedra, to desire him. Phaedra is convinced that concealing her feelings is the best course: calling on the nurse to 'hide' her head (245, 250) with robes, she also desires to keep silent (271, 273) about the cause of her sickness.

The governing concept for Phaedra is (in Greek) *aidos*, usually translated as 'shame', 'reverence', or 'respect' (see 385–6; as, indeed, it is for Hippolytus, see 78–81, 1258). None of these translations, however, captures the full range of a complex term that marks proper display (or concealment) of oneself before the public gaze.[37] In Greek culture, the anxiety of concealment is often insistently focused upon the genitalia, or *aidoia* ('things that should be treated with *aidos*'). But the word has a much broader remit than this. Ethical behaviour generally, including but not limited to sexual ethics, is covered by strictures of *aidos*: the term marks both the shame of sexuality and the modest reserve proper to civilized behaviour, particularly the veiling of the self and language.

Aidos is not a single concept, but a cluster of related ideas associated with concealment, with the dark interior, the feminine, the mysterious, the unknowable, the imperceptible. The French anthropologist Pierre Bourdieu would call such a cluster a 'habitus'.[38] Bourdieu's example is based around the symbolic structure of housing among the Kabyle people of Algeria.[39] The Kabyle house (which is gendered in strikingly similar ways to the Greek, tragic household) is only the most visible manifestation of an entire associative system that links the body, the self and society: it is the product of 'a world in which each object speaks metaphorically of all the others'.[40] The spatial organization of the home interlinks with a set of physical, physiognomical, gestural, sartorial and linguistic codes: it teaches the subjects to *embody* the principles of social propriety, at every level of their existence.[41]

In Euripides' play, however, despite Phaedra's attempts to conceal her passion, the nurse reveals all to Hippolytus. This exposure brings calamity upon the whole household. Hippolytus rages against his stepmother and promises to tell her husband and his father, Theseus; whereupon Phaedra kills herself, leaving a note accusing Hippolytus of attempted rape. Theseus discovers the note and banishes his son, who subsequently suffers a terrible fate: as he rides his chariot along the shore, a monstrous bull rises from the sea, panicking his horses and causing him to be mangled. Theseus is informed of the true course of events by Artemis, and is permitted a final reunion with the dying Hippolytus.

If Phaedra's problem lies in the exposure of her erotic feelings, Hippolytus' lies in their repression. His rejection of sexuality works at several levels. There is, in the first place, a strong genetic element. Hippolytus' mother was an Amazon, and Amazons – warrior women who lived apart from men – were associated particularly with barbaric denial of their 'natural' sexual function.

At another level, however, he represents a more general exemplar of the adolescent unwilling to leave adolescence. Athenian youths (or 'ephebes') undertook a ritualized rite of passage into manhood known as the *ephebeia*, a period spent in the mountainous borders before reintegration into the community as an adult. Although we have no evidence for the formalized ritual as early as the fifth century, there is a clear association in Greek culture between hunting in the mountainous woods and coming of age as early as the *Odyssey* (19.392–466). From this perspective, Hippolytus represents the adolescent's puerile desire for an infinite period sporting with his male companions, and his corresponding fear of the unknown (the female, sexuality). The impossibility of his desire to repress 'natural' urges is imaged in the figure of the bull, emerging from the sea (profoundly connected with sexuality, as the birthplace of Aphrodite) and the loss of control of his chariot. The reining of horses is a standard image for self-control in Greek thought (receiving fullest expression in Socrates' philosophical allegory in Plato's dialogue the *Phaedrus*). Hippolytus' very name suggests the freeing of horses.

Euripides provides the subtlest exploration of the emotional suppression demanded in a society that required, in the place of rule by others, self-rule from its citizens (see also chapter 12). Theatre, particularly Euripidean theatre, offered the citizens the opportunity to experiment, within licensed bounds, with levels of emotional release (both in the characters, and, through identification, in themselves) that they would have been denied in the normal run of life.[42]

Satyric Turns

Appended to the end of each tragic trilogy was a 'satyr' play, written by the same poet and (perhaps) performed by the same actors. Satyrs were hybrid figures, whose upper half was human and lower half goat (with a horse's tail); they were often represented as followers of Dionysus, and often represented with large erections pursuing the *maenad* ('ecstatic') women who accompanied him. The context for these representations is sympotic (see chapter 4) vases, which gives us a significant clue about the social function of satyrs: they represent an inversion of the normative expectations of self-control.[43] They show you what might happen if you let go (which is why it is fun to have satyrs on the *bottom* of drinking vessels, only visible when the vessel is drained). Satyr drama plays a similar game, filtering 'normal' literary narratives through the 'otherness' represented by satyrs.[44] Euripides' *Cyclops* (our only complete example, though a substantial portion of Sophocles' *Trackers* survives) takes the famous Homeric story of Odysseus' encounter with the terrifying ogre, condenses it, grafts on a chorus of satyrs, and turns it into a story about the discovery of wine. Like tragedy, the satyr play uses the tactic of *displacement*, focalizing the action through a body of commentators who represent antitypes to the audience; but whereas tragedy explores themes of political, cultural and psychological identity, satyr drama is orientated towards the baser instincts of the body. Satyrs are driven by the *appetites*.

Comic Turns

It is, however, with comedy that I wish to conclude this chapter. In antiquity, the three major poets of the classical period were held to be Eupolis, Cratinus and Aristophanes. These were the canonical poets of the so-called 'old' comedy. Of the vast, effusive wealth of comic talent, only eleven of Aristophanes' plays survive in their entirety.[45] From the following century, we also have one complete play and several large fragments of the 'new-comic' poet Menander (see also chapter 13, pp. 222–3), whose subjects of young love and intrigue follow a very different paradigm, closer to late Euripides than the old comic poets.

If tragedy is abstract, 'universalizing' and dislocated from Athens, comedy is specific, parochial and engaged, focusing on the day-to-day life of people. Although comic plots admit of wild fantasy (flying dung-beetles, or – even more extravagant – women in positions of political authority), comedies are set in Athens in the here-and-now, and its characters share the problems of the citizens watching: war, scarcity, political corruption, decadent youth, manipulative sophists. Like satyrs, comic characters are appetitive figures; sex and food are recurrent features in Aristophanes.[46] The utopian visions conjured up in comedy are fantasies of bodily indulgence, snubbing authoritarian social control.

Let us take an example. Aristophanes' *Acharnians*, the earliest of his surviving plays (produced in 425 BCE), represents the farmer Dicaeopolis ('Just-city') as an opponent of the war with Sparta (now six years old), which has caused him severe discomfort. Half the chorus is convinced, half unconvinced; but when Dicaeopolis argues his case against the general Lamachus (who embodies militarist values), they are all convinced. As a result, Dicaeopolis creates a private state of peace, which allows him to trade profitably with neighbouring cities. A Megarian sells him his daughters, disguising them as piglets (a slang term for female genitalia); a Theban comes loaded with the delicacies for which Boeotia is famous. These pleasures are for him alone; he refuses to share them with his fellow citizens. The conclusion of the play represents Lamachus as painfully injured in war, while Dicaeopolis is drunk and enjoying the company of two girls.

The *Acharnians* is one of a number of Aristophanic plays that pillory the establishment for its pernicious effects upon the lives of individuals. In *Knights* (424 BCE), the people turn their back upon the politician Cleon to claim a new favourite, a sausage-seller. In *The Clouds* (423), it is Socrates and the sophists who are attacked; their school is burned down at the conclusion, as the old man Strepsiades joyously liberates himself from their spell. *Wasps* (422) attacks the jury system at Athens; again it concludes with an old man (Philocleon) discovering there is more to life, this time exchanging jury service for drink and sex. In *Peace* (421), Trygaeus (like Dicaeopolis) becomes frustrated with the war, and puts an end to it on his own initiative; the play finishes with the marriage between Trygaeus and Opora ('Fruitfulness'), symbolizing the return of plenty.

But Aristophanic fantasy does not simply exchange public duty for private indulgence. Though they might oppose the status quo, Aristophanes' characters are not disaggregated and socially unassimilable, like an Achilles or an Ajax. The disagreeable aggression that is the stuff of the plays is the result of foolish policy or bad leadership, and it is rectifiable; the plays conclude with models of harmony and social reintegration. *Wasps* concludes with an ode enjoining the participants to 'come together' (1516); in the wedding-hymn concluding *Peace*, Trygaeus (or perhaps the choral leader) bids the guests 'follow me together' and eat cakes (1356). Most strikingly, the conclusion of *Lysistrata* – a play in which the women have refused their husbands sex until they put a stop to the war – portrays the male and female choruses coming together (1275–6).

The poet's claim to a socially constructive role within the city is specifically claimed by the chorus of Acharnians, in that play's *parabasis*, or 'stepping-aside' (628–718; a widespread feature of old comedy, whereby the chorus changes role and speaks more directly to the audience). The poet's enemies, the chorus says, criticize him 'on the grounds that he satirizes the city and insults the people' (631). On the contrary, the chorus responds, 'he is worthy of great reward from you, since he has stopped you from being overly fooled by the words of foreigners, from taking pleasure in being flattered, and from being gaping-mouthed citizens' (633–5). Comedy does have, according to the chorus, a positive function within the city – though this function is also paradoxically negative, namely to expose frauds. This conceptualization of comedy, however, depends upon a tendentious and self-serving understanding of who the frauds are. We might want to counter that comedy's *real* function is to construct a sense of solidarity at the expense of a limited number of outcasts, who – like scapegoats (*pharmakoi*) or executed criminals – are sacrificed for the sake of civic cohesion.[47]

Aristophanic comedy is a socially integrative genre. Unlike in tragedy, but as in speeches to the lawcourts and assemblies (see chapter 6), the people are directly addressed as 'you', 'the Athenians'. In this way, Aristophanes constructs an idealized 'imagined community' of Athenians. I take this phrase from Benedict Anderson's influential work on nation-formation;[48] but whereas Anderson's nation is imagined through more abstract and atomized phenomena (time, print media), Athens's imagined fiction of unity was tested in (among other contexts) the goldfish bowl of the theatre, where the entire citizen body was constituted by its visibility.

And as we have seen throughout this chapter, this – the making, unmaking and remaking of the citizen body – was the principal role of the Athenian theatre.

6

The Power of Speech

Doers of Deeds and Speakers of Words

In terms of action, not much happens in book 9 of the *Iliad*. Even so, it contains one of the most celebrated and powerful episodes in the whole poem. Rebuffing the peace-making advances of Agamemnon's envoys, Achilles delivers a long speech, a brilliantly constructed (and stylistically idiosyncratic) performance expressing his jaded sorrow and profound resentment (9.308–429).[1] His audience, the narrator comments, responded 'in silence, awed at the speech, for his riposte had been extremely vigorous' (9.430–1). Eventually, his old tutor, Phoenix, addresses him, in tears; only the reverend status of old age, admixed with the pathos of tears, can match Achilles' fearsome language. Phoenix and Achilles are subtly bargaining for verbal authority, and it is Phoenix who introduces the cunning twist: it was he, he claims, who taught Achilles to be a 'speaker of words and a doer of deeds' (9.443). If one person can trump Achilles' rhetorical performance, it is the man who taught him those skills.

Vocal prowess is – as one might expect in a poem rooted in oral culture – emphasized throughout the *Iliad*. 'Good at the war-cry' is a phrase used to praise heroes. In book 18, Achilles foreshadows his re-emergence into battle by displaying himself naked before the Trojan host; but rather than his visual aspect, it is his shout, 'as loud as the voice that is screamed out by a trumpet' (18.219), that drives 'endless terror upon the Trojans'. Twelve Trojans kill themselves at the mere sound of Achilles (18.230–1). When two warriors meet on the battlefield, they typically engage in what modern readers sometimes call 'flyting', the exchange of verbal insults; and the winner often vaunts over the body of his fallen foe. Doers of deeds, to borrow Phoenix' phrase, must also be speakers of words. Language is a crucial tool for the status-coveting Iliadic hero.[2]

But though the unadorned power of the inarticulate cry, and the aggressive provocations of flyting and vaunting, are appropriate to the violence of warfare, communities at peace must seek to remove violence from the public sphere. Or, perhaps better, to accommodate its inherent aggression within ordered, regulated structures. Speaking words is important to Homeric aristocrats not just in the theatre of war, but also in society itself. Decisions are contested and reached, identities are forged and impugned, through debate.

Sometimes, as in the case of Achilles and Phoenix, this occurs in private; but the stakes are often higher in the public sphere, or as Homer puts it 'in the middle' (*en messoi*). In the *Odyssey*, with its representation of life away from the Iliadic battlefield, the assembly is a crucial forum for the making and breaking of consensus and status. In book 2, Telemachus (Odysseus' young son) addresses the Ithacan assembly for the first time. It is a significant moment in the life of the young prince, as it publicly marks his coming of age. Taking the sceptre from the herald Peisenor, Telemachus excoriates the suitors for their craven greed. When he finishes, the response is dramatic:

> So he spoke in anger, and threw the sceptre to the ground,
> pouring out tears; and pity took all the people.
> Now all the others were silent, no one dared
> to respond to Telemachus with grievous words. (2.80–3)

As in the case of Achilles' address to the embassy in the *Iliad*, the audience's long silence signals the power and authority of the words. This speech is a performance of power: not just an 'expression' of powerful emotions, or indeed a powerful expression of emotions, but also a decisive claim staked to an empowered political identity within the community. This power is, as so often for Homer, predicated upon disguised – but nonetheless clearly intimated – force. No one 'dared' to reply, with 'grievous' words: to respond would be a risk, the risk of initiating a chain of events that would put at risk the civilized values of the community, and lead ultimately to violence. And indeed when the response does come, it is by Antinous, always the most provocative and brazen of the suitors. From here onwards in the *Odyssey*, Telemachus and the suitors are set on collision course, and one camp or the other must ultimately be destroyed. The suitors fear that Telemachus will plot death for them (2.325–30), and attempt to kill him first; but it is, of course, Telemachus who (aided by his father, the avenging Odysseus) will win out.

Theatres of Power

The Homeric assembly is a theatre of power. At stake is 'face',[3] and to lose face can be ruinous in the ongoing struggle for supremacy within communities. Any public space can be (or, rather, *must* be) a theatre of power, from a local church to a football match to a board-room; any dispute represents a contest for status, however apparently playful or trivial, from cock-fighting (in Clifford Geertz's famous example[4]) through to warfare. The Ithacan assembly of book 2 of the *Odyssey* is precisely such an event: what Geertz calls 'a metasocial commentary upon the whole matter of assorting human beings into fixed hierarchical ranks'. This public spat shows us how identities are being realigned in Ithaca. Telemachus is no longer a boy; no longer will the suitors be allowed to run riot in the household.

But if we are to view assemblies as theatres in which power is negotiated, we must be careful to define our concept of 'power' more carefully: this will have to be less a quality possessed more or less exclusively by one camp, and more a way of defining the relationship between two camps. Power is 'held' only for the fleeting moments of victory; thereafter it dissolves as the memory of the moment fades, and must be renewed through new challenges. The impotent silence of the other suitors marks Telemachus' empowered acquisition of mature manhood, but the subsequent response of Antinous indicates an ominous counter-challenge to Telemachus' newly won status. Like the warfare discussed in chapter 3, public speaking is a 'zero-sum game'. Although Homeric narrative certainly presents its characters as acquiring and developing expertise, guile, maturity and inner strength over time, power (in the narrow sense that we have identified) can be only asserted through face-to-face competition in public space.

Democratic Speech

The Homeric assembly is also a theatre of power in an extended sense. The right to speak is, crucially, restricted. It is, for a start, limited to men. 'Speech is for men', the rapidly maturing Telemachus tells Penelope in book 1 of the *Odyssey*, 'for all men, but me most of all'; he then sends her upstairs (1.358–9). Moreover, the sceptre, taken up by speakers (and hurled to the ground by Telemachus), is also the symbol of the *basileus*, the aristocratic lord. Speaking is central to the Homeric poems' culture of male, elite self-definition – which is why it is such a jealously protected privilege.

Let us fast-forward now to the classical period, to the fifth and fourth centuries.[5] It is no coincidence that Syracuse and Athens, two democratic states, drove the phenomenon (though as usual we have much more evidence for Athens, and so it is upon Athens that I shall concentrate). Where speaking in Homer had been rigorously limited to a select few, Athens constructed itself as a city of *isegoria*, of 'equal right to speak'. Every citizen possessed *parrhesia*, an entitlement to address the public freely, as instanced in the famous words spoken by the herald at the inauguration of every assembly meeting: 'who wants to speak?' Political enfranchisement and speaking were mutually definitive: you speak because you are a citizen, you are a citizen because you speak. Indeed, Pericles, in the funeral speech that Thucydides puts in his mouth, goes so far as to put down the citizen who does not contribute to the polity: 'we Athenians alone consider the man who takes not part in politics, not uninterfering, but un-contributing' (2.40.2).[6]

Exclusions still operated, of course: the category of 'citizen' excluded children, slaves, free men of non-Athenian birth ('metics', sometimes referred to as 'resident aliens'), and – most of all – women, who are repeatedly exhorted to silence (see further chapter 11). Ajax's consort Tecmessa reminds herself in Sophocles' *Ajax* of his words to her: 'Woman, silence brings glory to women' (293). More famously, Pericles' funeral speech offers a ringing paradox: 'great is the reputation of her who has the least fame among men, whether for virtue or blame' (2.45.2). The public sphere, where discourse is trafficked, is definitively male. When in Aristophanes' *Lysistrata* the women cast off the shackles of silence and invade the Acropolis, the absurdity of the comic inversion underlines the normal expectation.

There is no single word for 'rhetoric' in Homer; our word comes from *rhetorike*, a term apparently coined by Plato (who was a hostile critic), meaning 'the art of speaking'. In the course of the fifth century, with its move towards increasing intellectual specialization, speaking was repackaged as a skill, a technique, a resource that could be transmitted from person to person. Professional teachers, 'sophists', flocked to Athens, offering to teach the city's inhabitants, amongst other things, the ability to gain persuasive influence over their fellow-citizens through language. Theorists constructed schematic taxonomies of rhetorical form. The first authors of such 'handbooks' (though the term belittles the achievement) were held to have been the fifth-century Sicilians Corax and Tisias; the earliest surviving examples are the *Rhetoric to Alexander* attributed to Anaximenes of Lampsacus and Aristotle's *Rhetoric*. Practice speeches were composed by figures such as Gorgias, Antiphon, Alcidamas and Antisthenes, as examples to be imitated by students. By the fourth century, an established system of intellectual nepotism had emerged: like university professors, rhetorical superstars (like Isocrates and Isaeus) had their protégés, who responded with a recognizable mixture of gratitude and grudge.[7] Language was now more than just an instrument of power; speaking well had become a *discipline*, a central part of civilized humanity, a fundamental component of the art of living.

Community Models

Democratic Athens was, we have learned to say, a 'face-to-face community'. Not that it was small enough for each citizen to know every other: if the estimate of 30,000 citizens (i.e. excluding women, slaves, resident non-Athenians and children) is even approximately right, only the most prominent individuals can have had much recognition outside of immediate networks. It was, rather, a 'face-to-face community' in the sense that it *represented itself* as a single, unified totality that nevertheless acknowledged individuality.

Like theatrical performance (see chapter 5), public oratory played a crucial role in the maintenance of this self-image. Prior to the *ecclesia* (or 'assembly', where political decisions were taken), the 'Scythian archers', who maintained law and order in the city, rounded up stragglers and directed them to the meeting-place on the hill called the Pnyx. The decrees of the assembly were inscribed in stone and placed in the *agora*, the marketplace, for all to see (even if few could actually read them). Everything about the Athenian assembly suggested a radically new model of social inclusion, relative to (what was always the benchmark) the Homeric world. The democratic assembly was a 'theatre of power' in a sense that the Homeric theatre never could be: like the theatre of Dionysus, it fashioned the audience into a symbolically unified, undifferentiated group. The *demos*, or 'people', was at once the audience, the backdrop for the performance, and (in a sense) the spectacle itself.[8]

Another forum for democratic speech was the law court. One of the earliest descriptors of (one of the earliest forms of) the political system we now call democracy was *isonomia*, or 'equality before the law'.[9] The close association between democracy and law served to distance the city from the political regime it had ousted, tyranny; the sixth-century tyrants in fact introduced law courts as a populist measure, but allowed judges to preside over all cases without any scrutiny. In the democracy, a large jury was empanelled (from two hundred up to five hundred, sometimes more), selected from citizens who had enrolled themselves formally on a list of eligible jurors. As representatives of the Athenian people (they are frequently addressed as 'men of Athens' in speeches), the jurors bore the responsibility not only for true and false judgement, but also for maintaining the symbolic integrity of Athens as a community predicated upon consensus. Every case tried in an Athenian law court enacted (in Robin Osborne's phrase) a 'social drama', staging, exploring and resolving the challenges to the city's ideological fabric.[10]

Certainly, when an orator stood up to address the assembly or the law court, issues of real urgency were at stake: money, reputations, careers, citizenship, even life itself. Rhetorical speaking was language *in action*, energized by the make-or-break pressures of public competition. But their speeches, these fascinating records of intense interpersonal hostilities, tell us about more than local disputes: they are among our best evidence for the ideological issues that lay at the heart of Athenian culture.

Oratory, Power and Influence

Not that these new paradigms of democratic speech were free from tensions and dilemmas. In the democratic city, the ability to persuade was closely correlated with political influence: persuasion was power. 'Speech', writes Gorgias in his *Encomium to Helen* (on which more presently), 'is a great master: it can accomplish the most divine things with the smallest and most invisible body' (8; a famous utterance already by the time of Plato (*Phaedrus* 267a)). The persuasive power promised by rhetoric, and its teachers, made it suspicious, problematic – not least because those best advantaged were the rich, who could afford sophists' fees. In Aristophanes' comedy *The Clouds*, the foolish old man Strepsiades visits Socrates (here taken – though Plato would later protest to the contrary – as an arch-sophist) in order to learn how to wangle his way out of paying his debts. This is how he explains his plan to his son:

> This [Socrates' school] is the thinking-shop of wise souls;
> here live men who, in their discussions of
> the sky, persuade you that it is a bread-oven,
> and that it surrounds us, and that we are the charcoals.
> They it is who teach, if you give them silver,
> how to emerge victorious in speaking,
> over just and unjust arguments alike. (94–7)

Later on in the play, the personification of 'just argument' is defeated by the personification of 'unjust argument'. In this complex comedy, sophistry is presented as a pretentious, dangerous, anti-democratic force that elevates its initiates above others; but it is also presented, particularly by Strepsiades, as a means to transcend the constraints of poverty and realize a utopian vision for the individual (much as Dicaeopolis in the *Acharnians* manages to negotiate a private peace treaty and free himself from the sufferings of war – see chapter 5).

Outside of comedy, the orators themselves show awareness of the hostility that could be whipped up against formalized rhetorical training, which could easily be presented as a sign of elitism. Invective against political opponents is, of course, a common phenomenon in all ages, and it is not especially surprising to see charges of counter-ideological behaviour. What is particularly intriguing about this particular mode of attack on a rival's 'face', however, is that it is a high-risk strategy: for it is, in practice, unlikely that many public orators (and certainly none of those who have come down to us) were of genuinely sub-elite backgrounds. The accusation of rhetorical training can serve as a means of deflecting similar accusations away from oneself (what Jonathan Hesk calls 'the rhetoric of anti-rhetoric')[11] – but in doing so, the speaker opens up the possibility of a rebound attack.

Inventing the Politician: Demosthenes and Aeschines

The position of rhetorical expert, then, was an uncertain and problematic one. This is particularly evident in the case of Demosthenes. A crucial figure in fourth-century politics, and a hugely influential orator, Demosthenes began his career in the court, prosecuting his guardians for appropriating his inheritance. He studied under the celebrated and successful orator Isaeus. From 355 or so onwards, he began to devote himself to political oratory, and in particular carved out eternal fame for himself as a hawkish proponent of war against Philip of Macedon and his rapidly expanding empire. (Three hundred years later, the Roman orator Cicero styled his speeches against Marc Antony the *Philippics*, in imitation of his oratorical hero; and from there, the word entered the lexicon for good.)

Demosthenes the politician was attempting a difficult equipoise in Athens: he was constructing himself as a specialist purveyor of political advice to the people (*symboulos*, 'adviser', is the word he uses as a job descriptor), one who addressed the assembly with authority, but without any formal position (general, council-member or similar) within the city. This kind of political adviser had its roots in the fifth century, with specialist politicians like Pericles and his successors in the 420s, such as Cleon (best known through the hostile accounts of Thucydides in his *History* and Aristophanes' comedies of the period). But Demosthenes represented something new. His self-representation was arguably even more fierce, confident, and extreme.[12] The quality of his advice was (he claimed) guaranteed by his intellectual command of precedent, not by his practical experience.

Let us take, by way of example, a passage from the third of the three *Olynthiacs*, where he counsels the people to attack Philip of Macedon:

> The present situation, if any ever did, demands much thought and planning. I for myself do not consider the most difficult thing to be advising you what to do in the circumstances; what bewilders me, men of Athens, is the *way* I should tell it to you. For I am persuaded by what I know from both personal experience and hearsay that most of our advantages have escaped us because of your unwillingness to take the necessary course, or your failure to understand it. I ask you to tolerate my speaking with frankness, and to consider only whether I am speaking the truth, so as to improve the future. For you see that it is as a result of the flattering oratory of some that our situation has come to this wretched state. (3.3)

This is an ingenious strategy. Using the 'zero-sum game' technique (which we identified earlier in Homeric speaking), Demosthenes contrasts his own (supposedly) straightforward presentation of matters to the 'flattering oratory' of his rivals: his own 'face' is enhanced by attacking that of his rivals. His own expertise, he suggests, lies not in strategies of persuasion (or he would have persuaded the Athenians of the correct course long ago), but in political science. The opening sentence of the passage proclaims this confidence: 'The present situation . . . demands much thought and planning' serves as a recommendation to heed his own brand of political oratory, privileging it over that of his unnamed opponents. This self-representation as the expert dealer in unpalatable truth is backed up by the powerful language of obligation ('demands', 'the necessary course').

But it was this role that he arrogated for himself that left him most vulnerable to attack, for it implied a claim to superior status, a claim potentially repellent to Athenian ideology. In his biography, Plutarch (the moralist and biographer of the second century CE), writes of the criticisms levelled at him for labouring away in his study:

> As a result he had the reputation of lacking natural talent, and relying instead upon the powerful effects that come from labour. One strong sign of this was held to be that it was rare for anyone to hear Demosthenes speaking spontaneously; rather, he would often sit in the assembly not coming forward while the people called upon him by name, if he happened not to have given the matter thought and preparation. Many of the other politicians used to attack him for this, and Pytheas once mockingly said that his ideas smelt of lampwicks. To him Demosthenes replied, sharply, that 'My lamps and yours, Pytheas, are not party to the same practices'. (*Life of Demosthenes*, 8.3–5)

In a culture generally suspicious of the intellectual privileges of the elite, of surreptitious plotting and of nocturnal practices behind closed doors (symbolically opposed to democratic accountability, conducted in the public glare of daylight), Demosthenes' candlelit labours could be construed as dangerously counter-ideological. But the interesting point is that nothing is fixed or stable in this contest for rhetorical 'face': Demosthenes ingeniously turns the accusation against Pytheas, wittily accusing him of less salubrious nocturnal activities (references to lamps in Greek culture often suggest erotic encounters after dark). In political rhetoric, few activities or phenomena are intrinsically pro- or anti-democratic; rather, values are ascribed – provisionally, strategically – by rhetorical construction.

Rhetorical expertise could be 'spun' either way, as intellectual authority or dangerous calculation born of crypto-aristocratic elitism. The malleable nature of such identity-construction can most clearly be seen in the struggles for positional dominance between Demosthenes and his arch-enemy, Aeschines. The reasons for their disputes are complex, bound up in the difficult, convoluted relationship between Athens and Macedonia, and in the shifting roles of the two figures and their associates in the negotiations between the cities.[13] What interest me here more than the historical background are the struggles for positional dominance in the assembly and the courts, those democratic theatres of power, between these two very different self-authored public figures. Aeschines, so far as we know, lacked any formal rhetorical training (though he was unlikely to have been sub-elite); he certainly does not seem to have had Demosthenes' apprenticeship in forensic oratory or the patronage of a famous teacher.

In his speech *Against Ctesiphon*, Aeschines warns his audience of the tricks Demosthenes is likely to pull: 'So just as in gymnastic contests you see boxers contending with one another for position, so for the sake of the city, you must do battle with him all day long for position as regards his speech' (3.206). The pugilistic metaphor is not innocent: Demosthenes is constructed as an adversary of the citizens, using his expertise for aggressive purposes. What is particularly interesting, moreover, is that the boxer's aim, in the analogy, is not to floor his opponent outright, but to negotiate an advantageous *position*: rather than expecting a direct punch, the audience is to expect a constant shuffling around, a ground-shifting search for a suitable angle of attack. Elsewhere in Aeschines, Demosthenes is repeatedly presented as a 'sophist', a 'wizard', a practitioner of the 'unholy techniques of speech' (*On the Embassy* 56). In his reference to his adversary's 'techniques', Aeschines reminds his audience of the technical expertise that he himself lacked. The impugning of his enemy's artfulness serves the converse function of underlining the trustworthy spontaneity of the speaker.

Demosthenes, however, is capable of brilliantly countering such charges. In 348, before his enmity with Aeschines, he composed (but perhaps did not deliver: the case may have been settled out of court) the speech *Against Meidias*. Here he accuses the defendant (a political enemy) of having assaulted him in the theatre, while he was serving as *choregos*, or director of the chorus. Demosthenes construes this public attack upon his body while he was performing a public duty as an outrageous attack upon the public body.[14] In an oration that rests so heavily upon the speaker's ability to side himself with the interests of the people, it is crucial for Demosthenes to crush any suggestion that separates him out from the masses. For this reason, he predicts and defuses the kind of accusation that the defendant will use against him:

> Perhaps he will say of me 'This man is an orator'. If an 'orator' is one who advises you what he considers to be in your interests, and does this while falling short of harassing or coercing you, I should not avoid or disclaim this title. But if an 'orator' is like some of those speakers whom you and I see, shameless men who grow rich at your expense,

I could never be one . . . Perhaps he will also say this of me, that all my present words are thought out and prepared. I do indeed confess to having thought them out (I shall not deny it), and practised them to the best of my ability. For I would be a wretched figure if, after (and while) suffering such wrongs, I took no care over the things I was to say to you. (189, 191)

This is a brilliant move. Pre-empting the charge that he belongs to a sect of educated, manipulating elitists, Demosthenes turns the accusation back upon Meidias and his supporters. 'Orator' is not an insult, for Demosthenes, unless one means the kind of specious flatterer from whom he distances himself. Nor is the charge of having pre-pared and thought out one's speech; on the contrary, it is insulting to the people to do anything less. Demosthenes' expertise is here trans-formed from an ideologically suspect quality into a marker of his integrity as a politician and speaker.

And Demosthenes is also capable of accusing Aeschines of misus-ing technical virtuosity. The late speech *On the Crown* (330 BCE) represents the final phase in the complex struggle between the two men, a response to Aeschines' speech indicting Ctesiphon for propos-ing that Demosthenes be awarded an honorific crown for services to the city. In this masterpiece of political oratory, Demosthenes repeat-edly reminds his audience of Aeschines' background as a tragic actor (18.129, 209, 232, 261–2, 308), associating his performance not only with the calculating manipulations of a specialist but also with the visual artifice of theatre. But though he presents Aeschines as a tech-nically accomplished speaker ('practising his vocal exercises' before appearing in the assembly, 308), Demosthenes, interestingly, sees fit to mock the limitations of his skill: he is a 'tritagonist', or bit-player (129, 209, 262), 'imitating the speeches and flourishes' of others (232). Turning the tables on his accuser, Demosthenes simultan-eously exposes and contemptuously mocks Aeschines' own expertise.

The Trials of the City

In adjudicating the public conflicts between famous figures like Demo-sthenes and Aeschines, the city explored its own identity. Political oratory was very real, in that getting the decision wrong could have terrible consequences (Thucydides' history of the Peloponnesian war repeatedly presents the Athenians being misled by orators, as we shall see in chapter 7). But at the same time, it engaged the citizens on the imaginary level, asking them to consider what was the role of the political expert in the city, how they could countenance the concept of informed advice, and indeed how to manage the ever more involuted sequence of counter-accusations of artifice. The speeches of Demosthenes and Aeschines represent a truly prized archive of political-theatrical scripts, with each player in turn engineering an increasingly sophisticated arsenal of attack.

Nowhere in the corpus of private forensic speeches do we have anything quite like this rich, extended tapestry of interpersonal rivalry.[15] For a start, we never have more than one side of the case; and indeed we rarely have even any inkling of whether the speech convinced the jury (although it is arguable that only successful speeches are likely to have been preserved). But these speeches are no less valuable in cultural-historical terms, particularly for their insights into the ways that personal behaviour could be attacked and defended on ideological grounds. 'Personal' ethics should not, in this context, be taken to imply 'non-political'. 'Personal' conduct in classical Athens was subject to direct political scrutiny, for the privilege of citizenship was held to rest upon the individual male's ability to control himself, his finances and his household. Most famously, Aeschines' prosecution of Timarchus (predictably, a crony of Demosthenes) sought to strip him of his citizenship by demonstrating his addiction to sexual and other pleasures.[16] That Aeschines should pursue a political battle against Demosthenes through the private courts is further evidence that the two spheres intersect substantially.

The language used to evaluate private individuals was of a different order from that used to assess political action. When an adolescent was examined for his suitability for citizenship (at the ritual known as the *dokimasia*), for example, gossip about his private life thus far was admissible evidence.[17] The situation was no different in legal contexts. When making accusations of unethical behaviour, law court rhetoricians frequently appealed to rumour, to 'what everyone knows' about the individual in question – though of course this does not mean that everyone did know it, simply that the orator was presenting (or enforcing) an image of shared knowledge. Athenian courts lacked any judge to rule out certain kinds of evidence as inadmissible; insinuation and emotive *coups de théâtre* were permitted (though they might of course be attacked as such by the opposition). Much of the weight of persuasion was borne by narrative presentations, which served the twin purposes of exposition of events (as the side in question viewed them) and of *ethopoeia* or 'construction of persona'.[18] Modern accounts of Greek courts often stress the perceived weighting of character description over proof in the ancient texts (though admittedly such scholars are often strikingly naive in the implicit assumption that modern courts are unswayed by self-presentation).

In forensic oratory, just as much as in the assembly, the speaker had to assimilate himself to the *demos*, the Athenian populace: just an ordinary guy. In many of our extant speeches, however, this raises a complex issue. While in the normal run of things, many defendants and prosecutors (an unquantifiable number) will have spoken in their own voices, the rich could afford the services of a 'logographer', or speech-writer. Many extant law court speeches fall into this category. Because the texts that we have are written by the superstar orators of the day, moreover, they are likely to have been commissioned by particularly wealthy individuals. Did juries know when speakers were reproducing speeches written for them by the experts? Did they know that they were listening to words composed at great expense? It is prima facie unlikely that all jury members would have been fooled. But if so, did it prejudice their opinion? Did this awareness subvert any pretence on the speaker's part to be an ordinary guy? Or was it accepted as part of the process, thanks to a kind of culturally sanctioned, wilful myopia? These questions are impossible to answer, but also impossible to ignore. What *is* clear is that Athenian courtrooms were spaces where any claim to innocence could be treated with great suspicion, where cunning and sophistication were to be both expected and dissimulated.

Constructing Character: Lysias and the Courts

Let us take an example. Lysias (*c*.459–380 BCE) was the logographer par excellence, an amazingly successful orator, who hailed from Syracuse but practised in Athens (where he had the status of metic, or 'resident alien'). He specialized in creating characters for speakers, in concocting language that expressed the persona he was cultivating for them, while artfully dissimulating the artifice. In the third speech (*Against Simon*), for example, the speaker is a modest, unassuming, mature man, prosecuting a shameless younger figure. In the seventh (*On the Sacred Enclosure*), again, he presents a figure characterized by cleverness and cunning, one who could not possibly have committed the foolish crime of which he is accused (destroying a sacred tree).

But it is on the first oration, *On the Murder of Eratosthenes*, that I wish to focus.[19] This speech was composed for a certain Euphiletus,

accused of murdering a certain Eratosthenes. Euphiletus argues that
Eratosthenes was committing adultery with his wife, and so his
action constituted not murder but civic duty, a just exaction of the
penalty owed by all adulterers. The issues surrounding Euphiletus'
legal rights as a cuckold are complex and partly opaque. I forgo
detailed discussion here, except to say that the position he adopts
seems to have been tendentious but not absurd: an unsuspecting
husband catching an adulterer *in flagrante delicto* seems to have had
the right to exact summary justice.[20] Like most pre-industrial states,
Athens treated adultery with severity, and as a crime perpetrated by
one man against another; but in Athens, there was an additional
ideological dynamic, given that children had to be born of 'pure'
citizen blood (see chapter 11, pp. 186–7).

What interests me more than the legal niceties, however, is the
rhetorical strategy. Like tragedy, the courtroom enforces and explores
a separation between individual and community: the jury stands
for the Athenian people, the community; the defendant is separated,
isolated. In the opening words of the speech, Euphiletus asks the jury
to imagine themselves in his position, a tactic designed to reintegrate
himself into the community (1). This process is powerfully boosted
by the tactic of using the language of 'crime' only in relation to
Eratosthenes' adultery, and 'punishment' and 'justice' only in relation
to the murder. In this way, Lysias construes the adulterer Eratosthenes,
not the murderer Euphiletus, as the defendant in the case; Euphiletus,
as the agent of civic justice, is arrayed on the side of the jury. When
Euphiletus rejects Eratosthenes' supplication for his life (as Iliadic
heroes always do: every little guy has one big role in him), he does so
with the ringing words: 'it is not I who shall kill you, but the city's
laws' (26).

Lysias also needs to negotiate Euphiletus' social status. The defendant was presumably a wealthy man, wealthy enough at any rate to
afford a premium-rate logographer. The coy mention of a visit to his
'property' outside Athens (11) may refer to some kind of rural estate.
But otherwise, Lysias systematically erases any traces of Euphiletus'
elite status, constructing him instead as a wholly unexceptional figure.
In the narrative, Euphiletus is represented as intellectually naive and
unpretentious in his ethics and values – so not only unlikely to have
the wit or wherewithal of a vicious criminal, but also (and, arguably,
more importantly) a figure culturally and ideologically assimilable
into the collective.

This 'character-construction' (*ethopoeia*) is underlined with more
formal stylistic devices. Lysias was renowned in antiquity for his

elegantly 'simple' style, which perfectly suits the representation of Euphiletus he is building. Let us take an example from the narrative:

> Time passed, gentlemen, and I returned unexpectedly from the property. After dinner, the baby became upset and started crying – it was being deliberately aggrieved by the maid, so as to do this, since the man was in the house (I found all this out later). I told my wife to go and breastfeed the baby, to stop it crying. At first, she was unwilling, as though delighted to see me return after such a long time. But when I grew angry and told her to go, she replied, 'Yes, so that you can have a go at the slave-girl! You manhandled her once before, when you were drunk.' I laughed, and she stood up and went and locked the door, pretending it was a joke, and took away the key. I lay down, thinking nothing of it, with no suspicion, just glad to be back from the property. (11–13)

At first glance, this language is uncomplicated, direct, even repetitious in places. Euphiletus seems, perhaps, to be true to his earlier claim to present 'his circumstances, leaving nothing out, only telling the truth' (5). But as the critic Dionysius of Halicarnassus (who lived at the turn of the millennium) observed, Lysias' 'artless style is artfully constructed' (*Lysias* 8). This passage provides an ingenious web of suggestive insinuations. As early as the phrase 'I returned unexpectedly', alarm-bells are being rung: 'unexpectedly' *for whom*? For the dutiful Euphiletus, or for his up-to-no-good wife? The temporary separation of husband and wife activates with a well-known series of mythical narratives, strongly hinting at adultery: Clytaemnestra, in particular, quickly hooked up with Aegisthus in the absence of Agamemnon. The passage as a whole repeatedly overlays the simple narrative relayed by the gullible Euphiletus with titillating hints of the 'real' state of affairs. In narratological terms, it employs what we might call 'double focalization': the story is being told through the eyes of the actor in the story (Euphiletus the naive cuckold), but with interventions by the knowing narrator, who has the benefit of hindsight. Not only does the narrator interlace information that the actor at the time did not have ('I found all this out later'), but also phrases such as '*as though* delighted to see me' and 'with no suspicion' insist that there is more going on than Euphiletus the actor realizes. This ironic narrative strategy packs in a lot of rhetorical work: Euphiletus' simple character is further underlined, the jurors enjoy the pleasure of a comic cuckold, and Eratosthenes is assimilated to the standard stereotype of an adulterer.

Euphiletus' naivety is offset by the construction of others as sophisticates. The wife, sailing playfully close to the wind, full of deceitful artifices, monopolizes the narrative energy of the adultery plot, controlling her lover's access into and exits from the house. Presently, Euphiletus spots her wearing make-up (13); cosmetics figure the seductive artifices of woman at their most extreme. 'I was so naive', Euphiletus earlier claims, 'that I thought my own wife was the most virtuous of all in the city' (10). His self-representation as naive is dependent upon his construction of his wife as cunning.

The other major artificer of the text is Eratosthenes. The first wind that Euphiletus gets of the adultery comes when a slave approaches him with the grim news: 'It is Eratosthenes of Oe who is doing this; he has corrupted not only your wife, but many others. For that is his skill.' The word for 'skill' here is *tekhne*, a word with a range of meanings: here, 'profession' or 'art' might be the most appropriate translation, but the word certainly also connotes the ideologically problematic notion of educated technique or expertise. In the mouth of his supposedly witless narrator, Lysias inserts a highly sophistic-ated device: the representation of Eratosthenes' superior 'expertise' operates in the first instance in the sexual sphere, but simultaneously serves to distance Euphiletus from charges of manipulative rhetorical skill. This kind of disguised commentary upon the practice of rhet-oric is sometimes called 'metarhetoric'.

The claims to naivety that Lysias presses on Euphiletus' behalf, then, are part of a larger, calculated, integrated rhetorical strategy: a brilliant attempt to depict the identity of a simple, homespun guy floundering in a mire of artful deception. This character portrayal, this *ethopoeia*, is fully integrated into the ideological message of Lysias 1 as a whole, which seeks to reconfigure the court, constructing Euphiletus not as a defendant but as the righteous agent of the city's vengeance.

Oratory on the Edge: Socratic Rhetorics

Such ingenious strategies can be paralleled across a wide range of rhetorical texts in the period.[21] Socrates' defence against the charge of corrupting the young and introducing new gods is a case in point. The historical Socrates was tried and executed in 399 BCE. Two 'Apologies' or defence speeches, one by Plato, the other by Xenophon, have come down to us; and though it is doubtful that either is an accurate transcript of the words spoken by the philosopher in 399, both show a sophisticated awareness of the ideological pitfalls of the democratic court. Like Euphiletus, Socrates cultivates the persona of a rhetorical innocent. Near the beginning of Xenophon's account, Socrates is offered some advice by a certain Hermogenes:

> 'Shouldn't you have considered your defence speech?' 'Do I not seem to you to have lived my life practising my defence speech?' replied Socrates. 'How so?' asked Hermogenes. 'Because I have passed it all without committing any injustice – I consider that to be the finest practice for a defence speech.' (3)

The word used for 'practice', *melete*, is the standard word for rigorous preparation undertaken by orators; it also marks the kind of oratorical expertise that is often castigated in political speeches. Like Euphiletus, Socrates is being presented as morally good, but rhetorically underprepared.

In Plato's text, this device is integrated into the substance of the speech:

> From me you will hear the whole truth – for you will not, by Zeus, hear speeches prettified like those of the prosecution, nor tarted up with flamboyant expressions and words; no, you will hear words spoken spontaneously, using words as they come out. For I believe the things I say are just, and may none of you expect anything otherwise; for it would not do for one of my age to come before you making up speeches like a boy. (17b–c)

In Plato's writings (especially the *Gorgias*, the *Sophist* and the *Protagoras*), Socrates presents rhetoric as a false mode of teaching. Unlike philosophy, rhetoric has to flatter the vulgar caprices of the people; it cannot access the higher planes of intellectual enquiry. Socrates' rejection in the *Apology* of 'prettified', 'tarted up' speeches looks like another instance of this anti-rhetorical stance. And indeed, elsewhere in Plato's works, Socrates characterizes his own style as unrhetorical: in the *Symposium*, he expresses a reluctance to give a speech in praise of Eros, fearing (he claims) to embarrass himself in such exalted company (198b). But, as we have seen, the disavowal of rhetorical sophistication (and its attribution to others) is precisely a conventional ploy.

Is Socrates, then, a master rhetorician? Yes and no. Rhetoric is a medium that Socrates can use with great panache: in the *Apology* and the *Symposium* alike, he delivers his speech despite his protestations. But the *Apologies* of Xenophon and Plato dramatize a performance that any reader must know to be a failure, since Socrates was in the event convicted and executed. What is more, Socrates is an unconvincing *naïf*. The rhetorical success of Euphiletus in Lysias 1 depends upon the maintenance of the illusion of naivety; but Socrates, throughout his defence speeches, only shows up his intellectual sophistication. For example, in a famous episode, the Delphic oracle proclaims Socrates the wisest of men. Socrates dissents, but after testing a number of contemporary figures and finding them wanting, concludes that he must after all be the wisest, since unlike them 'I know that I know nothing' (Plato, *Apology* 20e–23b; abbreviated version in Xenophon 14). Though Socrates mimicks the ideologically expected line, denying expertise, he ends up exposing with relish his socially anomalous position as an intellectual. In Xenophon and Plato, however, this serves as a critique of the shortsightedness of the Athenian courts, and the democratic system underpinning it, rather than of the individual isolated and punished by it.

Athenian law courts provided a system for evaluating and punishing social deviants. But more importantly for our purposes, they provided a space in which the very concept of social deviance could be explored, challenged, determined, redetermined. How does a society built around a collectivist ideology deal with individuals? How can difference – be it social, cultural or intellectual – be absorbed? And what is the role of artful language in a context that demands unadorned truthfulness?

Oratory and the Public

In this chapter, we have considered what we might have distinguished as two distinct genres of high-octane, combative, public oratory: the political and the legal.[22] But 'genre', in this context, is not simply a literary or formal concept: these speeches gain their urgency and power from their surroundings, from the institutional and civic dynamics that frame these speeches. Oratory gives us arguably our richest insight into the language and thought of the Athenian masses. In the public spaces that housed these performances, the city spoke to itself, representing and celebrating its central ideologies. Not that the speakers and authors themselves were from the sub-elite; rather, it is the awareness that ultimately the people (the jury, the assembly) decide the outcome that dictates the heavily idealized vision of the city we encounter in these texts.

At the same time, however, the orators retain a measure of control, of manipulation. These are virtuoso displays of oratorical sophistication (the products of a confident, knowing and self-reflexive tradition), designed to support partial, partisan presentations of events. The oratorical texts do not simply *reflect* ideology; they play an active role in reconfiguring and shaping it. It is this aspect – the dynamic interaction with the city and its values – that represents their greatest interest to the cultural historian.

7

Inventing the Archive: Athens

Poetry, Prose and Intellectual Authority

Strabo of Amaseia (on the Black Sea) was an extraordinary man. Writing under the emperor Augustus, at the turn of the millennium, he produced a staggering volume of work: forty-seven books of *Historical Memorabilia* (now lost) and, most famously, the seventeen-volume work we call the *Geography*. This text is extraordinary not only in terms of ambition – it describes most of the known world, an intellectual map vying in scale with the Roman empire itself – but also in its claims about the status of prose literature.[1] Eratosthenes of Cyrene, his great predecessor in the third century BCE, had vaunted the superiority of his sophisticated, knowing geographical prose over the vague, opaque and mystifying poetry of Homer. 'You will find the location for the wanderings of Odysseus', Eratosthenes had declared, 'when you find the cobbler who stitched up the bag of winds' (Strabo 1.2.15). For Eratosthenes, poetry was simply the mumbo-jumbo of an earlier age. For Strabo, on the other hand, poetry was not only an earlier literary form, but also a better one:

> Prose (or at least artful prose) is, so to speak, an imitation of poetic discourse. For the art of poetry was the first to emerge into public prominence and regard. Then Cadmus, Pherecydes, Hecataeus and the like wrote, imitating them but abandoning the metre while retaining the other features of poetry. Then later generations successively stripped away some of these, and brought it down to the present state, as though from a great height. Similarly one might say that comedy took its structure from tragedy, but descended from its height into the state that is currently called 'prosaic'. (1.2.6)

Strabo's vision of the world is inherently ambiguous. On the one hand, he is a man of the present. With his synoptic panorama of the world – a world that his predecessors could never have known in such detail – he embodies the technological and intellectual achievements of his age. He is a hard-headed prose-writer. On the other hand, he remains fiercely loyal to the deepest and most ancient roots of Hellenic culture, which means poetry. Not for him the casual contumely of an Eratosthenes; Strabo's prose, though modernist, is reverent towards the past, almost apologetic. The passing of the age of poetic inspiration is a source of sadness for Strabo.

When did prose writings take on these associations with modernity and rationalism?

The Prosaic Turn

Almost all of the texts we considered up until chapter 6 were composed in verse forms. A great variety of verse forms, for sure: the Homeric and Hesiodic poems are in dactylic hexameters (a traditional metre, but flexible and expressive, ideally suited to oral delivery); sympotic poetry uses a variety of metres to suit the mood; comedy and tragedy use various metres (including lyric metres and dialect for choral passages). Some poetry comes close to prose: tragedy favours the iambic trimeter for spoken passages, 'the most colloquial of metres', according to Aristotle (*Poetics* 1449a). But Strabo was, ultimately, right: prose makes its entry into Greek literature relatively late.

Where, when and why did prose literature develop? A difficult question to answer, not least because (as we have repeatedly observed) 'literature' is a difficult term to define with precision. Is a decree inscribed on stone (such as began to appear in Athens in the 440s BCE) 'literature'? Or a table of laws? Or even – to take an extreme example – the accounting lists that provide our earliest evidence (roughly thirteenth century BCE) for a proto-Greek language, in the form known as 'Linear B'? Difficult questions these, and perhaps idle. What counts is not so much pinpointing a notional point of origin, as interpreting the historical moment when extended prose texts gained a widespread cultural value, and the opportunity to vie with verse for status.

This process began in the late sixth century, and intensified considerably in the fifth.[2] Towards the end of the sixth century, Ionia (the west coast of what is currently Turkey) saw an explosion of abstract theorizing, much of it conducted in prose: cosmologists like

Anaximander, Anaximenes and (in a different way) philosophers like Heraclitus revolutionized the way the world was imagined, substituting rationalizing material explication for Homeric and Hesiodic mythicizing. We have already seen (in chapter 2) the bold and provocative anti-poetic self-positioning of Xenophanes of Colophon (sixth century BCE): 'Homer and Hesiod have attributed to the gods everything that is shameful and culpable among humans: stealing, adultery and deceiving each other' (fragment 11).

These new claims to intellectual authority were bound up with the large-scale reorganizations of authority in the wider sense across the Greek-speaking world: as the concept of citizenship and collective enfranchisement spread, and as established status became less secure as a guarantee of political influence, so the intellectual authority of the 'masters of truth' – kings, law-givers, poets – was increasingly challenged by dialectic and debate. The choice of prose as a literary form presents itself as a strategic marker of distance between newer claims to 'objective', 'scientific' truth and older models of inspiration and regal authorization.

The earliest explicit statement polemicizing against poetry comes from a prominent fourth-century Athenian orator and theorist.[3] In his *Antidosis* ('exchange of property'), Isocrates compares his expositive prose (which he calls 'philosophy', though it is far from what we would recognize as such) 'to musical, rhythmic compositions' (46; cf. 47). In this text, he appropriates the traditional power accorded to poetry for himself; in his *Evagoras*, however, he offers a very different perspective (whoever demanded consistency of an orator . . . ?). The *Evagoras* presents itself as a generic innovation, a prose hymn. Poetry, Isocrates complains, has an inbuilt advantage, with the number of 'adornments' (8) it can adopt: lexical, figural and metrical tricks help them as they 'entertain' audiences (10). But these are merely superficial devices: 'if one were to leave the words and thoughts of the most respected poets and take away the metre, they would be revealed as much lesser than the respect in which they are currently held' (11).

Prose-writing bespeaks a new confidence in the power of the intellect to displace traditional, unquestioned certainties about the world.

The Discourse of the Archive

Prose is also the distinctive voice of the archive. Poetry necessarily invokes oral delivery (even when it is being read privately): the heavy emphasis it lays upon sonority and rhythm constructs every reading as a performance, and every reader as a performer. Prose can be performed – especially in the form of rhetoric – but the texts we shall be discussing in this chapter are born of a predominantly literate society's impulse to exploit the power of writing to monumentalize. And in this respect, they are wedded to their institutional contexts, to the travelling schools and academies springing up over fifth-century Greece, and in particular in Athens – and, once again, it is to Athens that we must turn for our most copious and richest evidence. Equally important inspiration for the new discourse of prose came from the institutions of the Athenian polity. From the 440s onwards, Athens saw a massive expansion in the role of writing within the city, to preserve and memorialize the decisions of the citizen body.[4] This body of inscriptions (primarily exploited by modern scholars for crucial historical information) served in contemporary society to democratize language, to make it accessible, accountable and permanently binding.

Literature too was subject to these processes of fixing in memory. Our best evidence comes in the field of Athenian tragedy, where throughout the fifth century a canon of 'classics' was established.[5] Already by the time of Aristophanes' *Frogs* (which won first prize in 405), it is evident that Aeschylus, Sophocles and Euripides are the three dominant tragic poets. The play represents the god Dionysus (patron of theatre) descending into the underworld, in search of a poet to save the city. His initial choice of Euripides (frequently teased by Aristophanes for his vulgarity and faddishness) is corrected to Aeschylus (a more traditional, austere figure, in this depiction at least); Sophocles plays a more withdrawn role (1516). In the fourth century, the tragic competition included performance of old plays alongside new. One fourth-century tragedian, Astydamas, bewails, in an epigram inscribed on his statue base, that the race for tragic pre-eminence has already been won.[6]

Prose literature shares in this rhetoric of stable permanence, of self-evident and fully public authority. In arguably his most famous pronouncement, the fifth-century Athenian historian Thucydides (to whom we shall return) differentiates himself from his predecessors by stating that 'this work has been composed not as a competition piece to be listened to in the immediate present, but as a possession for ever' (1.22). Oral performance is to be understood (so Thucydides tells us) as a transitory, occasional phenomenon; Thucydides' work, by way of contrast, because it subsists in the form of prose, expects to stand the test of time. It is, fundamentally, an *archival* text.

Herodotus and the Origins of History

But let us step back to the generation before Thucydides, to Herodotus of Halicarnassus (on the southern Carian coast).[7] Herodotus composed (probably) in the 430s and 420s, and perhaps anticipated an Athenian readership. The immense work we know as the *Histories* recounts the Greco-Persian wars of the early fifth century, culminating in the defeat of the invading forces in a series of key engagements (Marathon, Salamis, Plataea). But the *Histories* are much more than simply a military narrative. In his prologue, Herodotus states his aim, to give a general structural account of relationships between Greeks and barbarians (non-Greeks: see chapter 10):

> The researches of Herodotus of Halicarnassus are here put forth, so that the things which men have done may not be wiped out by time, and so that the great and marvellous works (some put forth by Greeks, others by barbarians) may not be lost to memory, nor (amongst other things) the reason why they fought one another. (1. proem)[8]

I want to spend some time upon these opening words, as they repay close discussion. So much here situates Herodotus firmly in a fifth-century context. The opening self-identification foregrounds the narrative authority of the author (and echoes Herodotus' major predecessor in prose history: 'Hecataeus of Miletus recounts as follows'[9]): this is a narrative that will be *accountable*, the perspective of one man. The word used for 'researches' here is *historie* (the Ionic form of the Attic *historia*); Herodotus' programmatic usage at the outset of his text is the reason that the name 'history' is attached to the genre we know by that name. But for Herodotus, the word does not refer to an already existent genre; rather, he is making a statement of polemical *difference* from literary models. To research, to enquire: these are the hallmarks of a new age, in which simply claiming divine inspiration no longer carries absolute conviction.[10]

An account needs to be verified, tested, proven. Central to Herodotus' self-representation is the idea of travel, of *opsis* or 'seeing with one's own eyes'. When discussing the Egyptian pyramids of Cheops and Chephren, for example, he pointedly claims to have 'measured both of them myself' (2.127); or again, discussing the god Salmoxis, 'as I myself discovered from the Greeks who live around the Hellespont and the Black Sea . . .' (4.95). Herodotus' authority is predicated on his faculties of observation, calibration and assessment; and on sheer leg-work. Narrative truth is not 'naturally' invested in the speaker; it needs to be striven for. Unlike Homer (and indeed to an extent exceptional among ancient historians), Herodotus foregrounds his sources (naming witnesses, where he has not seen the phenomenon for himself), sometimes evaluating, but often refusing to judge between them.[11]

New Directions

We can map Herodotus' self-conscious modernism most clearly if we trace his relationship with Homer.[12] The prologue cited above is strongly Homeric; this goes beyond the common (but in points of detail actually rather divergent) use of the Ionic dialect. More important is Herodotus' self-conscious emphasis upon the role of the text as a preserver of social memory: just as Homeric poetry offers its protagonists *kleos* (fame, glory) in return for their great deeds, so Herodotean history seeks to prevent the 'great and marvellous works' of the Greeks and the barbarians becoming 'lost to memory' (*aklea*, 'without *kleos*').[13] Notably, though, it is not the individual who is being commemorated, but the actions of Greeks and barbarians, macropolitical units. In orientating away from the aristocratic warrior as the focus of battle, and onto collectives, Herodotus both foregrounds the ethnographic element in his work and bespeaks the more enfranchising, citizen-based language of his day.

Another epic echo is the posing of the rhetorical question ('the reason why they fought' – probably an indirect question, though the syntax is difficult and debated) that will be answered by the text that follows. (Herodotus proceeds to offer the Persians' explanation, which he then renounces in favour of his own: see below.) Likewise, Homer asks his readers 'which of the gods inspired them [Agamemnon and Achilles] with contention to fight?' (*Iliad* 1.8), and then answers the question in the next line.

Yet Herodotus conspicuously wields the word *aitia* (*aitie* in Ionic), 'reason' or 'cause', a word that very much belongs to the vocabulary of fifth-century rationalism, and does not appear in Homer. It is helpful to draw a brief comparison with the fifth-century treatise *On Ancient Medicine*, one of the numerous texts attributed (almost certainly wrongly) to the doctor Hippocrates. The Hippocratic text lays great store by the knowledge of the cause (*aitia*) of each bodily dysfunction. The opening words of the treatise advertise the central topic of the essay, the 'principle underlying the cause [*aitia*] of disease and death' (1); and the author proceeds to assert the importance of accurate knowledge of 'what man is, by what causes [*aitia*] he is made and the rest' (20).

Herodotus' echo of the beginning of the *Iliad*, then, is not just pious homage to the founder of Greek literature. Homer's famous phrase has been recast in the light of contemporary rationalism: this will be not just a narrative, but an *explanation* for events. 'The whole texture of Herodotus' writing', observes John Gould, 'is soaked in the explanatory mode: the narrative connection is constantly made through inferential particles ('for', 'therefore', 'and so' rather than 'then', 'next').[14] Like the Hippocratic author, Herodotus seeks to understand scientific *reasons*.

There is another difference between the Homeric and the Herodotean passages. Homer answers the question 'which of the gods ... ?' immediately and decisively. It was 'the son of Leto and Zeus' who caused the strife (*Iliad* 1.9). Herodotus, likewise, offers an immediate answer, but it is only a provisional one: 'Now the Persian chroniclers, on the one hand [*men*], say that the Phoenicians were responsible for the dispute' (1.1.1). The Greek word *men* usually expects a balancing *de* (often 'on the other hand'). The reader is made immediately and powerfully aware that the Persian account is only one possible explanation (it is narrated in indirect speech, the syntax emphasizing precisely this point). Herodotus then proceeds to offer the Phoenician variant: 'The Phoenicians, on the other hand [*de*], do not agree with the Persians concerning Io' (1.5.2). This sentence again introduces an account in indirect speech. The 'cause' of the Persian war thus assumes the status of a mystery, the solution to which the reader is encouraged to await eagerly. The effect is reminiscent of what Barthes calls the 'hermeneutic sentence':[15] the enigma (what caused the Persian war?) is formulated and proposed, then the solution suspended by means of the interpolation of 'decoy' responses.

What is wrong with the Persian and Phoenician explanations for the war? The Persians, Herodotus tells us, believe that the war began with a series of tit-for-tat abductions: the Phoenicians abducted the Greek Io, the Greeks the Phoenician Europa and the Asian Medea, the Asians abducted the Greek Helen ... The Phoenician story differs only in that they claim that Io went willingly. Two features of this story, we might expect, would have appealed to Herodotus: the emphasis upon reciprocity (central to his historical explanations)[16] and the stripped-down, demythologized rationalism that transforms idealized heroic narrative into petty spats. In fact, we might conclude that the Persian/Phoenician account, a strikingly modernist rewriting of received mythical narratives, is not so much wrong as preliminary, a first step on the road to understanding. The author positions himself not so much against the Persian/Phoenician account, as beyond it, in the world of *knowledge* rather than speculation:

> But I [*ego*] am not going to say that these things occurred in this or any other way – for I myself know who first began the injustices against the Greeks, and shall reveal him, then proceed to the next part of my account, going through small and big cities of men alike. (1.5.3)

The promise of disclosure marks the culmination of a predominantly poetic formula styled by modern scholars the 'priamel': the revelation of the first person pronoun, 'I' (*ego* – visibly emphatic in the Greek), is dramatically delayed by the prior catalogue of opinions of others. The words 'who first began the injustices against the Greeks' pick up the Persians' claim that Io's abduction to Egypt 'was the first beginning of injustices' (1.2.1) – with, of course, the crucial modification that the Persians merely claim, whereas Herodotus *knows*. The reader has been educated in the art of interpretation: do not trust the first report; sift the available sources, and follow the most authoritative. This is perhaps also the moral of the famous story of Arion and the dolphin (1.23–4), which can be taken as programmatic: the tyrant Periander initially mistrusts Arion's story that he was saved by the dolphin, but after 'enquiring' (*historeesthai*) of the would-be murderous sailors, learns that it is true. Like all good 'historians', Periander understands the importance of source-criticism.[17]

Science and the Word

Herodotus' insistence on his own rightness in contrast to others – what scholars call his 'agonistic' (or 'competitive') approach – can be paralleled in a number of contemporary medical and scientific writers.[18] Like the scientists, Herodotus also advertises 'the prominence of the authorial ego, the prizing of innovation both theoretical and practical, the possibility of engaging in explicit criticism of earlier authorities'.[19] Herodotus' own claim to innovation lies in his application of 'scientific' procedure to the question 'who started the Persian war?' Questions about the beginnings of wars were frequently posed in the fifth century,[20] and so this particular form of authorial self-dramatization is likely to have struck Herodotus' audience as particularly modern – and thus pointed up all the more vividly the contrasts with Homer.

The prologue, then, establishes the expectation that the author will revise Homeric explanations of the causes of war in the light of the new scientific revolution of the classical period. The fundamental question 'what started the war?' can no longer be answered in terms of simple divine agency ('it was Apollo . . .'); what needs to be grasped is the history of political conflict, stretching back generations previously. There are, pointedly, no divine apparitions in Herodotus. An invocation of Apollo, for sure, miraculously brings rain to quench the flames engulfing Croesus (1.87); and according to Pheidippides (who ran the first 'marathon', from the battlefield of Marathon to Athens), Pan appeared to him en route (6.106; compare also 8.65). And what is more, dreams, oracles and other prognostications point to an ongoing trust in cosmically sanctioned order (very different in Thucydides, as we shall see presently).[21] But there is nothing in Herodotus to parallel the divine apparatus in Homer, with its councils, decisions and quarrels. Quite the opposite, in fact. In one particularly instructive episode, the Athenians are teased for being taken in by a fraudulent epiphany: Pisistratus' tyranny is endorsed by a woman dressed up as Athena (1.60). Divinity, for Herodotus, is not an *explanation* for phenomena, but an abstract embodiment of the natural, proper order of things.

Such conspicuous excision of divine or mythological elements in favour of more 'plausible' explanations also finds a parallel in the scientific texts of the period.[22] The Hippocratic text *On the Sacred Disease* (i.e. epilepsy), for example, begins by referring to the 'so-called sacred disease' (1), and the author's scepticism about its sacred origins is heavily emphasized in what follows:

> It is not, in my opinion, any more divine or sacred than other diseases, but has a natural cause [*aition*], and its supposed divine origin is due to men's inexperience, and to their wonder at its peculiar character. (1)

The author then proceeds to attack those 'magicians, purifiers, charlatans and quacks' (2) who attribute epilepsy to divine intervention.[23] The disease is, however, caused (n.b. *aition*, etymologically linked to Herodotus' word *aitie*) not by divinity but by humanity (3). Although its polemic is more implicit, the scientific language of Herodotus' prologue promises a similarly 'rationalist' explanation of the causes of war, with divine and mythological apparatus expunged. Herodotus invokes epic in order to signal his own intellectual differences. In the *Histories* and the Hippocratic corpus alike, rationalist authority is asserted in a form of agonistic 'zero-sum' game (see chapter 3), by impugning the naivety of his predecessors.

Cultures of Hybridity

I want to conclude my discussion of Herodotus by examining a rather different form of narrative authority. The tour of Persian and Phoenician views of myth demonstrates not only the author's versatility and source-critical capabilities, but also the range of his cultural experience. There are two points to be made in this connection. Firstly, as a resident of Halicarnassus in Caria (in what we would call southwestern Turkey), Herodotus must have grown up with an awareness of the city's eastern as well as its western orientation (Halicarnassus oscillated between Persian control and independence in the sixth and fifth centuries).

Secondly, and perhaps more pointedly, Herodotus' self-representation as a non-parochial, almost cosmopolitan thinker, intersects with contemporary intellectual thought. Cultural relativism, the belief that different cultures hold different beliefs, is an idea born of fifth-century sophistry. We shall explore these ideas more fully in chapter 10, where we shall consider Herodotus' startling story of the Callatian Indians (3.38). To pre-empt briefly: Darius I of Persia asked some Greeks what would induce them to eat their dead relatives; then the Callatians, whose custom it was to eat their dead, what would induce them to cremate them. The outrage of both leads Herodotus to quote and concur with Pindar, that 'custom is the king of all'. The historian's self-representation as a traveller, which we have already noted, is linked to the construction of his narrative authority: Herodotus' wisdom is predicated upon his travel, upon his grasp of multiple perspectives. (Like the Athenian law-giver Solon (1.32) and the Scythian sage Anacharsis (4.76), who both, according to Herodotus, derive their wisdom from travel.)

We can, of course, question the extent to which the cultural-relativist principle is applied in the *Histories*. Herodotus has an undeniable habit of conflating Asiatics, as though 'barbarians' shared common traits by virtue of the fact of their not being Greek. This process is already visible in the Persian account of the origin of the war, discussed above, where the Colchian Medea, the Phoenician Europa and the Phrygian Trojans are all rather assimilated, in cultural terms. His descriptions of the customs of others tend to assume that Greek practice is the norm from which deviation should be marked: the Lydians, for example, 'have similar customs to the Greeks, except that they prostitute their daughters [!]' (1.94). And the logic of the narrative (culminating in the defeat of the armies of Persian Xerxes) suggests the intrinsic superiority of Greek over barbarian. This is occasionally articulated explicitly, even by Persians. At 3.80–3, three Persians trumpet the merits of monarchy, oligarchy and – rather implausibly – democracy; at 7.102, Demaratus tells Xerxes of the wisdom and valour that allow the Greeks to keep their enslavement at bay.

What matters most of all, however, is Herodotus' positioning against his predecessors. Homeric narrative explains through divine agency; it is entirely self-authorized, claiming inspiration from the muses. Narrative authority is largely bound up with political and religious authority, with the unexamined rights of certain individuals to decree the way things are to be understood. Herodotus, by way of contrast, *works* for his narrative authority. His narrative truth is presented as assiduously compiled, asserted against competing versions, and accountable. In short, it partakes of what we have been calling the discourse of the archive: like a decree inscribed in public space, the *Histories* monumentalize both the truth they express and (crucially) the open methods by which it was reached. In this respect, they very much exhale the air of the political organization of the time, particularly in Athens.

Thucydides and Historical Realism

Herodotus' great successor in the art of historiography was Thucydides, an exiled Athenian general who died some time after 404 BCE.[24] Whereas Herodotus had chosen the glorious subject of the defeat of the Persians, Thucydides addressed the grimmer subject-matter of the wars between the Athenians and the Spartans, which Athens eventually lost (431–404 BCE).

Thucydides' famous repudiation of 'showpiece' history ('this work has been composed . . . as a possession for ever', 1.22), which we have already considered, is usually taken to be an implicit criticism of Herodotus. Prior to that comment, he has warned that 'perhaps the absence of any mythical element will make the contents seem less pleasurable to hear' (1.22); a polemical statement of difference, that this text will lack the genial digressions and exotic 'marvels' that Herodotus embraces. Thucydides' *History* (as we call it, though no convincing title survives) is an austere, forbidding work; a work of theory, perhaps, as well as narrative. In the place of Herodotean pleasure, Thucydides offers utility:

> Perhaps the absence of any mythical element will make the contents seem less pleasurable to listen to; but it will be enough if those who want to contemplate the clarity of past events, and of those that (according to human nature) are likely to recur in this or similar form, judge my work useful. (1.22)

Thucydides embraces the Herodotean logic of hypermodern rationalism, but develops it to an extent unparalleled in his predecessor. There are no 'mythical elements' here at all: not even Herodotus' oracles. Thucydides' narrative is always dominated by the naturalistic mode, what Roland Barthes calls the 'reality effect'.[25] Herodotus deliberately chops up chronology, pursuing his rhetoric of mastery over complex narrative. Thucydides' work, on the other hand, 'has been written in the sequence in which each thing occurred, by summer and winter' (2.1). Mimicking the seasons of natural time, this narrative seeks to disguise its own partiality, to present things 'as they really happened'.

Another 'realistic' device is the general avoidance of explicit source criticism.[26] Herodotus, as we have seen, often foregrounds the conflicts between different sources, sometimes adjudicating but sometimes refusing to pronounce. Thucydides tends, rather, to present his account as self-evidently true, suppressing his sources. Not that he presents himself as any less meticulous in gathering information:

> As for the events of the war, I decided to write them down not after learning them from anyone I bumped into, nor in accordance with my own impression, but both in events where I was present and in those I gathered from others by proceeding through every point as far as possible with accuracy [*akribeia*]. (1.22)

This word *akribeia* (accuracy) recurs throughout the *History*, a keynote for the work and for its realist strategy. The narrative is, we are led to believe, firmly grounded in accurate observation; and indeed so well grounded that there is no need for discussion. An exception to the general rule about the representation of sources will prove instructive. In book 6, in the discussion of the mutilation of the herms (ithyphallic boundary markers) in 415 BCE, Thucydides digresses into some ancient history: the story of Harmodius and Aristogeiton, traditionally the sixth-century slayers of the last tyrant of Athens, Hipparchus. In this narrative, we have four explicit statements of sources: three inscriptions (6.54, 55, 59), and one reference to spoken information: 'I know this with confidence, more accurately [*akribesteron*] than the others, thanks to an oral source' (6.55). The crucial points here, however, are two. Firstly, this event occurred in 514 BCE, around a century before Thucydides was writing (and indeed very nearly a century before the mutilation of the herms). The recourse to sources is central to Thucydides' handling of and authorization of older material.

The second point relates to the comparative form 'more accurately', which proclaims this version's superior authority relative to other accounts. Indeed, Thucydides introduces the digression with a justification, namely to show how the Athenians know nothing 'accurate' (*akribes*) about this particular episode (6.54). Who are Thucydides' targets? The story of the tyrannicides had been told by both Herodotus (5.55–6; 6.123) and Hellanicus, a fifth-century Athenian historian now largely lost to us.[27] Thucydides' exceptional strategy of foregrounding his sources serves in this context a polemical purpose, to vaunt his 'accuracy' as a historian over that of others.

Speech and Narrative

Like all 'reality effects', though, Thucydidean *akribeia* is a technical device, an artifice, rather than a straightforward window onto reality. The narrative of the *History* is not a mirror of life as it was experienced at the time, but a subtle and intricate construction with the carefully plotted coherence and teleology (and, to be sure, the fiendish complexity) of a brilliant novel.[28] Nowhere is this problem more evident than in his treatment of speeches. As he explicitly states, it is difficult (both for him and for his informants) to remember the 'accurate detail' (*akribeia*) of what was said. His solution is notorious:

> The speeches have been given in the way I thought each man should most properly speak in the circumstances, keeping as close as possible to the overall intention [*gnome*] of the words actually spoken. (1.22)

The methodology behind the speeches, that is to say, contains an apparent contradiction: they are *both* claimed as accurate, close to the words actually spoken, *and* as plausible fictions invented to suit the logic of the narrative. Scholars have agonized over this tension.[29] What can Thucydides have meant? Why does he so flagrantly refute himself? But the problem only really presents itself if we fool ourselves into believing that Thucydides *was* the father of scientific (that is to say, positivist) history. Modern historiography since the late eighteenth century has always driven a wedge between 'representation' and 'reality', insisting that the latter, with its fully independent, autonomous existence, is the historian's primary objective. Thucydides, it seems, had much greater faith in the power of representation, of *narrative*, to embody truth. The speeches in the *History* do not aim at 'reality' in the positivist sense, but distil the speakers' 'intention', or *gnome* – a key word for Thucydides, suggesting logical order, rationality, structure. The truth he aims at is not the actual words spoken, but their *meaning* in the narrative.

To show how speeches embody this narrative meaning, let us conclude on Thucydides with a conspicuous example. In book 2, the Athenian statesman Pericles delivers a coruscating 'funeral speech' (alluded to in the previous chapter; see also chapter 10) over those who have died fighting for Athens over the previous year (the 'real' speech would have been delivered in 431–430 BCE).[30] Over twelve extravagant chapters (2.35–46), this stirring oration forges links between the individual and the community, between personal tragedy and civic triumph. The commemoration of the dead is (as we saw in chapter 3) a function traditionally accorded to epic; but as ever, in collectivist Athens there is a substantial distance marked from the individualistic world of Homer.

In particular, in Pericles' speech *there is no naming*. In the democratic city, the individual is overridden by public identity: 'some of them were perhaps less good men . . . but they have done more useful work for the city by their public actions than they harmed it in their private' (2.42). What is praised is instead the polity, its freedom and values, the ways in which 'we differ from our enemies' (2.39). The funeral speech is a masterful performance of Athenian ideology. And I do mean *performance*, for the medium (sophisticated oratory) underlines the message, namely the intellectual, cultural and political superiority of the city: 'We love beauty but not extravagance; we love wisdom, but not softness . . . The whole city is an education for Greece' (2.41–2).

As was discussed in the previous chapter, speeches are a central feature of ancient, particularly Athenian, society: they constitute visible, public enactments of ideologies, representations to the city of its own identity. Yet (as the previous chapter also emphasized) speeches are also provocations, representing necessarily partial and partisan perspectives; and the space in which they are delivered is agonistic, uncertain, embattled. Athens, in particular, seems to attract diverse judgements. In the 'Mytilenean debate' of book 3, the contumacious Cleon and his opponent Diodotus present opposing views of Athens's proper treatment of its subject states. This theme recurs in the 'Melian dialogue', where the Athenians contest their brutal imperial vision ('the strong do what they are empowered to do') with the dignified but doomed islanders of Melos (5.84–116). In book 6, before the disastrous Athenian expedition to Sicily, the conservative Nicias (advocating caution) is verbally outflanked by the flamboyant general Alcibiades, who advances a more seductive vision of Athens's international obligations and powers (6.9–19).

Pericles' speech, on the other hand, is free-standing; there is no voice raised explicitly in opposition. But the speech *is* carefully contextualized in the narrative, and the context suggests alternative views of the state of Athens. Firstly, we have had the earlier speech of the Spartan king Archidamus to his troops, inveighing against Athenian arrogance: 'All Greece supports us and hates Athens . . . the Athenians think they have a right to empire over others' (2.11–12). Secondly, Pericles' speech is immediately followed by the graphic description of the plague at Athens in 430 BCE (2.47–55), which brings not just misery but also anarchy and moral collapse (2.53). This episode provides a stunning antithesis to the glorious imperial vision promoted by Pericles in the funeral speech: two wholly different responses to the phenomenon of Athenian death. This sequence is capped with the final speech of Pericles, in which he defends his policy and attempts to stiffen Athenian resolve in the face of the plague (2.60–4); and his death, followed by an encomiastic obituary in the narrator's own voice ('it was under Pericles that Athens was at its greatest', 2.65). When considered in context, the speech comes across not simply as an isolated expression of Athenian greatness, but as a forceful attempt to control public perceptions of the city in the face of rapidly changing circumstances.

The 'truth' of the funeral speech, for Thucydides, lies not so much in resemblance to the words really spoken, as in its aptitude to this particular narrative structure, with its ironies and reversal; and, of course, to the characterization of Pericles, the visionary but embattled leader of Athens in the early stages of the war.

Archival Thinking

Thucydides and Herodotus represent different responses to the 'discourse of the archive', the culture of accumulation and interpretation born of a shift towards greater literacy and, in the political sphere, the public accountability and social utility of truth. Herodotus advances a new, rationalistic, demythologizing approach to narrative; his work, with its complex strategies of self-authorization (particularly in the explicit shuffling of sources and the agonistic positioning against other thinkers), combatively asserts the importance of intellectual *process*. Thucydides, on the other hand, claims his work as a 'possession for all times', the narrative dramatization of a set of generalizable laws of human nature. Historical truth, for him, lies in the evident recurrence of narrative sequences.

What unites these two authors is a focus upon recording for posterity, upon *archiving*. Like the decrees and dedications that begin to proliferate in the public spaces of Athens, like the libraries that accommodate the city's poetical works, historical texts seek to preserve the past against the ravages of time, in the hope that a community can be improved by them. So far from being an intellectually rarefied, specialist activity aiming at an abstract, disembodied truth, fifth-century history was imagined as an organic part of the city's processes of self-reflection and (it was to be hoped) self-improvement. Understanding politics, and the theoretical principles that underlie it (the causes, the patterns), is politically useful.

Herodotus and Thucydides quickly became canonical figures. In the fourth century, history became a major genre: Xenophon of Athens composed two works on the Near East, the *Education of Cyrus* and the *Journey Up-Country* or *Anabasis* (in which the author features heavily), as well as a continuation of Thucydides, the *Hellenica* or 'Greek matters'. We have many other Greek historians surviving complete or substantially from later times: Polybius, Diodorus of Sicily, Dionysius of Halicarnassus, Arrian, Appian, Cassius Dio, Herodian – as well as fragments of numerous others. Eloquent testimonies to the ongoing value attached by ancient Greeks to the archiving of the past, which was seen in later times as a crucial repository for cultural memory, even for cultural identity. The following chapters will trace the development of that archival mentality, firstly in Hellenistic Alexandria, and then in Roman Greece.

8

Building the Archive: Hellenistic Alexandria

Greece and the World

Alexander the Great of Macedon died in 323 BCE. Within the thirty-two years of his brief life, the entire known world changed. The largest empire that the world had ever seen was created by the conquests of a single general, spanning from Greece in the West to the Punjab in the East, and extending down into Egypt in the South. There was no power sufficient to withstand the Macedonian forces. The Persian empire, for centuries the oriental bogey haunting the Greek imagination, was crushed. The city of Rome exerted influence locally, but as yet showed few signs of expansionism.[1]

With military conquest came cultural dissemination. Though Alexander's successors withdrew from the eastern boundaries of his empire, Greek influences can be discerned in the architecture, art and religious iconography of most of the Middle and some of the Far East. The period between Alexander's conquests and the battle of Actium in 31 BCE (when Octavian, soon to be Augustus, gained control over the Mediterranean) is known as the 'Hellenistic' period, when territories were 'Hellenized' (or turned Greek). To most eyes, the aftermath of Alexander's conquests showed the world becoming Greek.

But matters were not quite that simple. For a start, as a Macedonian, Alexander had questionable Hellenic credentials. Macedonia was ambiguously poised north of the Greek peninsula, between Greek Thessaly and barbarian Thrace; though the royals were patrons of mainstream Greek arts (Euripides and Aristotle both spent time at court), ordinary Macedonians were little understood by other Greeks. Alexander's namesake predecessor, Alexander I of Macedon, had (according to Herodotus) been barred from competing in the Olympic games on the grounds that 'the contest is not open to barbarians, only Greeks' (5.22.2). Alexander responded, Herodotus tells us, by claiming Argive ancestry, and was subsequently admitted – and won first prize. In antiquity as much as now, Alexander and the Macedonians could easily be attributed or denied Greek identity according to the exigencies of the situation.[2]

Moreover, as post-colonial studies have shown, political conquest entails a bilateral process of cultural exchange, not simply the forceful superimposition of a dominant cultural template onto another.[3] According to Plutarch, Alexander's biographer, the general taught Persian boys to use Greek letters and Macedonian weapons (*Life of Alexander* 47.6); but he himself also took the decidedly ungreek step of proclaiming his divinity (28.1), and wearing Persian dress (45.1). Why? Plutarch states that the last case, the adoption of Persian clothing, could have been intended simply to please his Persian subjects – *or* to introduce an oriental-style domination over the Macedonians. An arrestingly modern corrective to the simplistic, imperialist view of Hellenization dominant in the nineteenth century: conquest can transform the victor as much as the victim. When Greek culture became the dominant force in the Middle East, it changed native cultures, but also transformed itself.

The Contests for Identity

Alexander's cultural ambiguity is only the strongest example of a wider tension within Greek identity during the Hellenistic period, resulting from the processes of upheaval and dispersal that characterized the aftermath of the conquests. After Alexander's death, the empire fragmented, as his generals Antigonus, Antipater, Cassander, Lysimachus, Ptolemy and Seleucus vied for control. There followed a period of highly complex warfare and negotiations. By the middle of the third century, however, the major players were clear: Asia (governed by the Seleucids), Macedonia (the Antigonids) and Egypt (the Ptolemies). Pergamum (in Asia Minor), too, enjoyed spells of importance, under the descendants of Attalus. Each of these mini-empires competed not only for political but also for cultural dominance, attempting to arrogate to itself the valuable capital of Hellenic pre-eminence. Much art and literature of this period was, so far as we can tell, sponsored by the various courts, in their attempts to proclaim Greekness (even if the form of that sponsorship may have varied). Even before themes or content are considered, cultural production was invested with political significance, a counter in a wider struggle to usurp the title of leading Greek state.

The Hellenistic period saw the creation of some magnificent cultural centres. Ephesus, with its awe-inspiring streets dappled with fine statuary; Pergamum with its famous library and distinctive school of sculpture (the famous 'dying Gaul' statue formed part of the monument commemorating Attalus I); and, most of all, Alexandria, site of the famous library and 'Museum' ('Mouseion', shrine of the Muses), the power-base of the Ptolemies. It is on this city, which produced most of our surviving literature from the period, that we shall focus for the remainder of this chapter; and on the third century BCE, the most productive period in literary terms.

The name Alexandria commemorates its founder; the city was to be the Macedonian general's capital in Egypt. It was famed throughout antiquity for its resplendent opulence. In a novel of the second century CE, *Leucippe and Clitophon* (its author, Achilles Tatius, may have been an Alexandrian), the narrator describes 'the brilliant beauty of the city', and how his 'eyes were filled with pleasure'. Finally he addresses his own eyes: 'We are beaten, my eyes!' (*Leucippe and Clitophon* 5.1). The city was a spectacle. Arriving from the Mediterranean, the visitor would be confronted by the lighthouse on the island of Pharos (just outside the harbour). Achilles also mentions this 'extraordinary marvel': 'it was a mountain lying in the middle of the sea, touching the very clouds' (5.6). The island was connected to the mainland by a newly built causeway, which also served to create two artificial harbours, one on the east and one on the west. Alexandria represented to all comers the power of civilization to tame nature. The power and wealth of the city's rulers (though in Achilles' time, the Romans were now in charge) were proclaimed through the grandiosity of its architecture and design. This strategy of imperial self-representation owed much to, but vastly exceeded, the fifth-century building programme of Athens (see chapter 5).

The city itself was transected by two enormous streets, one running north–south, the other east–west. The 'quadrant' shape of the city also had the effect of creating zones, which gave ideological and cultural shape to the city. The bottom of the south-western quarter was the native Egyptian area. Here was sited the temple of Sarapis, an interesting figure: this god does appear in Egyptian religion (as a fusion of Osiris and Apis), but was taken over by the Macedonians, assimilated to Dionysus, and forcibly promoted as a symbol of the new unity of Greek and Egyptian. The Sarapeum also housed a second city library. In the far north-east was the zone for the many Jews of the city, whether their ancestors had settled in Egypt as early as the eighth century or had arrived after Ptolemy I conquered Palestine in 302 BCE. According to the historian Josephus (first century CE), Alexandrian Jews had identical privileges to the Macedonians (*Against Apion* 2.35).[4] Jewish scholars flourished in Alexandria throughout antiquity, the most famous being Philo. But the Ptolemies' policy was not simply liberal: the presentation of their city as a symbol of multicultural coexistence mirrored their grandiose aspirations to a world-empire.

The Library

Literature played a crucial role in the construction of this extravagant vision. In the western side of the north-eastern quadrant, overlooking the eastern harbour, was the 'Brucheion', the royal quarter. A small promontory, called Cape Lochias, housed the palace; to the south were other palaces, the gardens, and – notably – the famous Museum, and its library.[5] The patronage of intellectual learning was fundamental to the Ptolemaic bid for cultural centrality in the new world order. Other Hellenistic courts offered libraries and literary patronage (notably Pergamum in Asia Minor, and particularly Macedonian Pella, where the astronomical poet Aratus was supported), but this was the most celebrated and awe-inspiring. According to one ancient source, Ptolemy II mandated Demetrius of Phalerum (the Athenian philosopher, who had served as a Macedonian 'puppet' ruler of Athens between 318 and 308) to create the library by accumulating 'all the books of the world':

> Demetrius of Phalerum was employed to take charge of the royal library, and furnished with many different sums to bring together, if he could, all the books of the world. By buying and transcribing [or, perhaps, 'translating'], he brought the king's plan to fruition, so far as he could. In our presence, now, he was asked how many books there were. 'Over two hundred thousand, O king', he replied. 'Soon I shall endeavour to complete the collection with the remaining five hundred thousand.' (*Letter of Aristeas* 9–10)

This report is not worth much in strict historical terms ('Aristeas' is not a real eyewitness but a fiction, probably concocted in the late second century BCE). There is no solid evidence elsewhere for

Demetrius' role in the library, and Ptolemy II, the king here, is probably confused with Ptolemy I, the likelier founder of the Museum.[6] But what it does exemplify is the symbolic role of the library, predicated upon the ideological connection between the international aggregation of books and imperial power.

The question of translation from other languages is tantalizing. The specific word used here might simply mean 'transcribing', but the passage as a whole is designed to provide an explanation for how the Hebrew Septuagint was rendered into Greek. If we can trust this late and unreliable source, we can hypothesize an additional layer of cultural imperialism: the library centralized not just Greek, but all known learning, converting it into the master tongue of Greek.[7] The evidence is weak, but other sources testify that Hellenistic Alexandria presented Greek education as a universal lingua franca of civilized existence. The Alexandrians, according to one writer, were 'the educators of all the world, of both Greeks and barbarians'.[8]

The museum was not without precedent as an institution. According to some traditions, it was Aristotle who was the first to collect books. Aristotle was one of the forces behind the huge drive towards the codification of knowledge in fourth-century Athens, what we have called the invention of the archive; Demetrius of Phalerum was his pupil's (Theophrastus') pupil. For many observers, the Alexandrian Museum complex would have alluded, by a kind of architectural intertextuality, to the Lyceum, Aristotle's intellectual powerhouse in Athens. This was located, at least from Theophrastus' time, in a grove sacred to the Muses – so it was already a 'Museum' of sorts. As in the Lyceum, the scholars of the Museum covered an enormous range of specialisms, from (what we would call) science, through topography and antiquarianism, to poetry.

The Lyceum offered a prestigious precedent, then; but as with all intertextual allusions, it is just as important to see how the model is transformed. Sited in Egypt, away from the mother country, the Alexandrian Museum depended for its cultural valency upon the new symbolics of internationalism. But also – and equally crucially – it operated under royal patronage. Members benefited greatly from Ptolemy's favour: free meals, salaries, tax breaks and high social status. If Aristotle's Lyceum was the result of the fourth century's expanding vision for the possibilities of *paideia* – 'political' only in an abstract sense, in that it extolled the dominance of Greek culture – then the Museum represented a new attempt to concentrate its political capital in the hands of one man and the ideological system he represented.

The Language of the Archive

Most Alexandrian literary production – most surviving examples of which are concentrated in the first half of the third century BCE – is likely to have been conditioned by the Museum and the library. Many of the major literary players of the period are known to have held prominent posts. Callimachus of Cyrene (a Greek city in Libya, and part of the Ptolemaic empire), the most celebrated poet of the age, relocated to Alexandria, and soon found himself patronized by Ptolemy Philadelphus, the second Ptolemy (who ruled from 285 to 246 BCE; his influence looms over all the poets discussed in this chapter); it was Callimachus who compiled the first catalogue for the library (see below).[9] Apollonius of Rhodes, author of the epic *Argonautica*, was the second librarian, after Zenodotus (the renowned textual critic). He wrote several learned prose works, including *Against Zenodotus*, where he disputed his predecessor's suggestions for the improvement of the Homeric text.[10] Eratosthenes, like Callimachus a Cyrenaean, wrote in a prodigiously diverse range of genres, from poetry to topography, historical chronology, mathematics, science and Homeric criticism.[11] He was Apollonius' successor as head of the library. Among the major poets of third-century Alexandria, only Theocritus, the author of a number of short hexameter poems on rural and urban themes, has no obvious connection with the Museum and library.

Greek literary tradition had (as we have repeatedly seen) always been self-reflexive, articulating political and cultural change by signalling literary shifts. But this archival turn (anticipated, as we have seen, in the intellectual culture of classical Athens) represented something largely new in Greek culture. The construction of the archive entailed a 'classicization' of past authors, whereby their products offered themselves up no longer only to performance or reading, but also to sustained and rigorous study. The canonical poems of antiquity were engaged with not simply on the referential level, but also as intellectual problems, or as evidence for lost historical and cultural practice.

In *The Order of Things*, his work on changing patterns in the human sciences, Michel Foucault distinguishes an earlier phase in which literature was held to be 'composed of a signifying element and a signified content, so that it was proper to analyse it accordingly', and a later development: 'from the nineteenth century, literature began to bring language back to light once more in its own being'.[12] Hellenistic Alexandria, similarly, began to focus on literature and language 'in its own being', not just as representative of a reality. As we shall see in the following section, Alexandrian poetry shows a new awareness of technical treatises on (for example) poetic metre, the emendation of the text of Homer and lexicography.

Constructing the Canon

In the last two chapters, we have traced the emergence of prose discourse as a cultural phenomenon. In Athens of the fifth and fourth centuries, prose marked a new confidence in the permanence and authority of the archive, and hence in the power of Greek 'culture' (another translation of *paideia*) to transcend its narrow temporal and spatial limits. In Hellenistic Alexandria, the archival resources of the library dominated all literary production. In a sense, Callimachus' *Tablets*, his guide to the books in the library, epitomized what Hellenistic culture was all about: thorough to the point of exhaustion, minute, voluminous (120 books!), authoritative. Most of all, the *Tablets* represent not simply literature, but meta-literature: texts about texts, language about language. The *Tablets* are now lost, but comments in later writers allow us to infer that Callimachus subdivided 'all *paideia*', verse and prose, into genres. Within each genre, authors were listed alphabetically, and under each author there was biographical information and an alphabetical list of texts (with first lines, to prevent ambiguity).

The impulse to categorize, to taxonomize, was born of the archival mentality, an articulate expression of the literary consciousness of the age. But the *Tablets* were not simply an uninspired, functional exercise: they represented a monumental achievement, a confident bid for cultural authority in the present and infinite fame in the future. To understand the intellectual dynamics of the Museum, we need to recall the centrality to Greek cultural authority at every register – from Iliadic warfare to democratic rhetoric – of competition. The Museum was famous for its intense rivalries and hostilities. In a well-known poem, the sceptic Timon of Phlius (*fl.* third century BCE) satirized the scholars, comparing them to the animals in Ptolemy's zoo: 'Many book-scratchers are pastured in multicultural Egypt, squabbling endlessly, in the birdcage of the Muses.'[13] In this aggressive, agonistic context, the *Tablets* constituted a boldly provocative challenge, an attempt to reify the canon, and so to play gatekeeper to the subsequent reception of all literature. And it is instructive to note that many of the fragments we do have of the *Tablets* are preserved in hostile sources, questioning the title, attribution or biographical data supplied by Callimachus. Aristophanes of Byzantium, the fourth head of the library (and perhaps a pupil of Callimachus), wrote a text *Against* (or perhaps *In Reply to*) *Callimachus' 'Tablets'*, now lost except for one brief allusion.[14] The literary critic Dionysius of Halicarnassus, writing around the turn of the millennium, frequently refers to the *Tablets*, whether for praise or for blame.[15]

Cataloguing was only one means of ordering the sum of textual knowledge. As well as commentaries and lexicographical tables (such as the glossary produced by the influential poet Philetas of Cos, who flourished in the third century), Hellenistic Alexandria saw the first systematic attempts to 'correct' the texts of the classics, and particularly of Homer, with the aim of producing texts that cohered logically, culturally, syntactically and lexically. This was done primarily by emendation or deletion of lines. The key players here were the three librarians Zenodotus, Aristophanes of Byzantium (the author of the response to Callimachus' *Tablets*) and Aristarchus.[16] As with cataloguing, so textual criticism was a highly agonistic enterprise, born of (and ever anticipating) the incessant struggles for intellectual authority in the Museum. The rhetoric of this new critical approach is aggressively supremacist: texts were to be 'set upright', the *obelos*, or marginally inscribed 'spit', pointing to the offending lines that were to be gouged out.

The most extreme form of engagement with this burgeoning tradition was outright rejection: the satirist Timon of Phlius is said by one late source to have told his pupil, the poet Aratus, to use old copies of Homer, not those now 'corrected' (Diogenes Laertius 9.113). Within the Museum, however, scholars vied by proposing contrary interpretations, emendations and deletions. As with modern textual criticism (see chapter 2), those Alexandrians who reached the highest pinnacles of fame were those who (successfully) proposed the most far-reaching alterations to the text. The scholars Aristophanes and Aristarchus, notably, are said to have put the end of the *Odyssey* at line 23.296, thus removing a book and a half of the received text.

Though the Museum-library complex is often credited with the 'invention' of the protocols of scholarship as now understood, it is best to resist understanding the past in terms of its relationship to the present (this is often referred to as 'teleology'). Rather than viewing it as a stepping-stone from primitive to modern intellectual habits, let us consider it instead in its contemporary context, as a powerful transformation of established modes of engagement with Greek literature. Hellenistic Alexandria's literary technologies were first and

foremost attempts to root the spectacular city in the prestigious past
of Greece, to construct cultural continuity between the multicultural
capital of Egypt and the indigenous traditions of the mainland. But
the prevalence of second-order commentary (exegesis and criticism) on
earlier texts – what we might call the 'metaliterary' – simultaneously
marked the distance between present and past. It is this equivocal
position, between cultural continuity and cultural innovation, that is
repeatedly articulated in Hellenistic poetry.

Performance and the Book

Was Hellenistic poetry composed for reading or performance? Was
there still a living, vibrant song culture for which poets wrote, or
were these 'book-texts' produced in and for ivory towers? A difficult
question to answer. Certainly, Alexandria had its many festivals,
often revisions of mainland Greek institutions (such as the 'grand
procession' of Ptolemy Philadelphus, modelled on the Athenian Great
Dionysia).[17] But the question of the role of the surviving poems in
these festivals remains unclear. The beginning of Callimachus' *Hymn
to Apollo*, for example, conspicuously raises the question of a performance context:

> How the shoot of Apollo's laurel has shaken!
> And the whole roof, too! Begone, begone, any sinner!
> Phoebus surely steps on the doorway with his handsome foot.
> Can you not see? The Delian date-palm suddenly
> nodded, the swan sings beautifully in the sky.
> You yourselves, gate-bolts, draw back now;
> you yourselves, bars! For the god is not far away.
> Young men, prepare the song and for the dance. (1–8)

Nothing is known of any performative context for Callimachus'
hymns, or indeed whether they were performed at all.[18] Is this a real
cult poem? Does the 'Delian date-palm' imply that the poem was
performed on the holy island of Delos (itself the subject of one
of Callimachus' hymns)? Or is it an indication that the poem is a
fiction, dramatically set in a place far away from the scene in which
it would have been encountered in reality? (And also a knowing
literary allusion: Odysseus compares the young Nausicaa to the Delian
date-palm.[19])
    Between these two extremes, alternative possibilities can be imag-
ined: that it was performed solo in a festival to Apollo in Alexandria,

for example. Scholars have increasingly (and no doubt rightly) moved away from the view of these poems as ivory-tower productions, composed by the few exclusively for the few (like the literary games of dons in Victorian Oxford and Cambridge). There is no solid reason to doubt that poems like Callimachus' hymns were composed for a performance culture, although performance scenarios no doubt included (what we would call) more 'private' contexts, such as the symposia of the Ptolemies.[20]

But two caveats are in order. Firstly, the mere fact that a poem was (or may have been) performed publicly does not mean that it operated in the same way that the older, 'Homeric' hymns did, as expressions of the solidarity of a community. Alexandrian poetry (as we shall see presently) is preoccupied with divisions and hierarchies. Secondly, whether composed for performance or not, poems like this are aware that they (also) have a life as written texts. This gives an extra edge to the realist (or 'mimetic', as scholars call them) devices the poet adopts. The sensory overload (the shaking of foliage and architecture, the singing of the swan) becomes then tantalizingly evocative, but also recognizably and necessarily absent. 'Can you not see?' is a challenge to the reader: how powerfully can you imagine the scene? The god's heralded epiphany figures the aesthetic ambition of the text: Apollo 'is not far away', but he is nevertheless frustratingly out of view. The reader occupies an uncertain position in the poem's fictional scenario, between the initiates celebrating the ritual and the 'sinners' who are, according to the conventional mystery formula used here, banished far away. We might take this as a figure for the Hellenistic reader, uncertainly poised between 'authentic' Greek tradition and later, unauthorized imitation.

A poem like this confronts us with a profound question of identity. Do later readers belong to this intrinsically Greek world of initiates and neophytes? Are we part of it? Is it (still) our world? This question is treated in an even more complex manner in the same poet's *Hymn to the Bath of Athena*.[21] Here, the ritual described mimetically is specifically addressed to a band of girls from Argos. It is highly unlikely that many of Callimachus' readers or listeners would have been Argive virgins. The Argive cult has been (so the ancient commentators on the passage tell us) reconstructed by the poet from the (now lost) *Argolica* of Agias and Dercylus, authors he may have come across in compiling his works on *The Foundations of Islands and Cities, and their Changes of Name*, or *Names Used by Peoples*. The poet does not himself belong to the community of ritual practitioners; to describe the ritual detail, he needs historical sources.

What makes this poem doubly disturbing for the late, male voyeur spying on this ritual is its pair of embedded stories. The first tells of the blinding of the prophet Tiresias, for having unwittingly observed Athena bathing; the second (ostensibly a consolation to Tiresias' mother) of Actaeon's death at the hand of his hunting dogs for having seen Artemis bathing. This pair of narratives, stigmatizing the illicit viewing of females by males (and of gods by mortals), interacts with the mimetic device of the frame: are these cautionary tales for us readers? A frisson of dangerous pleasure . . .

Whether Callimachus' audience encountered his poems in an oral or written form (or both), these are texts that knowingly play with the reader's sense of separation from the religious world described (albeit perhaps only partial and intermittently experienced separation; nothing as strong as alienation or dislocation). These are hymns for a world that is conscious of the text as mediation, aware that its role is to create reality as much as to reflect it.

Insiders and Outsiders

Alexandrian poetry repeatedly confronts the reader with questions of membership. At issue is not just whether we belong to the religious communities evoked in Callimachus' *Hymns*, but also whether we belong to the knowing, learned community of super-educated intellectuals epitomized by the Museum. In a world in which literary production is limited to an elite, every poem is (in a sense) a *challenge*.

This is why Alexandrian poetry tends to be so difficult, involved and complex. The language is dazzling, a fusion of recherché Homerisms (*hapax legomena*, that is words found only once in Homer, are particularly favoured), allusive periphrases, ingenious etymologies and incongruous colloquialisms. This is language that promotes, as Foucault would have it, its status 'in its own being'. Even the poems of Theocritus of Syracuse that are notionally presented as the words of countryfolk are suffused with complex allusion.[22] The 'cup' that is offered as a prize for singing in *Idyll* 1, for example, is called a *kissubion* (27). Not only does Theocritus' goatherd offer an etymological derivation for this word (from *kissos*, ivy), but also the word is rare and Homeric, used most prominently of the cup from which the Cyclops drinks the wine that inebriates him (*Odyssey* 9.346). In poem 7, again, the rustic speaker refers to a certain Sicelides; the name is a knowing nickname for the epigrammatic poet Asclepiades (7.40). The most overwrought example of such complexity is perhaps

Lycophron's *Alexandra*, a poem in nearly 1,500 lines that 'prophesies' large tracts of Greek mythology in an impossibly dense idiolect. It is hard to believe that many readers would have been able to spot that the name 'Cerdylas Larynthius', for example, refers to Zeus (1,092).

The emphasis upon segregating insiders and outsiders, on creating and exploring boundaries, also partly explains the explosion in popularity of the epigram.[23] While it is difficult to generalize across the diverse range of forms that epigrams by Hellenistic poets exploited (funerary, erotic, sympotic, votive . . .), one feature is common: the simulation of a dialogue between text and addressee. Epigrams hail their readers, inviting them into an imaginary relationship. Here lies the distinctively Alexandrian challenge: are you comfortable with the role foisted upon you? Can you speak this language? Can you engage with this poem?

Let us take an example, from Theocritus:

> This bank allots equally to citizens and foreigners.
>   Deposit and withdraw according to your balance when the
>   account is set up.
> Let another man offer a pretext; but Caicus counts out foreign
>   Money at night, to those who want it. (14)

This epigram may or may not have been composed for a real bank run by a real Caicus. But whether or not that is the case, Theocritus surely wrote in full awareness that the poem would be circulated further afield, where the detail would not necessarily be understood. And when this poem is read out of context, it becomes a form of riddle.[24] Who is Caicus? Why does his bank open at night? Is there an insinuation that Caicus prostitutes himself to all comers? The point is that rather than seek to answer these questions (as though hypothesizing a fixed, original context would exhaust the poem's meaning), we should recognize the role of the poem's calculated enigma. The difficulty in making sense of these texts is part of their meaning. When we engage with them, we are already rising to the challenge, staking our own claim to join the limited club; but the very frustrating opacity of these texts makes decoding them a (deliciously) uncertain activity.

Past and Present

Callimachus' most famous poem is the *Aetia* or 'causes', a series of episodic narratives (spread over four books) united by the theme of explaining how things are the way they are. 'Aetiology' is nothing new in the Greek tradition. As we saw in the previous chapter, Herodotus and the Hippocratic writers both invest considerably in their ability to determine the 'causes' (*aitia, aitiai*) of phenomena. Narratives telling of the foundation of cities and races are widespread: the earliest elegiac poetry probably dealt with such themes (see chapter 4), which also resurface in the victory poems of the fifth-century Theban poet Pindar. Many of Euripides' tragedies conclude with the establishment of a ritual that his contemporaries would have recognized. In the context of Hellenistic Alexandria, however – an 'invented' city, with no indigenous ritual – such aetiology takes on a wholly different complexion.

Let us begin with the prologue to the *Aetia*, one of the most famous passages in Greek literature. Callimachus begins by attacking the dullards who criticize his poetry, whom he names the 'Telchines' (after the mythical race of primeval monsters), before proceeding to propound his own aesthetic principles: he privileges subtlety, lightness and sophistication of execution over the 'noisy song' (19), the 'asses' braying' (30) of his competitors. The poem clearly creates a barrier between cultivated and boorish literary critics.

Who are the Telchines? The ancient commentary on this passage names names (among them the epigrammatic poets Asclepiades and Posidippus), but presumably misses the joke in doing so. When you read this poem, *you do not know* who the Telchines really are; and, more to the point, you do not know whether or not you are one of them. This preface constitutes another Alexandrian challenge: Callimachus is drawing up boundaries of inclusion and exclusion, inviting the reader to side with him.[25] The Telchines are a (strategically and necessarily) non-specific group. It is also worth emphasizing that the relatively obscurantist name Callimachus gives his opponents (the Telchines are a fairly obscure bunch) is already erecting intellectual boundaries, testing the extent of the reader's knowledge and cultivation.

In the *Aetia*, Callimachus represents himself as the guardian of a sophisticated and deep-rooted intellectual heritage. When we read this text, we become aware of the extraordinarily rich vertical shafts of history that transect the horizontal plane of Greek geography and ritual. Let us take as an example the best-preserved section of the text, the story of Acontius and Cydippe from book 3 of the *Aetia* (see also chapter 11). The narrative itself is beguilingly simple: the young man Acontius falls for the maiden Cydippe, and tricks her into reciprocating. He rolls her an apple inscribed 'I swear by Artemis to marry

Acontius'. Cydippe reads the inscription (aloud), and thus formally binds herself to him. With its tension between the naivety of the young lovers and the sophisticated, self-referential emphasis upon the power of the text, this narrative encapsulates Callimachean poetics brilliantly. More important for our purposes, however, is the use to which the narrative is put, the nub of the aetiology. 'From that marriage', Callimachus writes, 'a great name was due to emerge' (50). The story explains how the Acontiadae (or descendants of Acontius) came to occupy the island of Ceos (as it would later be called). The 'aetiology' or explanation serves to root the identity of the islanders in an ancient, founding act.

What is particularly striking about this account is that Callimachus names his source: 'Xenomedes of old, who once set down the entire island in a mythological memoir' (54–5). Xenomedes is an otherwise obscure fifth-century chronicler. This kind of footnoting is common in prose (Herodotus uses it, for example), but unheard of in verse. This importing of the 'annotatory' voice into poetry is not just an example of Callimachus' literary experimentalism, but also underlines that the master-poet is a master-scholar. The poet presents himself as sure-footed, rational, commanding, in his construction of cultural links between past and present; but the scholar is also distanced from the past, needing an intermediary to provide him with this cultural know-how.

Callimachus is not the only Hellenistic poet to employ the aetiological mode. I want to conclude this section by looking briefly at the *Argonautica* of Apollonius of Rhodes, the only complete epic poem surviving from this period.[26] Apollonius' interest in aetiology can be glimpsed from the few surviving fragments of his *Foundations*, poems on the origins of cities.[27] His major poem, the *Argonautica* (the story of Jason's travel to the Black Sea to acquire the Golden Fleece), also has powerful aetiological elements.[28] Let us take an example. In book 2, the prophet Idmon dies on the Black Sea littoral, gored by a bull. The tomb built to him by the Argonauts 'can still be seen, even by late-born generations' (2.842). The heroic past is distant, but present yet: the traces it has left behind are visible on the contemporary landscape. Even so, Apollonius makes his readers aware of the massive gulf between the past and the 'late-born generations' of the present. Not least thanks to the addition of the particle 'even': *even* now (despite the passing of time) we can still see the tomb.

Like Callimachus, Apollonius constructs himself as an exclusive guardian of the past. Indeed, the contemporary inhabitants of the area, he tells us, have misidentified the tomb as that of Agamestor

(2.850). Apollonius knows better, 'if I must speak openly, under the influence of the Muses' (2.844–5). Engaging in some characteristically Alexandrian polemics (presumably directed against scholars who held this view, rather than the real inhabitants), Apollonius vaunts his ability to offer an accurate account, authorized by the Muses – who, in this context, must be imagined as the patrons of the Museum (literally the 'shrine of the Muses'). This is poetry that is ceaselessly aware of its own authoritative role in forging and maintaining links with the past.

Poetry and Patronage

Hellenistic poetry largely bypasses the more consensual, egalitarian poetics of democratic Athens. 'I hate everything common', Callimachus famously writes (*Epigram* 2.4). Though his principal objection is to intellectual vulgarity, there is a political component too: the word for 'common', *demosia*, denotes the sphere of the *demos*, the 'people' whose power was advanced in democracies. Intellectual, cultural and political elitism are all bound up together. Alexandrian poetry is – pointedly – anti-populist. 'Do not drive your chariot along the same tracks followed by others', Apollo advises the poet in the prologue to the *Aetia*, 'nor along the broad road; choose untrodden paths, even if the drive is narrower' (26–8).

   This is not simply a reflection of poetic or scholarly 'elitism': as we have seen, it is possible that Alexandrian poetry was composed for performance before the public. The point is, rather, that these texts articulate and disseminate a view of the role of culture and intellect as a justification for social hierarchies. To possess superior culture is to be more Greek, which is to claim higher status. 'Possessing' culture, however, does not simply mean practising it; it also, and more particularly, means patronizing it.

   At the apex of the social pyramid stood Ptolemy, the Alexandrian king. Theocritus' fifteenth *Idyll* describes the visit of two respectable but socially unremarkable women, amid a great throng, to the palace of Queen Arsinoe (the wife of Ptolemy Philadelphus). When they arrive, they marvel at the tapestries, and listen with pleasure to the performance of a poem. Although the poem is said by an ancient commentator to derive from a (now lost) mime by the fifth-century poet Sophron, it surely depicts a contemporary world, testifying both to the thriving song culture of Ptolemaic Alexandria and to the role of royal patronage.

Certain Alexandrian texts are directly political.[29] Callimachus' *Hymn to Zeus*, for example, celebrates the power of the king of the gods before drawing a direct comparison with Ptolemy ('our ruler seems to be testimony to this . . .', 85–6; see also *Hymn to Delos* 171–95; *Hymn to Apollo* 2.25–9). Theocritus' seventeenth *Idyll* praises Ptolemy directly. Both these poems adapt a number of traditional motifs from the archaic and classical poetry of kingship (see chapter 3). Callimachus lifts the phrase 'from Zeus come kings' (79) from Hesiod's *Theogony* (96); Theocritus reworks the fifth-century praise poets Pindar and Simonides, as well as Homer and Hesiod.[30] Such allusiveness falls squarely within the poetry's encomiastic compass, bestowing upon Ptolemy not just the prestige of association with famous figures from the poetic past, but also the intellectual and cultural aura generated by the process of unpacking intertextuality.

The traditional repertoire of monarchical praise, however, is inter-woven with wholly new themes. Theocritus 17 compares Zeus and Hera to Ptolemy Philadelphus and his wife Arsinoe, on the grounds that they are siblings as well as husband and wife (133–4). The *hieros gamos* ('sacred marriage' – that is, incest) was certainly a feature unfamiliar to the Greek tradition so far. Moreover, there are a number of traditional Egyptian motifs in the poem, serving to construct a pharaonic guise for the king: the representation of Ptolemy as the guardian of the Nile's fertile waters, for example (77–80), and as an embodiment of abundance (11–12).[31] In instances like these, we can see the complex work performed by Alexandrian encomium: this poetry located Ptolemaic kingship simultaneously in two political traditions, rooting it in traditional Greek idioms while adapting those idioms in light of the new cultural and political demands of the present.

Other texts are perhaps more obliquely political. Apollonius' *Argonautica*, dealing with the voyage of Jason to recover the Golden Fleece, can be read in ideological terms, as a clash between the Greek heroes and eastern barbarians.[32] Certainly there are contrasting im-ages of kingship: on the one hand, the terrifying Colchian king Aeëtes in book 3; on the other hand, the wise, benevolent and (not least) civilized figures of Alcinous and Arete, who protect Medea and the Argonauts from Colchian brutality. Yet the question of leadership between the Argonauts is not that simple. Jason is certainly a 'good' leader in that he respects the consensus and works for the collective; in this respect, he stands in opposition to the figure of Heracles, the violent individualist, the embodiment of primitive epic values (who is conveniently left behind at the end of book 1).[33] But he is also a problematic figure, constantly beset by 'helplessness', ever indecisive.

He is hardly a comforting paradigm for leadership. When confronted by the blustering Colchian Aeëtes, for example, he is described as 'helpless before this wickedness' (3.423).[34] The *Argonautica* is far from presenting a straightforward map of good and bad leadership.

Alexandria and its literary institutions represent a decisive new phase in the cultural history of Greek literary production. The poetry produced in this city is the product of a new, confident, highly textualized world-view, directed by a ruler with imperial ambitions. If classical Athens invented the archive as a model for Greek literary memory, then Ptolemaic Alexandria turned the archive into an expression of massively ambitious cultural power and technology. At the same time, however, we can see in the poetry of this period signs of tension, of an awareness that the relationship between the traditional Greek past and the new Greco-Egyptian present is not altogether straightforward.

9

Reading from the Archive: Roman Greece

The Invention of Achaea

Arguably, the most significant year in classical antiquity was 31 BCE. In early September, the naval forces of Octavian engaged those of Marcus Antonius and his Egyptian wife, Cleopatra, just outside the gulf formed by a promontory called Actium (in north-west Greece). Though the battle itself was nothing spectacular (the dominant modern image, Cecil B. DeMille's sequence in the film *Cleopatra*, is massively exaggerated), Octavian's victory had lasting consequences for Rome, Europe and the world. After Actium, with the last of his powerful Roman enemies subdued, Octavian commanded the entire Mediterranean. He changed his name to Augustus, assumed the title 'father of the fatherland', and invented a form of power that was wholly new to Rome. Appropriating aspects of Hellenistic Greek and oriental kingship ideology – but understandably resisting the title 'king', which carried despicable connotations – Augustus became the first Roman emperor.[1]

Augustus' accession had wider implications for the shaping of the Mediterranean world. In 27 BCE, four years after Actium, the territory of Greece was for the first time politically united, integrated as it was into the newly created province of Achaea. Rome had been engaged in military confrontations in Greece since the mid-third century BCE: wars with the Carthaginians (in modern Tunisia) had embroiled it in a complex series of struggles with Hellenistic Greek states and confederacies. Macedonia, Carthage's ally, had put up stern resistance, only to be annexed as a province in 147 BCE. Rome's expansionist policy was to prefer to cede formal autonomy in return for submission. At times, though, intervention could be less subtle, as the Corinthians discovered, when their city, the centre of the Achaean League, was razed to the ground in 146 BCE.

Despite the constant pressure exerted upon Greece over the previous centuries, however, the creation of Achaea represented something new. A province was an administrative unit within the Roman empire, run by a Roman governor who reported, ultimately, to the emperor himself. Now there was no possibility of any comforting masquerade of independence. Nor was there any differentiation on the political map of Greece. The diverse, independent city-states that had made up Greece were all now overridden by a larger political entity: not just Achaea, the administrative unit, but the Roman empire, a geopolitical structure that covered much of the known world, from Britain in the west (finally subdued in the mid-first century CE) to the Euphrates in the east; from north Africa in the south to Belgium in the north.

The choice of the name 'Achaea' to denote the province is significant. The word is Greek, and indeed reaches back into the distant removes of history. In the *Iliad* and the *Odyssey*, Homer employs the names 'Achaeans' and (to a lesser extent) 'Danaans' or 'Argives' to mark the group that later writers would style 'Hellenes', Greeks (see chapter 10). In choosing an archaizing name, Augustus and his advisers were concealing the radical act of unifying Greece behind a screen of deeply rooted tradition. Just as he claimed to be 'restoring the republic' at Rome when he inaugurated a wholly new form of government, so the invention of Achaea masked itself as the restitution of a traditional state.

Presenting Greece in such archaic terms, moreover, was itself an imperialist strategy. For centuries, Romans had constructed an image of Greece in exclusively cultural terms, branding it as a world of ancient ideas and images; in implicit opposition, of course, to the progressivist city of Rome, with its military vigour and political vitality (and, for sure, its own antiquities). In Virgil's *Aeneid*, the Latin epic exploring the monumental aspects of Augustus' vision for Rome, Anchises (Aeneas' dead father) speaks the following hortatory words: 'others may perfect the arts of sculpture, oratory and astronomy, but you, Roman, remember to rule peoples with empire' (6.851–2). Romans toured the ancient cities of Greece, studied in its academies, were initiated into their mysteries, grew beards, got themselves boyfriends, pillaged statues and artworks for their halls – but always, as Anchises advised, remembered that they were the rulers. Patronage – a relationship of political and/or economic dependence between a rich Roman and his 'client' – remained a powerful force throughout our period, so that many Greek texts and artefacts, irrespective of their subject-matter and mode of expression, acknowledged Roman domination even in their very being.[2]

The concession to Greeks of cultural primacy (the first work of Latin literature, after all, had been Livius Andronicus' translation of Homer's *Odyssey*), while far from unproblematic to some Romans, was a strategy of domination, a means of reducing a subject people to the role of suppliers of comestible products to the consumer city. All these strategies conspired to objectify Greece, to make it appropriable, *knowable*. Edward Said's comments on Europe's objectification of the Orient are pertinent here:

> [W]hat gave the Oriental's world its intelligibility and identity was not the result of his own efforts but rather the whole complex series of knowledgeable manipulations by which the Orient was identified by the West . . . Knowledge of the Orient . . . in a sense *creates* the Orient, the Oriental, and his world.[3]

To know, to understand, is to own; and, simultaneously, to deny.

But for all that Roman conquest created an image of Greece as a realm of pure culture, divorced from politics, civic life certainly continued to play a vital role within Greece itself. The epigraphical record for Greek cities in this period is the richest of any, attesting to countless festivals, decrees, votives, honorific dedications. The Roman strategy of imperial domination was based upon the principle of 'divide and rule'. Cities were permitted to govern themselves (within, of course, carefully circumscribed limits), and the elite were (slowly at first, and then more rapidly from the late first century CE) integrated into Roman citizenship. This strategy was largely successful. There is little evidence of any anti-Roman feeling in Greece. The Greek cities, too, metamorphosed into institutions that could effectively accommodate the distinction between Roman and non-Roman. All cities in this age were run as 'oligarchies', managed by a council of noblemen. In Athens, the public spaces where citizens had once congregated en masse were gradually but surely filled in with Roman monuments and artefacts.[4]

The struggle for personal status within the cities was intense. Again, public inscriptions help us to understand this: the huge volume of statue bases, records of public benefactions or entertainments, decrees of thanks, awards of citizenship and so forth attest an unparalleled preoccupation with self-advancement through civic recognition. The Greeks called this competitive desire for status *philotimia*, literally 'love of honour', and it is not hard to see how the games of publicly acknowledged 'honour' (*time*) and self-promotion played out on the Homeric battlefield had now been translated into the civic arena. After all, opportunies for military endeavour were now presented only by the Roman army. The rich and powerful militarist discourse bequeathed by Greek tradition was redundant, or needed to be shifted into a different register (a city's 'hoplite general', for example, was now in charge of grain supply). Civic politics provided that register.

The Politics of Education

But superior social standing was not always articulated in crudely social, financial or political terms. Class distinction was often paraded using a wholly different idiom, that of culture and intellect. The key term was *paideia*, an untranslatable word that simultaneously encompasses education, culture and social status. The elite were the 'educated', the *pepaideumenoi*; the masses were the 'idiots', the *idiotai*, the 'private citizens'. Modern scholars sometimes explain this mystification of social differentiation by recourse to Pierre Bourdieu's ideas of 'distinction'.[5] For Bourdieu, education is fundamentally a strategy to legitimize (and hence perpetuate) social stratification. Intellectual achievement is a form of 'symbolic capital', which can be converted to and from pecuniary capital; but it strategically conceals its relationship to the latter.

Paideia was indeed a strategy of distinction, but not just in social terms: education marked (and justified) the difference between slaves and free, women and men (sometimes, though there were educated women too), and – crucially – could in some circumstances differentiate between Greek and non-Greek. Learning and cultured, civilized behaviour were held to be differentiating markers of Hellenism, of 'Greekness'. 'I count as Greek', writes the polymath Dionysius of Halicarnassus, 'decent and benevolent deeds and actions' (*Roman Antiquities* 14.6.6). Even non-Greeks could 'become' Greek through education. In Philostratus' hagiography of the sage Apollonius of Tyana, the latter's sidekick, Damis, hopes that by associating with his master he will 'cease to be an unwise philistine [*idiotes*] and seem wise; cease to be a barbarian, and seem educated'; and hence to 'become Greek' (3.43). But there is, of course, a conscious paradox at work here; and Hellenizing 'barbarians' (such as the Syrian Lucian and the Gaul Favorinus, who are discussed in this and the following chapter) always occupy an ambivalent, contested position in Roman-Greek literary culture. If 'Greekness' was defined primarily through education, a question nevertheless remained over whether non-Greeks could 'become Greek'.

Romans too 'became Greek', as we have already noted. The second-century emperor Hadrian, in particular, was known for his Hellenophilia: he invested heavily in the cities of Greece, wrote poetry in Greek (as well as Latin),[6] and put up heavily Hellenized statues of his boyfriend Antinous. There were, however, powerful social forces within Roman society that stigmatized a too-heavy immersion in Greek culture (just as Victorian Britons sneered at those in the colonies who 'went native'). Hadrian himself was nicknamed 'little Greeky' (*Graeculus*). The Latin poet Horace famously complained of the paradox that a conquered state should command so much respect in Rome: 'captive Greece has captured its savage captor' (*Epistles* 2.1.156). The satirist Juvenal, again, makes a character say 'I cannot stand it when Rome goes all Greek' (*Satires* 3.60–1). Romans could adorn themselves with the booty of empire (like ethnic clothing in the modern West), but could expect stern reproval if they overcommitted themselves.

Greeks themselves, however, usually treated Roman receptivity to *paideia* as wholly positive. The most notable examples come in the course of Plutarch's *Parallel Lives* (late first–early second centuries CE), which pair famous Greeks and Romans, often concluding with a formal comparison between the two.[7] When he evaluates Romans, Plutarch often does so in terms of the degree of their education. At the beginning of the *Life* of Marcus Brutus (the assassin of Julius Caesar in the first century BCE), for example, Plutarch contrasts his subject with his ancestor, Junius Brutus: '[Junius] had a naturally hard character, unsoftened by reason [*logos*] . . . whereas [Marcus] mixed education [*paideia*] and reason [*logos*] into his character'; for this reason, he was turned towards 'goodness' (*Brutus* 1). One does not have to be Greek to benefit from Greek education. Indeed, there is nothing to prevent Romans from being more positively evaluated than Greeks, if their ethical behaviour is better. In the comparison between the Spartan lawgiver and his parallel, the Roman king Numa, Lycurgus is characterized by his 'austere' policy (2), while Numa is described as having a 'soft, benevolent muse' (1). For this reason, Plutarch writes, Numa is 'by far the Greeker lawgiver' (1)!

Plutarch's conscious paradox – a Roman who out-Greeks a Greek – is a clear sign of the tensions and complexities that arise when education is presented as the primary marker of social distinction. Elite Greek identity had now become a commodity, transferable onto other peoples too – albeit with a certain visible strain.

The Varieties of Education

Paideia was predicated upon engagement with the cultural past of Greece. The form that such implication took could vary widely. Symbolic capital could be accumulated through philosophy, music, athletics, poetry, oratorical declamation, religious initiation and many other genres. The vast majority of the *pepaideumenoi* of Roman Greece, however, focused their efforts upon reading, reproducing and reworking the prose literature of classical Athens. This was a 'prosaic' age, valuing clarity and authority over the mysticism of poetry (though there were some poets, most notably the epigrammatists of the *Greek Anthology*, the Cretan lyricist Mesomedes, and the didactic poet Oppian of Cilicia).[8]

Most prose was composed in a dialect modelled on the 'Attic' (that is, from Attica, the territory of Athens) of the fifth and fourth centuries BCE.[9] Not an arbitrary choice, this, for language *mattered*: it was the key to elite identity. Lexica survive from the period containing stern warnings about linguistic propriety. An example from Phrynichus' second-century lexicon addresses the pronunciation of the word for 'little pomegranate': 'the ignorant say *rhoïdion* with the diaeresis, we say *rhoidion*' (70). An almost embarrassingly pedantic point when viewed from a distance of two millennia, yet all modern readers will be aware from experience how central a role pronunciation plays in the deployment of social categories (*you say tom-ah-to, I say tom-ay-to . . .*). And accusations of 'barbarisms' or 'solecisms' could sting: the satirist Lucian, for example, writes a sarcastic defence against the pedant who picked him up for wishing him 'good health' rather than 'joy' one morning (*On a Slip in Greeting*).

Atticism presents itself as the antithesis of Asianism, an aesthetic of exuberance and alliterative word-play. But as ever for authors of this period, linguistic style is a political issue as well as a formal feature of language. In the preface to his work *On the Attic Orators*, Dionysius of Halicarnassus (late first century BCE–early first century CE) associates Atticism closely with traditional Hellenic purity. Explaining the long dominance of Asianism over Atticism until the latter's resurgence under Roman guidance, he comments:

> The Attic, ancient, autochthonous muse has taken up clothing that marked its dishonour, exiled from her own property. But the other muse, which arrived just the other day from one of the pits of Asia – she is Mysian, or Phygian, or some Carian abomination – she thought fit to inhabit Greek cities, driving the former out of their public affairs:

the ignorant Muse driving out the philosopher, the madwoman the self-controlled. (1.6–7)

Using the strong, polarizing imagery so common in the period (especially in cases like this of female personification), Dionysius valorizes the Attic dialect as older and hence more Greek. Appropriately enough for a dialect originating in Athens, he even uses the term 'autochthonous' to privilege the one mode over the other: the term refers to the Athenians' belief that their founder was born from the very soil of their land.[10]

But who were the 'Asianists', and why do we not have any of *their* manifestos? Were there in fact any authors who actively espoused this style? The answer to such questions must be carefully nuanced. If Dionysius is right, and his generation saw the eclipse of Asianism by Atticism, then we will have lost all of our evidence in the vacuum of rhetoric from the Hellenistic period. It is, moreover, unlikely that it was ever codified into precepts, as Atticism was: Atticism was the dialect of the prestigious institutions of Greece and Rome, and shared in their powerfully normative drive to centralize and systematize. On the other hand, certain texts of the Roman period do indeed harness the jangling sonority and perky rhythms of poetry. Longus' erotic novel *Daphnis and Chloe* is an example (to be discussed later in this chapter). But the choice of Asianizing style there is a judicious one: in a salacious, titillating genre, a risqué, luxuriant style was appropriate.

The ruling cult of Atticism, however, could be taken to great extremes. In one of his dialogues, the satirist Lucian has a character mock a 'hyper-Atticist' writer called Lexiphanes (the name means 'word-flaunter') as follows:

Can't you hear how he talks? Abandoning us, who converse with him now, he talks to us from a thousand years ago, twisting his tongue, combining these alien elements, and taking himself very seriously in the matter, as if it were a great thing for him to speak a foreign language and debase the established currency of speech. (*Lexiphanes* 20)

For Lucian, this attempt to claim a literary identity has a self-destructive effect: though he tries to speak the best Greek, the speaker actually fills his words with 'alien elements' and speaks 'a foreign language'. Paradoxically, however, all of Lucian's texts (including this one) are themselves saturated with Atticisms, even if he does not drive his practice to the extremes of a Lexiphanes. And, indeed, it is Atticism, an artificially cultivated dialect for *all* second-century practitioners, Greeks and non-Greeks alike, that has permitted the Syrian Lucian to become Greek. As so often in satire, the criticism also rebounds upon the satirical persona's identity. When the satirist attacks literary pretension and social climbing, no one escapes unharmed.

The 'Second Sophistic'

Modern commentators sometimes refer to the period of Greek culture occupying the first three centuries CE as the 'second sophistic'. Though it does have an ancient pedigree, the coiner of the phrase, the third-century polymath Philostratus of Lemnos, uses it in a much narrower sense. For Philostratus, the 'second sophistic' was a style of oratory fashionable under the empire, but invented by the Athenian Aeschines in the fourth century BCE (*Lives of the Sophists* 481, 507). The currency of the term among moderns often springs from a desire to emphasize the derivative, 'secondary' aspect of these texts at the expense of a more positive engagement. By linking a historical period to a cultural form (sophistry), moreover, these commentators arguably continue the Roman, imperialist practice of reducing Greek history to consumable culture.[11] As though this period of Greek history were significant for nothing more than its 'sophistry'.

But oratory was certainly central to the world of *paideia*. The style that Philostratus names the 'second sophistic' involves the impersonation of famous figures of history, or fictitious figures confronting some kind of crucial decision. Fundamental to the cultural value of sophistry was the competitive experience. Across the empire, from Rome to the Near East, members of the Greek-speaking elite gathered to watch eminent men put their status on the line in the high-risk, energized forum of sophistic theatre. A highly attuned audience would pick up on the slightest flaws. To make the process even more difficult, performances would often be improvised, the audience suggesting topics. In the status-driven world of elite *philotimia* ('ambition'), sophistry presented an opportunity to risk all in front of one's peers.[12]

The second century CE was the high point for sophistic display. Men such as Polemo, Favorinus, Scopelian and Herodes Atticus were figures of enormous power and influence. In part, this subtilization of sophistry sprang from imperial beneficence. This century saw the Antonine dynasty in power at Rome, emperors who built their public image around the embracing of civilized Greek values: the bearded Hadrian (grieving for his drowned boyfriend, Antinous), the gentle

Antoninus Pius, and the philosopher Marcus Aurelius. Tax breaks could be awarded to sophists and philosophers, sophists could serve as ambassadors from the Greek cities to Rome, and they could also attain prestigious positions such as Greek secretary to the emperor or the chair of philosophy or rhetoric in Athens.[13]

The shift of oratory's centre of gravity away from civic politics and the courts (see chapter 6) towards 'sophistry', that is historical and fictional subjects, at one level reproduces the Roman imperialist attempt to depoliticize Greek culture. (Not that political oratory ceased entirely: among the orations of Dio Chrysostom, for example, are several polished addresses to his fellow-citizens in Prusa, north-west Asia Minor.) At another level, however, sophistry remained a forum for negotiating in the abstract all manner of issues, issues that were (on the broader definition) eminently political. Though we possess very few actual speeches (unsurprisingly, given the central importance accorded to oral improvisation), the titles can themselves be eloquent. A huge weighting towards the fourth-century icons such as Demosthenes and Alexander the Great implies a desire to relive the glory days of Greek autonomy, and to mimic the now-defunct rhetoric of xenophobic militarism.[14]

At a more sophisticated level, however, different sophists provided different, varied models for manly Hellenism; the challenge, and the pleasure, for the audience lay in contemplating and evaluating the complex pluralities of identities before them. At one point in his *Lives of the Sophists* (a collection of biographies), for example, Philostratus narrates an encounter between the glamorous, world-famous sophist Polemo and Marcus of Byzantium, who 'wore his beard and hair scruffily, which led to most people thinking that he was too rustic to be intelligent'. When Polemo asks the audience to propose a theme for his declamation, they look to Marcus, which draws the sophist's ignorant contempt. Marcus' vigorous response reveals his identity: 'I shall propose a theme, and I shall declaim' (529). Two very different approaches, then, to sophistic performance.

Though he looked boorish to Polemo, Marcus may well have designed his image with care. The passage contains subtle allusions to Odysseus ('you would have called him sullen and foolish; but when the mighty voice emerged from his chest, and the words like snow-flakes . . .', *Iliad* 3.220–1) and Socrates (whose ugly, satyr-like exterior conceals a divine interior: Plato, *Symposium* 215b). The contrast between the urban sophisticate and the unkempt rustic figure confronts the audience with two competing claimants, and two competing kinds of claim, to cultural authority. Exceptionally among sophists,

Marcus uses the Doric dialect to declaim, a dialect associated with rusticity, but also (and particularly) with the ancient Spartans. Though Polemo is not Athenian (he is from Laodicea in Asia Minor) and Marcus is not a Spartan, the famous conflict between Athens and Sparta in the fifth century BCE still underlies this conceptual polarity articulated some 600 years later.

Sophistic oratory was a forum for exploring and sharing concepts of masculinity, Hellenism and elite identity. But what is more striking is the variety of forms these constructions could take: in what was fundamentally a competitive context, identity was ever open to reinvention and reinterpretation.

Travelling Wisdom

It was not only the texts of Roman Greece that were filled with reminiscences; the very landscape, too, reverberated with the ghostly echoes of voices. Sanctuaries, shrines, ruins, temples and statues were freighted with history and memories. Philostratus' *Heroic Tale* (again a third-century text) presents a dialogue that takes place on the Chersonnese (the narrow lip of land overhanging the north-western coast of Asia Minor) between a Phoenician sailor and a vine-grower. During the course of the conversation, it transpires that the latter has frequent meetings with the hero Protesilaus, the first of the soldiers who accompanied Agamemnon to die on Trojan soil. The cult-site (as described by the vine-grower) is ancient, ruined, but still inhabited by awesome, numinous powers:

> You see how little of the sanctuary is left. But back then it was lovely and not small, as can be made out from its foundations. This cult statue stood upon a ship, since its base has the shape of a prow, and the ship's captain is set there. Time has worn it away and, by Zeus, those who anoint it and seal their vows here have changed its shape. But this means nothing to me, for I spend time with him and see him, and no statue could be more pleasant than that man. (9.5–7)

Religion is closely interlinked with cultural identity. A prayer to a hero or god to appear invokes the continuity of traditions, representing an attempt to reanimate the numinous power of the cultural past in the Roman present. (An analogous process to Hellenistic aetiology: see chapter 8.) At a later point, the Phoenician asks when it was that the heroes were seen on the plain of Troy. The vine-grower replies by correcting his interlocutor's tense: 'They *are* seen, I said, they *are still* seen by cowherds and shepherds on the plain. They are great and divine, and there are times when their appearance spells trouble for the soil' (18.2).

The *Heroic Tale* is centrally about the power of the mythical heroes of the past to affect the present. Hector drowns a Syrian boy who mocks his statue (19.5–7); Achilles responds with equal violence to the Thessalians who fail to keep up his cult (53.22). But such issues are invariably focused around a feature of the landscape: a cult-site, a statue or some other site of memory.

Antiquity's most famous traveller was a Greek (probably from Lydia, in Asia Minor) called Pausanias.[15] Pausanias travelled extensively in mainland Greece during the later part of the second century CE, probably under the reign of Hadrian (whom he praises intermittently). Because of his no-frills style and pared-down narrative technique, which tracks the eye of an imaginary voyager ('turning to your left, you see . . .') and records local histories and legends, he has in the past been considered an unsophisticated observer, to be judged by the criterion of accuracy alone. For more recent critics, however, the *Description of Greece* (as the text is sometimes called – we have no authentic title) has been reclaimed as the product of a skilled writer, the author of a rich and complex 'imaginary Greece'. At one point, he programmatically records his desire to capture 'everything Greek' (1.26.5); and it is the multiple forms of Pausanias' Hellenic confection that constitute both the brilliance of the text and the challenge for interpretation.

Though he does occasionally include explicit narratorial judgement, Pausanias' most eloquent and (arguably) powerful passages are those where he allows juxtapositions, both temporal and spatial, to resonate without comment. In his account of Sicyon, for example, he writes: 'The sanctuary close to the temple of Persuasion is now dedicated to the Roman emperors; it was once the house of the tyrant Cleon' (2.8.1). He then proceeds to tell the story of Aratus, 'who performed the greatest deeds of the Greeks of his day' in uprooting the tyranny established by Cleon. It is a fine example of Pausanias' narrative style, which repeatedly interweaves geopolitical description and historical experience, anchoring the present in the prestigious past. But what does it *mean*? Is Cleon to be conflated with the Roman emperors? Are we to pray for a new Aratus, heroically ousting the new tyrants? The narrator declines to comment. It is up to the readership to decide.

The structure of the *Description of Greece* as a whole is meaningful. The highlight of the first book is Athens, and that of the final Delphi;

the central portions are occupied by Olympia. These are significant places, the most famous tourist sites of the day, and their significance is underlined by their prominent positions within the architecture of the text. But the text is not just about destinations, it is also about the spaces in between. The famous tourist sites present only one face of the polyhedron that constitutes 'everything Greek'. The final book provides an excellent example of this. The description of Phocis is, as one would expect, dominated by Delphi. The oracular sanctuary is a world-famous symbol, and Pausanias is careful to stress this site's openness to appropriation by other peoples. This is how he begins his description of the city:

> As you enter the city, there is a sequence of temples. The first of them is ruined, the second empty of statues of both gods and men. As for the third and fourth, the third has statues of a few Roman emperors, and the fourth is called that of Athena of Foresight; in its front is a dedication from Marseilles, bigger than the statue inside. (10.8.6)

The description of the sequence of temples is (as usual for Pausanias) focalized through the eyes of an imaginary traveller ('as you enter the city'): a series of puzzles, with no omniscient narrator to explain. Why the ruins, why the despoliation? What is the story? And the 'sequence' itself demands a narrative, like the cases in a museum: what links these four temples? It is a classic case of Pausanias' strategy of allusive juxtaposition, which allows – but does not commit – the reader to associate the pillaging of Delphi with Roman imperialism, with its status as an international symbol.

Despite its cosmopolitan appearance (a dedication from Marseilles in the passage above), Pausanias' Delphi has an irreducibly Greek core, protected by divine will. Foreign attempts to sack the site are a recurrent theme of this account: 'it seems that right from the start the sanctuary at Delphi has been the subject of attacks by numerous people' (10.7.1). The most substantially narrated invasion is that of the Gauls in the third century BCE (10.19.5–23.14), who are – tellingly – repulsed by a series of prodigies: an eclipse, caused by mist rolling down from the mountains (10.22.11), and 'portents from the god, swift, and the most conspicuous we know of' (10.23.1), including continuous thundering and lightning and manifestations by long-dead heroes. Religious sensibility buttresses Pausanias' vision of Delphi as a site of distinctive Hellenic importance. History matters too. The pass by which the Gauls attack, Thermopylae, is freighted with historical significance: this was the site of the heroic Spartan defence against Persian invasion in the early fifth century BCE (and Pausanias explicitly connects the two events by comparing the numbers involved, at 10.20). History too contributes to the idealization of this site.

Delphi is a curious mix, then, of benign and hostile interference, on the part of both Greeks and non-Greeks; but the site maintains its numinous power, beyond the glossy, visitor-friendly superficiality. Significantly, however, Delphi does not mark the end of Pausanias' journey. The next site immediately after Delphi is the Corycian cave on the slopes of Parnassus: though the ascent is difficult, this is 'the most worthy of beholding of all the caves I have seen' (10.32.2). This cave prompts a digression upon the variety and splendour of caves, including the Themisonian cave – with 'no entrance, and lit by little sun, the roof for the most part close to the floor' – where locals hid from invading Gaulish armies. Caves are presented as places of refuge from foreign predation: mysterious, eldritch locations, enfolded under the crust of the landscape. The relative inaccessibility of these caves invites contrast with the bustling traffic of the grand sites such as Delphi. All these locations contribute equally to Pausanias' map of 'everything Greek'; but there are powerful hints that the caves, naturally formed and shaped but rudely by human hands, preserve something more primevally Greek (even pre-Greek) than the locations that are better known, and hence more subject to foreign takeover.

The Inner Eye

Travel literature offers one model of distinguishing between levels of knowledge: the superficial aspect of the landscape is open to all, but the knowing eye penetrates the surface to understand and access the inner core of its being. Pausanias' narrative technique dramatizes the value of *paideia*, of deep understanding, in action: only the educated can fully comprehend the rich shafts of religious and myth-historical significance that run through places and monuments. This structure clearly reproduces the strategy of social 'distinction' discussed above, playing out a division between educated and uneducated travellers and viewers. As Lucian puts it in his speech *On the Hall*, 'in matters of sight-seeing, the same convention does not operate for ordinary and for educated people' (2) – the words he uses here for 'ordinary' and 'educated' being precisely *idiotes* and *pepaideumenos*, which (as we have seen) standardly denote respectively a member of the mass and of the elite.[16]

The field of travel literature, however, is not the only one where the division between superficial and intrinsic knowledge operates. The literature of Roman Greece often presents a profound and self-conscious orientation away from the public-dominated conceptions of the self that we find in classical Athens. In the satires of Lucian, again, superficial paraders of *paideia* are repeatedly pilloried for paying more attention to appearance than to substance.[17] In *The Uneducated Book-collector*, an unidentified target is attacked for ostentatiously reading his expensively turned books without understanding their content. In *The Sale of Lives*, philosophers present themselves to be bought like slaves on the basis of their appearance.

Two texts associate this commercialization and banalization of *paideia* particularly with Roman consumerism. In *Nigrinus*, the eponymous philosopher berates educated Greeks in Rome who 'philosophize for a salary and set out their virtue for sale, as if it could be bought from a market-place' (25). *On Salaried Posts in Great Houses*, meanwhile, attacks those educated Greeks who subject themselves to the indignity of Roman patronage. It is not even, Nigrinus writes, as though the patron appreciates *paideia*:

> He does not want you at all for that purpose [i.e. instruction]; but because you have a long beard and a serious appearance and you are dressed modestly in a Greek cloak and everyone knows that you are a grammarian, rhetorician or philosopher, it seems good to him for such a man to be mixed in with his retinue and escort. For this will make him seem a lover of Greek knowledge and altogether a man of taste when it comes to education [*paideia*]. As a result, my friend, there is a danger that you have hired out your beard and cloak, rather than your splendid speeches. (25)

The educated Greek, according to this passage, serves only to advertise to the world the great man's 'taste' and 'education': the content of his speeches is irrelevant. (Similarly, Philostratus reports that the emperor Trajan, processing in his chariot with the philosopher Dio Chrysostom by his side, once turned to him and said: 'I do not know what you are saying, but I love you as I love myself', *Lives of the Sophists* 488). Lucianic satire, with its proclaimed ability to see through the superficial concerns of society, presents itself as a corrective to this reductive commercialization, a true distillation of Greek values.

It is arguable, however, that this pose of righteous aloofness self-destructs. Not only is Lucian (self-consciously) a non-Greek himself, a Hellenized Syrian (see chapter 10), but also his claim to be above all this display and money-seeking is suspect. *The Apology*, a companion piece to *On Salaried Posts*, defends the author against a charge of hypocrisy, the accusation being that after writing the attack on Greeks who flog their wares to Romans, he himself proceeded to take up an office in the Roman establishment. Whether or not we are convinced by Lucian's defence (and not all readers have been), the example shows how easily the satirist's weapons can be turned upon himself. Satire, particularly Lucianic satire, presents a world of masks and poses, and even the author is an adept manipulator, with his proliferation of textual surrogates and personae: the dialogues, particularly, present suggestively quasi-Lucian figures like Lycinus (Lukinos, close to Loukianos), 'The Syrian' and Parrhesiades ('Free-speaker'). Ironically, so far from being a solution to the Roman-driven superficialization of *paideia*, satire exposes itself as a symptom of it.

The reverse side of this critique of superficiality and display is a new privileging of the inner person, an emphasis upon the varieties of self-scrutiny and psychic therapy that Michel Foucault has termed 'the care of the self'.[18] Plutarch's *Lives* place character at the centre of historical investigation, evaluating both Greeks and Romans according to the ethical state of their souls.[19] Contemporary philosophers iterate their indifference to physical subjection: the horrors of exile, the fear of death, torture and oppression, the loss of a loved one – all these calamities can be managed by inner strength and resourcefulness. Favorinus, a second-century Greek-speaking Gaul, comments as follows in his consolatory speech on exile:

A good man takes even less notice of the value of wealth, human honours, ancestry, rank, and public opinion. For those things mentioned earlier are extrinsic: a fatherland, children, kinship, friends, and all the rest are not mine to the extent that they are not under my control. I certainly do, however, lay claim to and call my own the ability not to crave these things (for that *is* under my control). Since everything that is not under our control is extrinsic, all this business about honours, opinions and wealth is the most extrinsic of all. (19.1)

Across a wide range of texts we come across this rejection of 'the extrinsic'. Despite his apparent rejection of the trappings of the external world, however, Favorinus is playing a powerful political game. He has (or so he tells us) been exiled by the emperor Hadrian: his paraded ability not to be bothered by that exile marks the superiority of the inner, intellectual (and, fundamentally, *Greek*) power to determine what is 'under my control' over the emperor's authority over the mere body. Here, being philosophical means showing indifference to the overweening authority of the Roman emperor.

Modern readers may well immediately think of early Christian and Jewish martyrs in this context: these religions, too, privileged inner being over external social identity, and defined themselves in terms of resistance to the Roman state. But it would be simplistic to think of any supposedly unilateral 'influence' of Christianity and Judaism over pagan culture. It is preferable to imagine these genres as sharing in the same sociocultural drive to resist the centralizing power of the Roman state.

After all, pagan Greek culture had its own stock of stories, including the 'acts of the pagan martyrs', as they are often called: papyrus finds have uncovered a number of these popular stories telling of Greeks defying domineering Romans.[20] And then there was pagan Greece's most famous story of heroic resistance to state pressure. In 399 BCE, Athens had put to death its most prodigious intellectual, Socrates, on a charge of corrupting the young and introducing false gods. The figure of Socrates, as iconized by Plato and Xenophon (and generations of successors), represented a powerful model for men like Favorinus who sought to privilege inner integrity over state power. The first-century Stoic philosopher Musonius Rufus was even known as the 'Roman Socrates'.

There is, however, a crucial difference between Socrates and his Roman-Greek descendants. Socrates was an Athenian citizen, and claimed only to have left the city twice, on military service. According to Plato and Xenophon, his defence speech (see chapter 6) presented him – however ironically – as the model of an Athenian citizen. Socratic ethics offered a new model for citizenship. Roman-Greek Socratics, on the other hand, rejected (or presented themselves as rejecting) state identity. What was held to matter now was exclusively the inner self, not any external identity as a citizen: ethics meant being true to yourself, not sacrificing yourself for the state.

This culture of introspection and meditation is sometimes difficult to engage with. A prime case is Aelius Aristides' *Sacred Tales*, an extraordinary text detailing the orator's illnesses and commands for cures given by the god Asclepius in dreams. The articulation of intimate detail in the context of a public, rhetorical performance is wholly alien to twenty-first-century eyes, brought up as we are to consider illness as something to be hidden away. How are we to read a sentence such as 'But now I wish to reveal to you the matter of my belly' (48.2; cf. 51.67)? In a well-known book, E. R. Dodds claimed that the second century was an 'age of anxiety', and that the 'hypo-chondria' (as he put it) of figures like Aristides expressed their spir-itual emptiness.[21] Dodds's anachronistic retrojection of modern pathologies and his Christianocentric teleology are easy to dismiss. A more satisfying explication is proposed by Judith Perkins, who sees continuities between pagan and Christian idealizations of bodily suffering.[22] The body – its interior, its surface, its orifices – has now become the primary focus for public debates over identity and power. A truly cultivated Greek has an inside, as well as a public face. And while it would be debatable to argue that psychology is 'invented' in this period – it is already evident in fifth-century tragedy (chapter 4), even in Homer[23] – it is certainly focused upon with a new intensity.

Novel Trajectories

The one major generic innovation of Roman-Greek literature, the novel, provides ample evidence for this new orientation.[24] The five complete novels that we have – the *Ephesian Story* of Xenophon of Ephesus, Chariton's *Chaereas and Callirhoe*, Longus' *Daphnis and Chloe*, Achilles Tatius' *Leucippe and Cleitophon* and Heliodorus' *Ethiopian Story* – centre upon the passion of a young girl and a young boy, their trials, separations and reunions. The focus upon recipro-cal, heterosexual love intersects with the new value in the period given to consensual, heterosexual marriage, which will be discussed further in chapter 12.

For now, though, I want to focus on the idea of sexuality as a site of self-determination: it is crucial to the young lovers that they can *choose* with whom they spend their lives, even in the face of the threats of rape and abduction. Bodily suffering and inner dialogue are as central to the novels' narratives as they are to Aristides' *Sacred Tales*. In Achilles Tatius' novel, for example, Leucippe, the female protagonist, is molested by the bullying Thersander. When she refuses his advances, he turns to anger:

> 'You wretched slave, you really are love-sick! . . . You do not think it a great blessing to be kissed by your master? No, you pretend to be shocked, and put on an air of desperation. I reckon you are a whore: after all, you *are* in love with an adulterer. Alright then, since you are unwilling to try me as a lover, try me as your master!'
>
> 'Even if you want to be tyrant over me,' replied Leucippe, 'I am happy to be tyrannized, if only you refrain from violence against me.' (6.20)

'Tyrant' is an accusation that resonates loudly in an imperial context, dominated as it is by the iconic image of the emperor (and his various subordinates, the governors and judges of the imperial bureaucracy). In the following exchange, Leucippe expresses her contempt even for torture, a passage that strongly evokes the pagan martyrs' principled resistance to Roman oppression:

> 'Prepare the tortures! Someone bring in the wheel and stretch my hands: here they are! Someone bring in the whips, too, and beat my back: here it is! Someone bring in fire and burn my body: here it is! Someone bring in a blade and slice up my skin: here it is! You will behold a novel kind of contest: one woman competes against all your tortures, and conquers them all!' (6.21)

The novels are filled with sexual predators, assailing the virtues of the female and the male protagonists alike. The narrative structure systematically strips the young lovers of any power to determine their future: they are kept apart by their families, constrained by protocols, defamiliarized in foreign lands, captured by bandits, sold into slavery. Only cunning resourcefulness can help them; the only power they maintain is over their sexual virtue.

Novels also lay strong emphasis upon the play between social convention and inner being. Because of the particular narrative form adopted in most of the Greek novels – external 'omniscient' narration – readers can access the deepest thoughts of characters, even when those characters are attempting to disguise them. In Chariton's *Chaereas and Callirhoe*, for example, the Persian king's henchman tries to persuade Callirhoe to submit to his master's passion:

> At first, Callirhoe felt the urge to dig out, if she could, the eyes of this man who was attempting to corrupt her; but then, since she was an educated [*pepaideumene*] and thoughtful woman, she swiftly considered her place, who she was, and who was speaking. She transformed her anger and in what followed gave the barbarian an ironical reply. (6.5.8)

Callirhoe's *paideia*, her cultivated Greekness, consists in the ability to keep her feelings hidden for pragmatic purposes, to disguise her initial response of disgust. The reader is permitted access to her thoughts: 'we' arrayed on the side of the educated Greek against the hoodwinked 'barbarians'. The educated may, indeed, recognize another way in which Callirhoe's response is characteristically Greek: mastering his first thoughts was precisely the technique adopted by

Odysseus to defeat the Cyclops, in a famous Homeric scene.[25] In this brief passage from a love story, we have a crash course in how to be Greek in the face of an authoritarian threat to your body: you disguise yourself, confident in your inner self.

In a more general sense, the novels repeatedly stage a clash between public expectation and private intrigue. One of the generic set-pieces places a love-sick character (usually a male, for women are still shielded from the glare of publicity) in a convivial gathering, desperately trying to force his expression into one of congeniality. 'Dionysius was wounded [by desire], but sought to conceal the wound, as befitted an educated [*pepaideumenos*] man who laid especial store by virtue' (Chariton 2.4.1). Ruses and subterfuges drive novelistic narrative: in this particular dramatization of cultivated behaviour, of *paideia*, the reader is permitted to access both the public performance (open to all) and the machinations behind the scenes (more restricted).

One of the five novels, however, presents a very different take upon *paideia*. Longus' *Daphnis and Chloe* tells of two babies exposed in the countryside by their urban parents. As they mature, they are struck with desire for one another.[26] But so extreme is their rustic naivety that they fail to understand what is happening to them: 'they wanted something, but did not know what they wanted' (1.22.4). Even when advice is offered, they are too innocent to understand it. 'A kiss, an embrace, and lying down next to one another with naked bodies' (2.7.7), though well-intentioned, is simply too euphemistic to allow them to relieve their passion. When Daphnis is finally initiated by a city-dweller called Lycaenion, she forewarns him of the blood that will follow Chloe's defloration. Daphnis, however, misinterprets, thinking he will wound Chloe; and so he resists putting to use his new-found knowledge (3.19.2–3). Longus defers his lovers' consummation not (as other novelists do) through separation, but through ignorance.

Crucially, this ignorance is presented as want of *paideia*. Philetas, the over-euphemistic adviser alluded to above, is said to provide 'education' (2.8.1, 2.9.1), as is Lycaenion (3.18.4, 3.19.1). Indeed, in the very prologue the narrator offers to 'remind him who has loved and *educate* him who has not' (preface 3). Despite the suggestion that inexperienced readers might be educated by *Daphnis and Chloe*, however, it is impossible that anyone could match the naivety of the protagonists. The text presumes an 'educated' reader, both sexually and intellectually. Intellectually, because this is a beautifully constructed tale, saturated with intertextual resonance (particularly to Sappho, Plato and Theocritus) and mythical allusiveness. The ironic focalization of the narrative through two ingenuous *naïfs* only underlines how impossible is this hermetically secluded rustic fantasy – and, of course, dramatizes the knowing superiority of the cultivated, urban reader.

The literature of Roman Greece develops and broadens the institutionalized, intertextual self-consciousness of Alexandrian literature. *Paideia*, education, is its controlling concept, born of a complex of interrelated factors: Rome's construction of Greece as a cultural marketplace, Greece's desire to anchor identity in the prestigious past, the necessity of creating a new discourse of social distinction to stratify the new, Romanizing ruling classes, the privileging of the probing insight of the insider over the superficial gaze of the tourist, and the new orientation towards the interior self. As we have seen particularly in this final section, though, the cult of *paideia* was not simply a functional response to social circumstances; it was also a powerful motivating principle underlying some of the most ingenious and coruscating literary texts produced in classical antiquity.

Part III
Conflicts

10

Inventing the Greek: Cultural Identity

Apollonius of Tyana, the Greek sage of the first century CE, was an impressive figure.[1] A Pythagorean philosopher (some said a miracle-worker), he dressed, according to his third-century biographer Philostratus, in linen. He abstained from meat and wine. Five years of his life were passed in silence. But most amazing of all, he travelled to three of the known world's four corners: to India, Ethiopia and Spain. (The cold, barren wastes to the North clearly offered no attractions to a philosopher.) In these exotic locations, he variously conversed with local sages and analysed biological and geophysical phenomena. A globe-trotting superstar, Apollonius, beyond any other ancient sage, encapsulated the drive (particularly prominent in Hellenistic and later philosophy) towards cosmic, universal wisdom.

In Greek philosophical circles of Roman imperial times, parochial views on the world were disdained. Travel itself was not necessary. The philosopher Musonius Rufus (first century CE) – a Roman who wrote in Greek – professed himself, while exiled on the tiny Aegean island of Gyara, a 'citizen of the city of Zeus' (fragment 9).[2] 'Cosmopolitanism', citizenship of the cosmos, was the name of the game.

The Indian Brahmans, according to Apollonius (who was greatly taken with them), lived 'both on the earth and yet not upon it' (Philostratus, *Life of Apollonius* 3.15). Their physical levitation, to the Greek sage, figured their transcendental state: they were both of this world and above it. In Philostratus' account, the Indians do much to correct his narrow, Hellenocentric perspective: where Greeks consider self-knowledge a difficult thing, the Brahmans know everything (3.18); they decry the Greeks for considering that abstaining from injustice makes for justice (3.25). Here, at the edges of the known world, the readers of Philostratus' biography learn how narrow and culture-specific their own perspective is.[3]

This episode in Philostratus' narrative looks to be a world apart (literally) from the narrow ethnocentrism of the earlier Greek world. And yet – this is the crucial point – it is not. Philostratus' India, notwithstanding its exoticism, is mapped out using entirely Greek reference points. The Indian Brahmans, we read, look like Spartans (3.15); their hill is the height of the Athenian Acropolis (3.13); their spring looks like the Dirce in Boeotia, and their song sounds like a Sophoclean paean (3.17); their tripods resemble those of Pythian Apollo, and their cupbearers Ganymede and Pelops (3.27). The Indian king, moreover, lives in a city with Greek-style walls (2.20) and an Athenian street plan (2.27); its inhabitants wear cloaks that look like old-fashioned Attic ones (2.40). Although at one level Philostratus' India offers a profound challenge to the reader's (supposedly) narrowly Greek view of the world, it also underlines the inability of voyagers to shed their ethnocentrisms. Greek literature always commits to a Greek view of the world – even if, as the *Life of Apollonius* shows us, the exact constitution of Greekness can be subject to radical questioning.

Identity Parade

What do we mean by 'Greek' literature?[4] What, indeed, do we mean by 'Greece'? A question that even now retains its urgency, but was all the more involved in a world without defined geographical borders, without passports or centralized nationalism, without indeed (until the Roman period: see chapter 9) any centralized government. Is Macedonia part of Greece?[5] How Greek are the islands of Lesbos, Lemnos and Cyprus? What of the Greek cities of Ionia, now the western coast of Turkey? Or *Magna Graecia*, the Hellenized south of Italy? Impossible questions to answer conclusively, primarily because the criteria for defining Greekness are themselves elusive. In the case of Macedonia, for example, different fourth-century Athenian authors present it as, respectively, Greek and 'barbarian' (that is to say non-Greek, an 'other'), depending upon their political relationship to Philip the Great (the father of the celebrated Alexander).[6]

In Herodotus' *Histories*, famously, the Athenians refer to four factors that are definitive of Greekness: community of blood, language, religious buildings and religious ritual (8.144). This assertion, however, is not a straightforward statement of contemporary dogma, as is sometimes assumed. The terms of the formula are dictated by the larger narrative. The Spartans have advised the Athenians to reject an approach by Alexander I of Macedonia (a Persian vassal), who seeks to broker a treaty between them and the mighty eastern empire of Persia; in the passage under consideration, the Athenians are stating that they have indeed rejected the proposals, and that they are siding instead with Sparta. In emphasizing the role of common blood in the determination of Greekness, there is an implicit snub to the Macedonian king, whose status as a descendant of true Greeks is a matter of debate. Earlier in the *Histories*, the same king was refused entry to the Olympics, on the grounds of not being Greek (5.22; a refusal, albeit, successfully challenged by appeal to the king's supposed genealogical relationship with the state of Argos).[7] So the four Herodotean factors should not simply be taken as describing a received set of criteria, but as a pointed intervention in a debate; a stage in the ongoing *exploration* of the meaning of Greekness. This process persisted, unresolved, throughout antiquity.

What *did* it mean to be Greek?

Inventing the Other

Identity definition is determined at borders. It is, after all, only at immigration control that we are asked for passports; and, in general, it is when identities are challenged or embattled that they are most stridently asserted. If we wish to understand the ways in which Greekness might be asserted, it is best to begin by returning to the theme of travel, so central to Philostratus' biography, as indeed it is to many Greek texts.

It is often said that travel broadens the mind, but this is a simplification. The traveller is required to engage in a *dialogue* with the visited culture, and dialogues can be carried out in many, varied ways.[8] Let us take, for example, the figure of Odysseus, Greek literature's earliest traveller. In the opening lines of the *Odyssey*, he is identified as the 'man of many turns, who wandered far and wide . . . many were the men whose cities he saw and whose habits he came to know' (1.1–3). Described in this way, Odysseus emerges as an accumulator of knowledge, one whose travels lead to him to a broader objective experiential base. But knowledge of a foreign culture is not innocent: as Edward Said has influentially argued, the discovery of others is also a form of mastering them; describing others is a form of subjecting them.[9]

Understanding otherness means learning to integrate it into our own conceptual universe, often subduing it in the process.

The *Odyssey* is an early example of a travel narrative that uses cultural discovery to map out a set of moral, cultural and political values.[10] This aspect of the text appears to be closely related to the project of Greek colonization that began in the early eighth century BCE.[11] Let us take a well-known example. In book 9, Odysseus describes to his Phaeacian hosts his encounter with the Cyclops Polyphemus, who serially cannibalizes Odysseus' crewmen, before the survivors blind him and escape by trickery. Before narrating that part of the episode, however, Odysseus provides an ethnographic description of the Cyclopes:

> From there we sailed onwards, grieving at heart,
> and came to the land of the overweening,
> lawless Cyclopes, who do not put their trust in the immortal gods,
> nor do they plant with their hands, nor plough;
> everything grows unsown and unploughed,
> wheat and barley and the vines that bring them
> wine from the large clusters. Zeus' rain makes them grow.
> They lack any forum for decision-making, and laws;
> they live on the peaks of lofty mountains
> in hollow caves, and each sets the laws for his own
> children and wife. They have no heed for each other.
> . . .
> . . . the Cyclopes have no scarlet-prowed ships,
> nor are there among them any shipwrights who might labour at
> well-thwarted ships to take them to
> the various cities of humankind, in the way that men
> often cross the seas in ships to visit each other.
>   (Homer, *Odyssey* 9.105–15, 125–9)

This description communicates information that was not yet available to Odysseus at this stage in his journey (as he approached the island, he was unaware at the time of the Cyclopes), but that he now supplies retrospectively as a narrator. It has, then, been placed here carefully by Odysseus (and by Homer), to frame our reading of the following sequence. The dominant theme it communicates is *lack*: the Cyclopes want for law, religion, agriculture, politics, communality and seafaring.[12] The description of the Cyclopes, then, presumes (and hence naturalizes) a set of expectations about 'normal' society. Odysseus' identification of a series of absences invokes a checklist of necessary conditions for civilized living.

These absences, moreover, make for a radically unsocialized population: not only does their insularity cut them off from humankind, but even among themselves there are no collective institutions. They live in mountains, which Greeks throughout the ages imagined as marginal space (Greek cities often occupy plains). This race is organized only at the level of the family unit, which is required to exercise the kinds of function one would normally expect of a macro-community ('each sets the laws for his own children and wife'). Again, this identification of a social perversion rests upon, and hence shores up, the received understanding of the mechanics of social order.

When Odysseus acquires knowledge about the various forms of social practice across the world, he does not simply *discover* it (in the sense of dis-covering, of revealing pre-existent facts); he *invents* it, interpreting it and plotting it on his culture's own normative map of social and cultural values. This is why cultural difference figures primarily as absence or excess (the Cyclopes are 'overweening'): the Other is being accommodated into a ready-made ideological schema.

Broadening the Mind

Perhaps the most interesting example of this practice is Herodotus' fifth-century text the *Histories* (see also chapter 7), which bears the strong imprint not only of the *Odyssey*, but also of the cultural relativism of contemporary sophistry. This long prose work incorporates what we would now regard as two separate genres, historiography and ethnographical narrative. For Herodotus, however, these two forms combine to serve a single purpose, namely the analysis of Greece's relationship to the non-Greek, or 'barbarian', world (though, as we shall see presently, Herodotus can also imagine transcending this division). The Greek–barbarian polarity reaches its most urgent expression, for Herodotus, in the Persian wars of the fifth century, where a largely united (albeit fragmented by internal dissensions) Greek force beat off the superior numbers of the Persian invaders. In the earlier books, however, the process of polarization is explored through different media, including the narrative of Herodotus' own travel abroad.

In book 2 of the *Histories*, Herodotus presents his famous and extraordinary description of Egypt.[13] For Herodotus, as for many since, Egypt is a land of wonders: a landscape overshadowed by pharaonic follies, a people habituated to absolute domination, a massive river, with unknown sources, that (exceptionally) floods in the summer. But among the greatest fascinations, for Herodotus, is their habit of deviating from Greek practice:

> I am extending my account of Egypt because it is the land with the greatest number of wonders, and phenomena that go beyond description can be found in every area. For this reason, I shall give a lengthier account of it. Not only are the heavens different in Egypt, not only does their river act in a manner that suggests a different nature to other rivers, but also many of their customs and habits are exactly the inverse of those of other peoples. (2.35)

If Odysseus' primary trope in describing cultural difference was *absence*, Herodotus' here is *inversion*. The Egyptians, we read in the following sentences, do everything the wrong way around. Of the many examples: women go to market, while men stay at home weaving; they relieve themselves inside, and eat outside; their priests have short hair, rather than long; they knead dough with their feet, and clay with their hands; they write from right to left. Egypt is a topsy-turvy country, at the level of both ethics and geophysics. Here, the historian invokes a principle central to contemporary medical thought, that climatic and geophysical factors are related to the ethical status of the inhabitants. The Hippocratic tract *Airs, Waters, Places* (late fifth century, in all probability), notably, argues for a rigidly environmental-determinist model of ethics, attributing the superiority of Greek customs to the geophysical situation of Greece in the natural centre of the world, balanced between the extremes of North, South, East and West.

Yet unlike the author of *Airs, Waters, Places*, Herodotus is not committed to an absolutist view of Greek superiority. In the first place, his views are not narrowly environmental-determinist. The dominant principle in the passage cited above is of analogy (geophysical inversion is *like* cultural inversion), not of cause and effect. Moreover (and this is my main point), in general he focuses upon the role of culture rather than nature, upon *nomos* ('convention'), which (citing an otherwise unattested phrase from Pindar) he calls 'the king of all' (3.38).[14]

In the episode capped by that quotation, Herodotus exemplifies the principle that all peoples consider their own customs to be the best with an anecdote about the Persian king Darius (3.38). Darius, so we are told, brought together some Greeks and some Indians called Callatians (whose practice it was to eat dead relatives), and observed the horror of the one group at the concept of necrophagy, and of the other at that of cremation. The cultural-relativist moral to this story is clearly inspired by debates in contemporary sophistry, and particularly the famous doctrine of Protagoras of Abdera that 'man is the measure of all things'.[15] And, indeed, a citizen of Halicarnassus, a city on the coast of Asia Minor that oscillated between Greek and Persian control, might be expected to take a broad view.

How do we reconcile this cultural-relativist position with the Greek-centred perspective he adopts in, for example, his list of Egyptian inversions? It is sometimes suggested that we should not ask for consistency from such an accumulative writer, but such readings are ungenerous. The important point is that *cultural relativism is not a culturally neutral position.* (No more than multiculturalism is in the modern world: a set of beliefs exclusive to the rich West.) It is as a fifth-century Greek, with all the intellectual sophistication and insight implied by that, that Herodotus disavows parochialism. Like Philostratus' *Apollonius of Tyana*, written some six and a half centuries later, the *Histories* do not simply reject a Greek-centred view of the world; rather, they redefine what a Greek-centred view of the world means.

Inventing the Greek

Let us turn now to another privileged site for thinking about the meaning of Greekness, namely the earliest Greek texts. As Thucydides already noted in the fifth century (1.3), however, Homer has no all-embracing word for Greeks. The poems are, for sure, composed in a language we call Greek,[16] and they seem to presume a common set of cultural reference points that we would identify as Greek. But the word *Hellen* ('Greek') appears only to a very limited extent in early epic. In the *Iliad*, only the Myrmidons, the tribe from Thessaly (in the North) commanded by Achilles, are referred to as *Hellenes*, and then only briefly in the midst of a huge 'catalogue of ships' (a list of forces fighting for Agamemnon: see *Iliad* 2.684). *Hellas* occurs more frequently, but again always linked with Thessaly.[17]

In the *Iliad*, the terms *Hellas* and *Hellen* do not consistently refer to the territory and people that we call Greece and the Greeks. But do there exist alternative names for the same phenomena? The collective name Homer uses for the host of allies fighting against Troy is 'Achaeans', less frequently 'Argives' or 'Danaans'. The first two names are generalizations of local identities, the specific territory of Achaea being located in south-west Thessaly (in the north), and Argos being a famous city in southern Greece. The name 'Danaans' is more promising if we are in search of a collective identity for the host, since it denotes the offspring of Danaus. Danaus is one of a series of three related mythical figures who give their names to races: Danaus begets the Danaans, Aegyptus the Egyptians, and Phoenix the Phoenicians. Here at last we do have a concept of shared ethnicity among the host, or at least a hint at a myth of shared descent from a single figure.

Even if there is a deeply underlying concept of the ethnic unity of 'Greek' peoples, however, on the cultural axis they are largely undifferentiated from the Trojans, at least: the latter speak the same language, worship the same gods, and practise the same customs as their assailants.[18] The differentiation is not between Achaean and Trojan but between Achaeans and Trojans, on the one hand, and on the other a dimly perceived series of Near-Eastern peoples allied to the latter. The Trojans' Carian allies, notably, are 'barbarian-voiced' (*barbarophonoi*, 2.867).

In the *Iliad*, there are only the vaguest hints of a proto-Greece, a territory occupied by an ethnically united people; and in the cultural sphere, although there are certainly normative expectations of 'civilized' behaviour, these are not invoked to differentiate Greeks from Trojans (indeed, Odysseus and Menelaus are said to have visited the Trojans before the war and enjoyed cordial relations of reciprocal hospitality: see 3.207–8). In the *Odyssey*, on the other hand, there seems to be a stronger, emergent sense of *Hellas* (the adjective *Hellen* does not figure). Odysseus' fame has spread broadly 'through Hellas and the midst of Argos' (1.344, 4.726, 816), and Menelaus asks Odysseus' son Telemachus if he will travel the same route (15.80); Achilles' ghost asks if his father is still honoured, or now dishonoured 'through Greece and Pythia' (11.496). Hellas is now something physically larger and conceptually much more significant than a one-stop town in Thessaly.

What that entity is, though, is a more complex question: the most popular suggestion is that 'Hellas' refers to northern Greece (including, but not limited to, Thessaly), and 'Argos' to the south.[19] But 'Hellas' could equally well refer to the Greek mainland as later understood, the phrase as a whole meaning 'throughout all of Hellas, even into the depths of Argos'. This expanded meaning can be found in another early poem, the *Works and Days*, where Hesiod refers to the 'Achaean' expedition 'from holy Hellas to Troy with its beautiful women' (653). Here we see an explicit statement that never appears in Homer: the assault on Troy constructed as a clash between Hellas and a different people.

But if we want to know whether the Homeric and Hesiodic poems show awareness of a concept of Greece, we shall always find ourselves up against questions of composition. On most opinions, these poems are woven together from older and younger strands, with centuries separating them (see chapter 3). Modern scholars hypothesize – the reasoning is plausible, but it is impossible to tell for certain – that in the older parts of the text, *Hellas* refers to a place in Thessaly, but that the term gradually takes on wider and wider connotations, signalling first the northern mainland and then (what we call) Greece as a whole. But this cannot be the whole story. There are even mentions of Panhellenes ('all the Greeks together') in the seventh century, in Archilochus, and in the texts of Homer and Hesiod.[20] It is possible to explain away these lines (using the usual scholarly expedients: textual corruption, or later interpolation) – but who can tell?

The period of composition of the early epic poems ranged over a unique period in Greek history, when the concept of Hellenism was being phased in. Parallels can be drawn from contemporary history. The eighth century saw the foundation of panhellenic festivals (notably the Olympic games), and cult-sites such as the Delphic oracle; while these may have started out as local cults, they gradually developed 'panhellenic' significance, significance for 'all the Greeks together'. Epic poetry itself may have played an important role in this process of panhellenization, through performance at panhellenic festivals (chapter 3). Although vestigial traces of local bias can be detected, the Homeric and Hesiodic texts seem to come to embody the values of the entire Greek world.

Mapping the Territory

Despite this terminological haziness, early epic does nevertheless play a fundamental role in the formation of Greek cultural identity. In the first place, it provides narratives that inspire the culture-defining narratives of later generations. So, for example, Athenian tragedy of the fifth century repeatedly 'reads' the *Iliad* as a battle between Greeks and non-Greeks (that is, barbarians);[21] and the *Odyssey*, as we have seen, is a crucial reference point for later travel-writers such as Herodotus. Homeric and, to a lesser extent, Hesiodic narrative have cultural significance not just in terms of what they *are* (or, at least, what modern scholars think they are), but also in terms of what they *represent* to subsequent thinkers.

Secondly, and perhaps more immediately important for our purposes, Homer and Hesiod invent what we might call 'maps' of Greece. A distinctive feature of Greek oral poetry is the catalogue, a long list of elements that serve, taken together, to define a macro-structure. We have already met, for example, the list (almost 300 lines long) of the host under Agamemnon's control (and the Trojan allies too), the so-called 'Catalogue of the Ships' in book 2 of the *Iliad*. The Iliadic catalogue divides the men by provenance, so each party from each *polis* has its own entry. This catalogue, then, becomes a textual representation of geopolitical space, an index of all the Greek polities.

Thanks to the authority of the *Iliad*, this map became canonical. But traditions exist to be reinvented (see chapter 2); and we find a number of more or less subtle attempts to rewrite the catalogue in accordance with the priorities of the later Greek world. The *Iliad*'s vision of (what would later be called) 'Greece' seems particularly favourable to Thessaly: it is Thessaly that is (in the Homeric poems) the original *Hellas*, and of course the poem's protagonist, Achilles, is Thessalian. (Another early epic hero, Jason, came from Iolcus in Thessaly.) Other cities, understandably, sought to enhance their own roles: Corinth, for example, which is mentioned only twice in the *Iliad* (2.570; 13.664). The poet Eumelus, in his *Corinthian Epic*, sought to identify his native city with the shadowy Homeric Ephyre, thus at a stroke more than doubling the number of references in the text.

Athens seems to have been equally aggrieved. Only two Athenian leaders are named, Menestheus, leader of 'the people of great-hearted Erechtheus, once nurtured by Athene the daughter of Zeus, though it was the grain-giving earth that bore them' (2.547–9; he also appears at 4.327–48; 13.195–6; 13.689–91) and Iasos (15.337); neither is anything like a central figure. Pisistratus, the sixth-century Athenian tyrant (sometimes credited with sponsoring the first written text of Homer), is said to have added a line to the so-called 'Catalogue of the Ships' in book 2, positioning Ajax alongside the Athenian squadrons (a line still printed in most editions of the text as 2.558). This trick (if the reports are right) may have fooled some of the people for some of the time, but not the eagle-eyed Alexandrian editor Aristarchus (third century BCE), who acted to delete the line.

Another form of mapping, of time rather than of space, proceeds by 'genealogy' (the Greek word means, literally, 'narration of descent').[22] In Homer, the identity of an individual is constituted by his or her genealogy. Thus, for example, when the Greek Diomedes encounters the Glaucus (a Lycian, allied to the Trojans) on the battlefield, the former asks the latter who he is, to which he replies 'why do you ask me about my ancestry?' (*Iliad* 6.145); he then proceeds to a narrative of his father's exploits. Glaucus interprets the question 'who are you?' as a request for family history.

It is among the works attributed to Hesiod, however, that we find the most intensely genealogical poem of all early epic; and it is here, moreover, that genealogy is put to its most active culture-defining use. The poem in question is the *Catalogue of Women* (fragments 1–245), of which large sections survive intact (and many more on partially damaged papyrus). What is immediately noticeable is the central role accorded to Hellen, the 'eponymous' (i.e. name-giving) founder of the Hellenic people.[23] Hellen was the son of Deucalion, who (like Noah) was a survivor of a devastating flood. The sons of Hellen, according to this poem, were Dorus, Xuthus and Aeolus: of the three tribes of Greece, the Dorians spring from Dorus, the Aeolians from Aeolus, and the Ionians from Xuthus' son Ion. So the Hesiodic *Catalogue* has an identifiable agenda, namely to construct a myth of ethnic integrity to unify Hellas, perhaps even the known world. Like the so-called 'Catalogue of the Ships', though, the *Catalogue of Women* seems dimly to reflect the imperialist aspirations of Thessaly:[24] Deucalion and Hellen are both Thessalian figures, just as Hellas in the *Iliad* is under the sway of Thessalian Achilles. Myths of cultural unity are never innocent.

And as with the 'Catalogue of the Ships', so the Hesiodic catalogue was subject to later revision. The fragments of Hecataeus of Miletus (sixth–fifth centuries BCE) seem to suggest a pro-Aetolian rewriting, and those of Acusilaus of Argos (fifth century) a pro-Argive one. These rewritings are not simply wilful distortions: it is in the nature of genealogy to be flexible and adaptive. In predominantly oral societies like those of early Greece, genealogy certainly functions as a kind of collective record-keeping, a memory bank for disparate peoples with limited opportunity for communication; but unlike a census, it retains the ability to shift across time and space, to present a view of the world that reflects its maker's interests.[25]

Genealogy remained a fundamental means of defining identities of and relationships between cities throughout Greek antiquity. This was particularly important for colonies, which often depended upon the activation of links with the mainland for political, military and economic support.[26] The poems of Pindar (the fifth-century Theban lyric poet) demonstrate this clearly for the classical period. His fourth Pythian ode, for example, is addressed to Arcesilas, king of Cyrene (in north Africa), on the occasion of his victory in the chariot race at

Delphi. The narrative included within this poem details the foundation story of Cyrene: descendants of the Argonaut Euphamus ended up in Cyrene, via Sparta and the island of Thera. Interestingly, the same poet's fifth Pythian ode, addressed to the same king, gives a different foundation story for Cyrene (and still others are known). Narratives of foundation, like all genealogies, can be redesigned in accordance with the requirements of a specific situation.

The genealogical mode persisted throughout antiquity. In the Hellenistic period, poets frequently wrote on the origins, foundations and descent of cities (chapter 8). Later still, in the Roman period (chapter 9), the emperor Hadrian founded an institution based in Athens called the Panhellenion (131/2 CE).[27] This prestigious body included among its members only those deemed to be truly Greek, Greekness being defined on genealogical grounds (cities needed to be able to show descent from the founding fathers of the tribes: Aeolus, Dorus and Xuthus). Some of the cities were obvious: Athens, Sparta, Argos, Epidaurus, Megara and so forth. But beyond the geographical limits of Greece, there were many cities of Asia Minor admitted to the Panhellenion, and the claims of some of these (such as Sardis, historically the capital of the Lydian empire) to Greekness were certainly not obvious. Among them was Cibyra, which other Greek writers refer to as a non-Greek settlement. Whatever the strategic reasons for this city's admission to the Panhellenion (it was an assize centre, thus of administrative importance to the Roman empire), the inscription commemorating admission celebrates the achievements of a mythographer, Publius Antius Antiochus, in rewriting ('renewing', the inscription actually says) the Perseus myth so as to construct a plausible genealogy.[28]

For the duration of Greek history, literary genealogies provided a device for mapping the concerns of the present onto mythical time. Early epic, with its catalogue devices, created the 'language' through which such political and ideological concerns might be articulated; but like any tradition, such catalogues were open to periodic reinvention.

Usurping the Tradition

'Greekness', then, was not a given or fixed concept, but a contested, embattled term; and literature was one of the primary media through which such battles were fought. As the discussion above has shown, Greek identity was manipulated in different ways by different individuals, with different affiliations. Greece was, always, inherently, a contradiction: *both* a collection of discrete, heterogeneous polities *and* the assertion of a transcendent unity. The consequence of this contradiction was an irreducible plurality at the heart of Greekness: all city-states agreed that it existed, none agreed what it was.

The power of representation, then, was crucial. Greek literature was a vehicle not simply for the expression of an individual author, but also for the political identity of a community. This is why, for example, democratic Athens invested so much in the visual splendour of art, architecture, public inscription and the theatre (chapter 5); why the courts of Sicily and Macedonia were reportedly so keen to attract intellectuals like Aeschylus, Euripides, Plato and Aristotle; why the Ptolemies of Hellenistic Alexandria invested so much in patronizing the library and museum (chapter 8); and why generations of Romans patronized Greek poets, such as Cicero's client Archias. To facilitate the production of literature is to stake a central claim to Greek identity – and also, crucially, it bestows the ability to redefine the nature of that identity. Literature was not the only vehicle for articulating Greek identity (others included athletics and music) – but it was certainly a privileged one.

The best-attested and most spectacular example of this process is democratic Athens. Athens's patronage of culture was closely tied to its exclusivist policies. The festival known as the 'Great Panathenaea', notably, enacted a symbolic link between the two every four years. The central participatory event was a civic procession through the city. Topography is never innocent, and the route taken articulates a preoccupation with cultural origins and cultural progress. The procession began outside the city in the Potters' Quarter, at the spot where the first Athenian, Erechtheus or Erichthonius, was held to have been born from the soil of Athens (impregnated by the semen of the limping smith-god Hephaestus, who ejaculated when pursuing Athena). This commemorates the mythical process known as 'autochthony',[29] which in the Athenians' eyes gave them exclusive right to inhabit the land. The myth of autochthony gained power after Pericles' citizenship law in 451/0, which stated that Athenian citizens (i.e. males) must be born of an Athenian mother and father.[30] Law and myth supported each other: Athenian identity was now to be construed as pure, untainted, entirely endogamous.

Entering the city through the grand Dipylon gate, the citizens wound their way through the *agora* (the commercial and political heart of the city), up to the Acropolis. Here was the sacred heart of the city, but also the strongest expression of Athens's identity as a cultural superstate. The theatre of Dionysus was visible on the slopes of the

Acropolis; the grandest architecture surrounded them (the frieze that they could glimpse high up on the sanctum wall of the Parthenon – the 'Parthenon frieze', some of which is now in the British Museum – is even held by many to represent the Panathenaic participants). This symbolic journey, from the humble Potters' Quarter outside the city to the glittering emblem of Athenian power and civilization, fused mythical past and politicized present into a rich and meaningful continuum.

The Potters' Quarter was a significant location for another reason. Those citizens who died in war defending the fatherland were, in an annual ritual, cremated and buried here, symbolically returned to the ground from which the first Athenian sprang. Athens's proprietorial approach to identity, and in particular to the Greek tradition, is nowhere more visible than in the institution of the funeral speech, delivered by 'the best' citizen, in praise of these heroes.[31] A number of these speeches survive, including the famous one given to Pericles in book 2 of Thucydides' *History* (chapter 7). Let us take, by way of example, that attributed to Demosthenes, the fourth-century Athenian orator. Intriguingly, he *never refers to Athenians* at any point in the course of the speech, only to 'Greeks'. It is as though – and this is surely his strategy – he were attempting to conflate the two, to the extent that the Athenians are the true Greeks. And the *only* true Greeks too, for Demosthenes uses the theme of autochthony to promote in the strongest terms the exclusive claims of Athens:

> For alone of all men, these inhabited the fatherland from which they were born, and passed it on to those born from them, so that one might justly consider those interlopers who enter cities and are called citizens of them to be similar to bastard children, while considering our citizens the children of the fatherland by legitimate birth. (60.4)

The Athenians *alone* are legitimate; all others are bastards. A problematic assertion, for it is not even true that the Athenians were the only Greek people who pronounced themselves autochthonous. But what matters most of all is the force of the rhetoric, which proclaims, insistently, that the Athenians are the only 'true' Greeks.

With this construction of Greek identity as exclusively Athenian goes the self-proclaimed right to evaluate and update the panhellenic literary heritage. Athens was staking its claim to be the true guardian of the Greek heritage, a heritage which it was instrumental in defining: for the classical Athenians, to be Greek meant to engage in sophisticated cultural practice, including art, music and literature. Although this 'cultural' definition has now become widely naturalized – it is a cliché to associate 'ancient Greeks' with literature and art – it is crucial to recognize both the specific reasons for its genesis (its roots lying in Athenian propaganda), and the alternative models against which it was competing (most importantly, the Spartan militarist tradition).

Culture and Identity

Classical Athens's claim to be the principal state in Greece depended upon both its rhetoric of genetic purity and its (largely successful) attempt to monopolize the patronage of culture. In Athens, we might say, the genealogical mode of identity-definition was fused with a new mode, which is sometimes called the 'cultural' mode.[32] Athens invented the idea that the keepers of the Greek literary, intellectual and artistic heritage were the true Greeks. This new, 'cultural' mode of identity-definition, however, was capable of taking on a life of its own, independent from the genetic myth-making of Athens. In the fourth century, the Athenian speech-writer and pamphleteer Isocrates writes in his *Panegyric* that

> Athens has so surpassed other men in thought and speech that its pupils have become teachers of others, and it has made it seem that the name of 'Greeks' belongs more to cast of mind than to descent, and that it is those who share our education who are called 'Greeks' rather than those who share our common nature. (50)[33]

Here, the orator is claiming that culture *on its own* can make one a Greek, even without ethnic ancestry; and, particularly, that Athens is the guardian of Hellenism. This is a view that persists throughout the Hellenistic and Roman periods, when the Greek customs and language (in a form derived from the 'Attic' dialect used in Athens) gradually became the lingua franca of the entire Near East. The definition of Greekness by 'culture' was congenial to those who were 'ethnically' un-Greek. But it did not, as some scholars maintain, replace the 'ethnic' or 'genealogical' paradigm:[34] the two stood in tension with each other, as parallel and occasionally competing models for cultural definition.

I want to conclude this chapter with an example, from the second century CE, of a non-Greek who could claim to have 'Hellenized' or turned Greek through his prodigious mastery of the Greek tradition. This is Favorinus, a Gaul from Arelate (modern Arles). His *Corinthian*

Oration is a protest against the Corinthians' removal of his statue, spoken as if by the statue itself.[35] The statue argues for the importance of Favorinus as an example to all of what you can do if you put your mind to it: Favorinus has 'emulated not only the voice but also the mind-set, life and style of the Greeks' (25). In particular, he stands as an example to indigenous Greeks of the principle that 'being educated is no different from being [Greek] by nature, as far as appearances go' (27).

At one level, Favorinus is simply repeating Isocrates: the 'ethnic' mode of Hellenism is being displaced by the 'cultural'. But there is more to it than that. Firstly, the stress on 'appearances' is a new phenomenon: is being Greek, then, just about seeming, about style? (Perhaps this is what a hollow, bronze statue *would* say...) Secondly, there is a naughty tweak here. Corinth, as Favorinus well knows, was sacked by the Romans in 146 BCE, and refounded by Roman settlers under Julius Caesar. Its own claims to Hellenism are only skin-deep. Appearances can be deceptive...

Education – *paideia* is the Greek word – is the central marker of elite Greek identity in this period (see chapter 9). When Favorinus exalts the power of 'being educated' into Greekness (the Greek word he uses is cognate with *paideia*) over that of nature, he is invoking a set of assumptions that he would expect his audience to share, in broad outline at least. At the same time, however, to place the cultural and the genetic models in such stark opposition is to be deliberately provocative. Genealogy was still a powerful force: Favorinus was declaiming under the emperor Hadrian, the founder of the Panhellenion, which (as we saw above) defined a city's membership of the Greek community on the basis of genealogy.

The occasion for Favorinus' speech was the removal of his statue: clearly not everyone was equally convinced by his case for Hellenism. Nor, arguably, was he; as we have seen, the *Corinthian Oration* is playful and slippery in its treatment of Greek identity. The point, then, is not that the cultural mode came to replace the genetic, but that the two presented themselves as different forms of self-definition, sometimes coalescing and sometimes (as in Favorinus' case) clashing.

The Greek literary tradition was, throughout antiquity, a means of communicating Greek identity. What I hope to have shown in this chapter, though, is that that identity was not a self-evident, recognized 'given' but a locus of conflict. Numerous writers venture to delineate Greekness, but none of these should be taken as per se authoritative: they are all strategic, all self-interested attempts to control a radically elusive concept.

11

A Woman's Place

Gender Trouble

Much of this book has circled around the role of literature in the definition and contestation of masculine identities. In chapter 3, we encountered the concept of the 'zero-sum game' in the context of Homeric warfare: heroic status is acquired by competition with others. Chapter 9 explored the competitive demands of rhetorical speaking, which often requires the speaker to promote his 'face' at the expense of that of his opponents. Greek literature, and indeed Greek society, was intensely male-dominated; and while there were (of course) continuing anxieties about what it meant to be a man (we shall explore some of these in the next chapter), an androcentric focus is usually presumed.[1]

Women, on the other hand, were subject to protocols of silence and confinement.[2] Even the one sphere in which expression was approved, public lamentation, seems to have been increasingly regulated (in fifth-century Athens, at any rate).[3] But although women are repeatedly marginalized in Greek literature, they never disappear. The silencing of women is not a fait accompli, but (as feminist literary criticism has shown)[4] *a process* that can be exposed (and even, arguably, reversed) in the reading of literary texts. In particular, vying against the ongoing attempts within Greek literature to fix women securely within the household, we can point to the recurrent anxiety about the *mobility of women*, and their refusal (or inability) to remain 'in place'. In a virilocal society (i.e. a society in which marriage requires the transfer of the woman from her father's house to that of her new husband), women are objects of exchange; but, as the French anthropologist Claude Lévi-Strauss observes, they can never be *reduced* to the status of exchange-tokens, for they possess language and the active power to influence.[5] It is this active, self-determining status of women, and the fear it inspires, that Greek literature repeatedly explores.

The *Iliad*, for many the definitive text of macho war culture, is a story of gender trouble: the campaign against Troy springs from Helen's relocation from her first husband (Menelaus in Sparta) to her second (Paris in Troy). The idea that wars start with the movement of women later became canonical: the 'Persian story' beginning Herodotus' *Histories* (fifth century BCE; see chapter 7), notably, explains the East–West conflicts as the result of a series of abductions (Herodotus himself, though, is sceptical, on the disturbingly familiar grounds that 'they would not have been abducted if they had not wanted to go', 1.4.2). In the *Acharnians* (425 BCE) of the comic poet Aristophanes (chapter 5), the chorus blames the current war with Sparta upon the abduction of a prostitute (523–9).

Despite the overwhelming focus upon men and war, women do appear at crucial points in the *Iliad*. Agamemnon's destructive dispute with Achilles is fired by a quarrel over women, an echo of the original abduction of Helen; though for Agamemnon and Achilles, now living in tents by a shore, it is not a question of wives – and the civilizing institutions and structures that go with them – but of two slave-girls, Chryseis and Briseis. As so often, the role of women is constructed as that of object of desire, and the type of woman desired defines the type of men. The Argive host – so this episode implies – has lost touch with ordered society, quarrelling as they are now over mere commodities and tokens of honour.

The Trojans, on the other hand, have an ordered society, including households and wives. It is when women refuse to limit themselves to that role, when they breach the boundaries of gender definition, that social stability is placed at risk. In book 6, Andromache, the wife of Hector (the Trojan champion), confronts him at the gates, entreating him to look after the family rather than go out to fight. Andromache is the model of a dutiful wife, but her presence is no less troublesome for that. The gates occupy an ambiguous position, between inside the city and outside – a significant context, for Hector's ambiguously dual identity (as a warrior, on the one hand, and a husband and father, on the other) is here being probed. Hector's epithet, in Homer, is 'of the flashing helmet'; it is precisely that helmet that he removes, because it terrifies his baby son (6.471–3). But just as it seems as though he will reject his identity as a warrior to become a father, he orders her back into the household to her weaving: 'war will be for men, all men, but especially me' (6.492–3). This brusque command serves as a brutal reassertion of gender divisions, in the face of the ambiguity that has developed: he must go outside to fight, she must go inside to weave.

The map of sexual identities imposed by Hector, delimiting both space and social roles by gender, was (as we shall see) to have a long history. For Greeks in general, the attainment of adult identity was constructed differently for men and women. Marriage marked the coming of age of women, and – at least in the classical period – the first military campaign marked that of men (though marriage was certainly important for them too). Jean-Pierre Vernant writes, apophthegmatically, that 'marriage is to the girl what war is to the boy':[6] both were institutions with vital identity-defining roles in Greek society. What is interesting about the Homeric passage, however, is that it exposes the *process* of distribution, and the brutal authority that underlies it: identities are at risk in the passage cited, and only Hector's forceful, even arbitrary intervention re-establishes order between the genders.

Travelling Women

The archetypal travelling woman is Helen.[7] Narrative economy demands that, as the catalyst of the most important literary war in Greek literature, she occupy an exceptional position. As the daughter of Zeus and Leda, she is semi-divine (in this respect a female counterpart of the text's other main actor, Achilles); and as the wife of two men, one Argive and one Trojan, she occupies a problematically dual role. In book 3 of the *Iliad*, she is found at the gates of Troy (an ambiguous, liminal position – as we saw in the case of Andromache), responding to the questions of the Trojan elders about the principal Argive warriors (3.146–242). Helen reproaches herself for having come to Troy, and the narrator describes her desire for her homeland and former husband (139–40); but still, she presents the Trojans with her insider knowledge of their enemies. As one with a stake in both camps, she is fully committed to neither.

This theme is brilliantly (but disturbingly) explored in a passage in book 4 of the *Odyssey*. Odysseus' son Telemachus is visiting Menelaus and Helen (now reunited) in search of news of his father. Helen slips a drug into the others' drinks. It is a benevolent drug, removing their pain (4.220–1) – but surreptitious drugging is nevertheless hardly the practice of a regular wife. Helen proceeds to tell Telemachus a story of how she entertained Odysseus when he slipped into Troy in disguise

(4.235–64). This story, representing Helen in a positive light, is balanced by a far less flattering one told by Menelaus (4.265–89): when the Argive soldiers were huddled in the Trojan horse, she circled the edifice, calling out to them and imitating the voices of their wives. In both stories, Helen exploits her uncertain position, between the Greek and the Roman camp – the difference is that Menelaus' account appraises the story less favourably. We are left, finally, with a question: which side is she on? How do we read her?[8]

Men's difficulty in reading women is a recurrent theme of Greek literature (we have already met this idea in our discussions of Semonides and Anacreon in chapter 4). Even Penelope in Homer's *Odyssey* is characteristically inscrutable. The very model of a faithful, constant wife (no travelling here), Penelope is – exceptionally for a woman in the Homeric poems – said to possess 'fame' alongside her husband.[9] Yet her motives are not always clear. In some cases, certainly, her trickery can be seen as a form of loyalty to the household: she deceives the suitors because she does not want to remarry, and even when she tests the revealed Odysseus it can be argued that she simply wants to establish for certain that he is who he says he is. But some of her other actions are more difficult to assess. Why does she beautify herself before appearing to the suitors? Why does she weep when a dream portends their death? What, as Freud might have put it, *does the woman want*?

Sappho and the 'Personal Voice'

We know what one woman, at least, wanted. Or, at least, we think we do. Sappho is one of antiquity's most fascinating figures, but also one of the most mysterious.[10] Practically nothing is known of sixth-century Lesbos, where she flourished, and what is known is mostly hypothesized from fragments of her poetry and that of her contemporary, Alcaeus. Even these fragments are sparse: we possess only two complete or near-complete poems by Sappho, which owe their survival to citation in later Greek literary-critical texts. Despite this almost complete lack of any context, however, scholars and commentators have throughout history often been drawn to fill in the gaps with spurious biography.[11] In antiquity, she was supplied with a male lover, Phaon, and made to leap to her death when her love was unrequited (there is a letter, in Latin, purportedly from her to him transmitted with the works of the Roman poet Ovid). At the turn of the twentieth century, the famous German scholar Ulrich von Wilamowitz-Moellendorff claimed that Sappho was a schoolmistress, whose concern for the women in her company was entirely pedago-gical.[12] Both narratives are – to modern eyes, at least – hopelessly crude attempts to deal with the issue of sex between women (which will be discussed in the following chapter).

Sappho's poetry, composed in a variety of lyric metres (and most famously in the stanza now known as the Sapphic), focuses upon relationships and emotions, dramatizing the inner space of reflection, representing an idiomatic 'personal voice', offsetting that against the public world of men.[13] Her poetry continually returns to moments of quiet intimacy beyond the watchful gaze of the world. How we *inter-pret* this phenomenon, however, depends on what kind of contexts we supply. If her poetry was directed towards a small group of friends, then we can consider this private poetry. But if – as certainly seems the case with at least some poems – they were for performance in social or ritual contexts (such as weddings), then her poetry can be seen as a form of voyeurism, exposing a 'private' world to 'public' view. If the latter is assumed, then we might conclude that her poetry offers her readers teasing glimpses of a world from which they are necessarily separated. Different readers will have different views. My working hypothesis (which is, of course, ideologically invested) will be that Sappho's work is not simply private poetry; rather, it ex-plores the *dialogue* between public and private, always aware of the masculinist tradition and repeatedly marking *difference* from it.

Sappho Reading Homer

Sappho is the earliest reader of Homer's gender politics. The frag-mentary poem 16, beginning with three substantially intact stanzas, offers the most powerful example:

> Some say that a force of cavalry, others a force
> of infantry, others a force of ships
> is the best thing on the black earth, but I say that it is whatsoever
> one loves.
>
> It is altogether easy to make this intelligible to anyone,
> for Helen, who surpassed mortals
> by far in beauty, leaving her excellent
> husband,
>
> sailed and went to Troy,
> and heeded not at all her son or
> dear parents . . . (16.1–11)

This passage is the first example in classical literature of a device known as the 'priamel', a series of alternatives rounded off with the poet's own preference. But this formal device also serves a cultural-political function, to contrast Sappho's choice with those of the un-named 'some' who prefer military sights. The poem presents her as an individual, even idiosyncratic figure. Societal and literary norms parade the values of war; Sappho, by contrast, celebrates the erotic. In the final two stanzas (now fragmentary), Sappho links this polarization of war and sex directly to her own situation in the here-and-now, stating that she would rather see the absent Anactoria than 'the chariots of Lydia or the armour of infantrymen' (19–20). The poem thus turns away from the grand, cosmic, heroic, universal themes of traditional epic, to embrace instead the immediacy and specificity of one individual's desire for another.

The poem invites a 'metapoetic' reading, as a programmatic statement of Sappho's literary self-positioning: traditional poetry, she implies (though this is arguably an ungenerous implication), has focused exclusively upon martial themes, but this will be a new form, focused not upon competition and power but upon the desiring self. But this is not all. Sappho goes further, 'rewriting' the *Iliad* as a poem motivated by female desire. Helen, who (as we have seen) plays a limited though important role in the *Iliad* (primarily in book 3), becomes in Sappho's revision a central narrative agent.[14] And, indeed, an active desiring *subject*: it is Helen who chooses to leave for Troy, she is not abducted or seduced. In the received myth, Aphrodite offers Helen to Paris as an inducement to judge her the most beautiful of the goddesses; Sappho's version, by way of contrast, turns her into the prime mover of the *Iliad*. One final point on this poem: it is striking how Helen (a positively validated figure in this poem) rejects the bedrock of the patriarchal value system. 'Leaving her excellent husband', Sappho writes, '. . . [she] heeded not at all her son or dear parents.' Hardly the traditional Greek view of feminine propriety. This is a poem that confronts, even affronts, the male-centred literary tradition.

Fighting Talk

Sappho's rewriting of Homer also operates at the semantic level. Her poetry is suffused with Homeric language, but military imagery is repeatedly employed to describe the effects of love.[15] In poem 1, for example, Sappho begs Aphrodite not to 'subdue' her soul (3), and asks her instead to become her 'ally' (28). It is indeed a feature of the Greek language in general that the discourses of war and sex overlap. But although critics conventionally write of Sappho's use of 'military metaphors', this description is implicitly loaded, constructing the military as primary ('literal') and the erotic as secondary ('metaphorical'). Sappho disrupts such certainties. Which came first, the military or the erotic? Why do we not rather write of the *Iliad*'s adoption of 'sexual metaphors' in military contexts?[16]

As we have seen, Sappho self-consciously sites herself within the slowly emergent Greek literary tradition, undertaking a highly creative, even confrontational, engagement with its originary texts, the Homeric poems. Sappho presents a challenge to the norms of that tradition, particularly but not exclusively in terms of gender (her poems also oppose the miniature to the grandiose, the private to the public, East to West). These poems present (or present themselves as) the first deliberate challenge to Greek literature from the margins.

The Tragic House

It is, however, in the Athenian tragedy of the fifth century that we see the most powerful development of epic anxiety over female mobility.[17] As a context for literary performance, democratic Athens represented a radically new cultural and ideological frame; and (as we saw in chapter 5), the theatre of Dionysus provided a central focus for the exploration of issues that lay at the heart of the community. In Athens, the idealized division of labour and space according to gender (such as we have seen attributed to Homer's Hector) became the subject of powerful norms. Fifth-century Greek houses seem to have been designed to shield the females of the house from male guests.[18] The female goddess of the hearth, Hestia, inhabited the innermost portion of the house, while the male god Hermes oversaw the threshold, the point that separated inside from out.[19] Architecture and ideology conspired to locate women in private space and men in the public world beyond (though of course they were expected to be masters of their households too).[20]

Tragedy, in particular, genders the viewing experience. Scholars still debate whether women were permitted to attend performances at the theatre.[21] If they were, the numbers are likely to have been small; and although their presence (if accepted) would imply a fascinating, if irrecoverable, alternative perspective (what would they have made of these texts?), it seems as though the primary function of drama was conceived of as the education of citizens – that is to say, men. Dramatic space reproduces the contours of the public/private gender ideology discussed above (see also chapter 5 on dramatic space).[22] The *orkhestra* or 'dancing area' on which the action was performed was partially enfolded into the semi-circular space where the citizen audience watched; at the back of it lay the *skene* (literally 'tent'), the set building that is put to a variety of uses, but the norm (and the expectation) is that it will represent the house. In the centre of the audience's field of vision lies the door, the central focus for much of the action, the site of transition between the two discrete worlds of public and private.

Transgressions

These spatial dynamics are put to terrifying use in Euripides' *Medea* (431 BCE). This play portrays Medea's revenge against her husband Jason, who is attempting to remarry; famously, she murders her own children. (This would have come as a shock to those familiar with the traditional story, although scholars think the infanticide motif had been introduced by an earlier poet, Neophron.) Infanticide is a particularly strong form of rebellion against anticipated gender roles.

The drama opens with Medea wailing incoherently inside the house, conforming to the stereotype of a demonical barbarian. When she appears from the house, however, she delivers a magnificently eloquent oration on the subject of reputations, and particularly upon the lot of women, confined to the house and entirely dependent on husbands (214–66, especially 244–51). The (transgressive) action of emerging from the house substantiates the message of the oration: that she will now take action, no longer tolerant of her enforced passivity.[23] And indeed, as is often noted, Medea takes on much of the language and character (determination, self-righteousness, isolation) of a traditional male hero.[24] Although Medea does periodically revert to the role of traditional wife, she does so only to deceive her preening husband ('Jason, I beg you, forgive me for the words I spoke . . . I am what I am: a woman, not an evil', 869–70; 889–90). Her revenge is not only upon Jason, but also upon the gender role forced upon her.

This powerful sense that Medea cannot be placed as a woman is underlined at the end of the play. After her murder of her children has been revealed, Jason claims that she is 'a lioness, not a woman', he wails, 'with a nature more vicious than Etruscan Scylla' (1342–3). What kind of being, then, is she? At this stage, she has appeared on a flying chariot (or, as some believe, on the roof of the house), while Jason stands outside, a brilliant but chilling perversion of the expected spatial dynamics of the house. The gendered separation is maintained, but Medea is no longer *inside* but *above* the house, transcending both Corinth and its constraining sexual economy. Is she a woman now? Or an animal, as Jason claims? Or a witch? Or a goddess? Her refusal to adopt the anticipated woman's place in the house leads to a radically uncertain status.

Tragic plots return repeatedly to the theme of transgression of space and (hence) gender roles. Most tragedies stage narratives of kinship violation, of the failure of relationships within the household.[25] Kinship violation is driven particularly by the misplacement of women within the social economy. In Aeschylus' *Agamemnon* (458 BCE), it is Clytaemnestra's adultery that impels the calamitous events. Aeschylus seems to have innovated in devolving the primary narrative energy to the woman; in the canonical version (repeatedly) narrated in Homer's *Odyssey*, it is the men who take the lead.[26] In Aeschylus' account, Clytaemnestra is stigmatized from the very start as a transgressive figure, a woman (exceptionally) with political authority: 'that is how the manly-devising, expectant heart of the woman wields her power', comments the watchman who speaks the prologue (10–11). The juxtaposition (in the original Greek) of the words 'woman' and 'manly-devising' is striking: in assuming 'power', the woman Clytaemnestra exceeds the proper limits of her sex. Exceptionally, in this case we have the entire tragic trilogy, and critics have traced the 'dynamics of misogyny' that link the three plays, concluding with the final trial scene in the *Eumenides* (or 'Furies').[27]

Here, Apollo presides over the first homicide court at the Athenian Areopagus, summoned to judge Orestes' killing of his mother (Clytaemnestra) to avenge his father (Agamemnon). The law courts were central to Athens's sense of itself as a democracy, institutions that managed the ideological and ethical life of the city (see chapter 6). This particular case, though, revolves around the issue of *gender*, and does so at two levels. Firstly, the prosecuting Furies are female, though they are not women; they are 'contemptible monsters, hated of the gods' (644), natural, elemental forces, embodying all the earthy foulness and impurity that a misogynistic tradition associates with the abject female.[28] The court's choice is, then, between a young man (with all the implicit idealization that goes with young men in Athens) and nameless, formless female figures saturated with the repulsive horror.

At the second level, Orestes' matricide is being weighed against his avenging of his father. With which parent should the court side? In the event, the answer is not so simple as might have been expected: the jury is hung, so the casting vote goes to Athena. At lines 657–73, Apollo attempts to sway her by delivering a striking speech in which he describes the 'so-called mother' as 'not the parent of the child, just the nurturer of the newly-sown fetus' (658–9); the man is the true parent. This speech seems to mimic the language of contemporary medicine, but his evidence is far from clinching: as testimony, he cites the (hardly standard) case of Athena herself, born directly from the head of Zeus. For all that its conclusions chime with Athenian sexism, this is an argument that perhaps could only ever fully convince Athena herself. As it does: Apollo's arguments carry the day.

Adultery, Gender and the City

The centrality of gender transgression to tragic narrative is no accident. Athens was a city that was rapidly evolving its own racial eugenics. In 451/0, as we saw in the previous chapter, Pericles introduced his famous citizenship law: for a child (male, of course) to be a citizen, he needed both parents to be Athenians. Pericles' innovation placed a massive new premium upon endogamous gender relations. Aeschylus' *Oresteian Trilogy* was staged seven years before the citizenship law, but already manifests the paranoid fear of adultery. In the Homeric narrative, it is the male usurper Aegisthus who is blamed; in the Aeschylean, the adulterous mother Clytaemnestra.

The *Oresteian Trilogy* has a further connection with Athens's new emphasis upon the purity of its bloodline. When Apollo argues that the father is the true parent and the mother a mere vessel, he is implicitly invoking the myth of autochthony (see chapter 10). The first Athenian, Erechtheus (or Erichthonius), was (so this narrative runs) born from the earth when Hephaestus' semen fell upon it. The myth of autochthony expresses the 'dream of a world without women'.[29] Nicole Loraux has famously argued that autochthony's exclusion of any female reproductive role was part of an overall drive to exclude Athenian women from any sort of social status.[30] The argument is overstated, in that the woman's role as guardian of the bloodline does appear to have been acknowledged in Athens, in some contexts at least.[31] But it is certainly the case that the misogynist dream of a male-only world is expressed in tragedy. In Euripides' *Hippolytus*, the protagonist (a young man unwilling to effect the transition to adult sexuality) wishes vehemently that children could be bought from temples, without the need for women (616–24); Jason in the *Medea* utters a similar wish (573–4); Eteocles in Aeschylus' *Seven against Thebes* also wishes he could live apart from women (182–95). Execration of the female is nothing new in the Greek tradition (already in the archaic period, Hesiod and Semonides were engaging in it);[32] what is new here is the specific wish to deny women their role in *reproduction*, which has gained powerful new urgency from the contemporary discourse of autochthony.

The Comic Woman

Aeschylus' Clytaemnestra became instantly one of the best-known icons of the fifth-century stage, with an influence that reached beyond the generic confines of tragedy. Aristophanes' play *Lysistrata* (411 BCE) was the first of his three plays (the others being the *Women at the Thesmophoria* (also 411 BCE) and *The Assembly Women* (392 BCE)) showing women unshackling themselves and taking control. It was also, probably, the first comedy to feature a female lead character (though the part was played, of course, by a man).[33] Lysistrata (apparently based upon a well-known contemporary priestess, Lysimache) organizes the women of Athens to unite with those of Sparta and elsewhere, take over the Athenian acropolis and to refuse to have sex with the men until a reconciliation is reached in the war between Athens and Sparta. In keeping with other plays of Aristophanes (*Acharnians*, *Peace*), it presents war as inimical to the indulgent pleasure of the comic world (see chapter 5); and like all of his plays, it concludes with a joyous restoration of the 'natural' order, of bountiful harmony.[34]

Modern commentators have sometimes branded this a 'feminist' play. Tony Harrison's version, *The Common Chorus*, was tellingly set in the Greenham Common peace camp. In the play, however, the 'emancipation' of the women is presented not as a desirable end in itself, but as an abnormality, a symptom of the men's pathologically destructive desire for war. The play concludes with the cancellation of this perverse state of affairs, and the reintegration of women into the proper structure of the household, symbolized by a dance of reunion: 'let husband stand beside wife, and wife beside husband' (1275–6). The inversion of city's (and the house's) normal gender hierarchy is followed by a renewal and celebration of the traditional state of affairs. If the *Oresteian Trilogy* finally tames the challenge of

the transgressive woman by recourse to law, Athens's ideological
state apparatus par excellence, then the *Lysistrata* does so with a
massive party: more fun, perhaps, but no less ideologically freighted.

For readers expecting a feminist play, this ending is disappoint-
ingly conservative. Indeed, there are misogynistic stereotypes to be
found even within the earlier narrative. The women, Lysistrata herself notwithstanding, are presented as driven primarily by lust for
sex and drink, a standard joke. The women's compact is sworn by a
drinking cup (209–37). At one point, Lysistrata has to prevent sex-
starved women from breaking out of the Acropolis and heading back
to their husbands (728–80).

But for all its jolly conservatism in relation to sexuality and sexual
stereotypes, the play does present a number of challenges that are not
so easily resolved. In particular, macho male stereotypes are just
as vulnerable to Aristophanic assault. At one point, the women are
approached by a civic official, a *proboulos* (a board of ten *probouloi*
had been created two years before the play was performed to deal with
state emergencies). After blustering and demanding that the women
abandon the Acropolis, he engages in a dialogue with Lysistrata, in
which he makes it clear that he cannot comprehend the notion of
women forming intelligent plans:

> [Lysistrata:] We shall be your saviours.
> [*Proboulos:*] *You??*
> [Lysistrata:] Exactly: us.
> [*Proboulos:*] That's disgraceful!
> [Lysistrata:] That is how you will be saved, whether you like it or
> not.
> [*Proboulos:*] What a terrible thing to say! (497–9)

In what proceeds, the *proboulos* threatens the women with violence,
and in particular seeks to control their *speech*. 'Speak quickly, or
you'll find yourself weeping' (503); 'Keep your cawing to yourself,
old woman; [to Lysistrata] *you*, speak' (506). Lysistrata's words that
follow, putting forward the women's plan for salvation, also return
to the notion of the silencing of women: 'we kept our silence' (507),
'you did not even allow us to squeak' (509), 'my husband would
say "Won't you shut up?", and I would shut up' (515). When she
questioned her husband's decisions, Lysistrata says, he threatened
her with physical violence if she did not return to the loom, citing
Hector's famous words (discussed above), 'war will be for men' (519–
20). This allusion is more than just an appeal to Homeric authority;

it also recalls the precise context of the scene between Hector and Andromache, where the warrior re-established the boundary between the proper spheres of activity of woman and man alike.

It is commonly claimed in democratic Athens that, in the words of Sophocles' Ajax (as reported by Tecmessa), 'silence becomes a woman' (*Ajax* 293). Citizen wives were not allowed to speak in court, or even (it appears) be mentioned by name.[35] The funeral speech that Thucydides attributes to Pericles (in book 2 of the *History*) is mostly devoted to the virtues of men, but as an afterthought, the concluding words acknowledge women: 'great is the renown of her who has the least fame among men, whether for virtue or for culpability' (Thucydides 2.45.2). This is a striking phrase, a self-conscious paradox – renown is won by avoiding fame – that later was privileged to receive an essay-length rebuttal from the second-century CE polymath Plutarch (in his *Virtues of Women*).

But the Aristophanic passage exposes both the brutality and (as would be claimed by Plutarch, an advocate of the education of women: see the following section)[36] the foolishness of the silencing of women. By putting these words into the mouth of a protesting woman, Aristophanes invokes the memory of Medea's opening speech in Euripides' play of that name (discussed above): both confront the Athenian audience with a challenge to their repressive treatment of women. The allusion to the Iliadic encounter of Hector and Andromache, moreover, also strategically marks the *difference* between the two scenes: the *Iliad* represents the tender affection of husband and wife, the *Lysistrata* brutal violence; the *Iliad* a complicated compromise overshadowed by the impending death of Hector, the *Lysistrata* the dozy ignorance of the male. In Aristophanes' play, the silencing and depoliticization of women are presented as springing from blind machismo, not fatal heroism.

The *Lysistrata* takes over the tragic paradigm of the transgressive woman, and adapts it to the different requirements of the comic theatre. As in tragedy, Aristophanes' play constructs a powerfully normative role for women within the household, as submissive to men. This is not a 'feminist' venture; the repeatedly stated aim of the women is to save the city, not to transform it. But comedy attacks extremism, and the extremist repression practised by the men who silence women, who stick to their plans inflexibly, who will not listen to alternatives, is also ruthlessly pilloried. It is the women who come up with the ideas, the women who control the narrative energy, and the women who manage the transition to the comic utopia that concludes the play. Even if the potential threat posed by that unexpected

burst of female activity must be dissipated by the return to established gender hierarchies in the utopian ending, the *Lysistrata* nevertheless remains a play that radically interrogates the Athenian ideology
of female silence – while simultaneously defusing any real threat by
turning it all into a joke.

Changing Paradigms

Historians sometimes point to an increased relaxation of the
constraints operating on women in the Hellenistic (*c.*323–31 BCE;
chapter 8) and Roman (*c.*31 BCE–400 CE; chapter 9) periods.[37] It is,
however, impossible to quantify 'liberation'. Free-market capitalism
encourages modern subjects to regard 'freedom' as a self-evident quality, namely the absence of state control; by implication, then, the
history of the West has been one continuous progress towards emancipation. But not all western subjects, and many fewer non-westerners,
accept that the world has become straightforwardly and progressively freer. We should be wary, then, before subscribing to any simple
historical narrative of 'liberation' over time. Post-classical literature
demonstrates *changes* in the treatment of women, not necessarily (or
not *simply*) progress.

Our texts provide an inconsistent range of evidence about female
mobility. From one perspective, texts from the Hellenistic period seem
to suggest more mobility for women. In Theocritus' fifteenth *Idyll*
(early third century BCE), two women go unchaperoned to the palace
of Arsinoe in Alexandria to see the fine tapestries and hear a performance.[38] The only male criticism they incur is for their broad
accents (15.87–8). In Herodas' *Mimes* (probably also third century),
women apparently work as pimps (1), visit temples and discuss the
artworks there (4), beat slaves for having sex with another woman
as well (5), discuss the supply of dildos (6), visit the cobbler who
makes them (7) and have breakfast together (9). The women of
Herodas 1 seem to be prostitutes, so are perhaps exempt from the
usual constraints on female behaviour; but all the others are married
property-owners. This focus upon middle-to-low-life women is undoubtedly comical, and probably aimed at the gratification of a male,
elite audience. But it is the titillation of eavesdropping on private
woman-to-woman conversations (Herodas' characters like to claim,
ironically, to be alone: 1.47–8; 6.22–5) that provides the frisson
here, not the fear of women leaving the house. There is no apparent
anxiety over these mobile women.

Other sources, however, suggest that little has changed. In the so-called 'new comedy' that dominated the stage of Athens in the Hellenistic period (and the stage of Rome, via the Latin versions of Plautus and Terence), plots of love, rape and abduction depend upon the availability of women in public space; but except at religious festivals, the women in question are almost never citizen women.[39] That citizen women could take part in religion is a telling exception: this was the one form of public participation open to them in democratic Athens, too.

Similarly, in Callimachus' *Acontius and Cydippe* (a poem that appeared in the third book of his *Aetia* or *Causes*, third century BCE; see also chapter 8), the lover Acontius glimpses his beloved at a festival, and tricks her at a temple (by rolling her an apple incised with the words 'I swear by Artemis to marry Acontius', which she proceeded to read aloud). As in 'new' comedy and (from later periods) the Greek novels and Musaeus' *Hero and Leander* (fifth century CE), citizen men glimpse citizen women only in religious contexts. It is equally notable that in Callimachus' tale (at least, in the fragments we have) Cydippe is entirely passive. Acontius plots to get her, her father arranges the succession of marriages that fail (because they contravene her oath). There is no indication that she shares Acontius' passion; indeed, the only words (again, so far as our fragments can tell us) she utters are those incised on the apple, that is, those scripted by the male Acontius.[40]

Elite women were certainly more likely to be educated in later periods. There are references to a number of female intellectuals, from the early Cynic philosopher Hipparchia (fourth century BCE; see Diogenes Laertius, *Lives of the Ancient Philosophers* 6.7) to Hypatia of Alexandria (fourth–fifth century CE). Julia Domna, wife of the Roman emperor Septimius Severus (193–211 CE), is said to have cultivated a circle of Greek intellectuals.[41] But such figures are significant as exceptions to the general, ongoing male-centredness of Greek literature.

There were certainly philosophers, particularly in the Roman period, who argued that women should receive an education as much as men: Plutarch wrote an essay *That Women too should be Educated*, now largely lost; and the Stoic philosopher Musonius Rufus (first century CE) wrote short pieces called *That Women should also Philosophize* and *Should Daughters be Educated Alongside Sons?* (fragments 3 and 4).[42] These tracts would seem to propose an opening up of traditionally male prerogatives to women (though their polemical nature presupposes that the issue is contentious and debated). Despite the initial promise of equal terms, however, it soon becomes clear that women are to be educated so that they can perform better their 'natural', domestic tasks: 'one should allot the tasks that are most appropriate to the nature of each . . . perhaps it may be that some human tasks exist in common, and are shared by both men and women . . . but some tasks are more fitted to the nature of one, and some to that of the other' (*Should Daughters be Educated Alongside Sons?*). So much for equality.

Greater access to literacy for women (among the elite, to be sure), however, certainly did have positive results. In contrast to the earlier Greek tradition (from which we have only Sappho), there are from the Hellenistic period a number of small poems written by women from the early Hellenistic period, specifically by Erinna, Nossis, Anyte and (probably from this time) Corinna.[43]

Many of these detail intense relationships of kinship or friendship between women; in this respect, they site themselves in a line with Sappho (Nossis explicitly: *Palatine Anthology* 7.718), albeit adopting new forms. As a result of a lucky papyrus find, we now have a fragment of Erinna's most famous and admired poem, *The Distaff*. It is not clear from the fragment we have why the poem was so titled, but the reference to weaving fits well the poem's concern with private life between women. This complex text refers to her 'memories' of youthful play with Baucis: the children's game 'tortoise', playing with dolls, the stories of Mormo (the Greek bogey-woman). A recent critic has argued – subtly, though necessarily speculatively – that the poem centres on the thematic polarity of mobility and stability, and thus explores the constraints that operated upon women in society.[44] On this interpretation, Hellenistic women's poetry continues (despite the increase in female literacy) to articulate the confinement of women to their 'place' in household and society.

What did men in the Hellenistic period think of the phenomenon of female poets? In Herodas' mimes, one woman refers to 'Nossis, the daughter of Erinna' as a recognized user of dildos (6.21–2). At one level, this is just a cheap laugh at the expense of two prominent poetesses, a crude attempt to put women who dare to impinge on the masculine sphere of poetry back in their place by sexual defamation. At a more abstract level, we might take the dildo as a metaphor for the poetic voice. Women lack the phallus just as they lack the power of self-expression: like the dildo, female poetry is an artificial attempt to mimic what men have 'naturally'.

We should be wary, then, before assuming progressive 'emancipation' throughout antiquity. The narrative of sexual liberation itself, as we noted earlier, is ideologically suspect. More importantly, our sources give out mixed signals. There are signs of increased mobility, literacy and intellectual expression; but there are also powerful attempts to defend the received gender hierarchies.

Novelties

One genre of the post-classical age that has always been associated with women is the Greek novel (discussed in chapter 9), in which reciprocity and fidelity between women and men are prized, and women often take a central (and dynamic) role.[45] It was once accepted that these texts were written for bourgeois women and men (one critic refers infelicitously to 'the poor-in-spirit . . . naive readers').[46] This view rests upon the anachronism that the readership was similar to that of eighteenth- and nineteenth-century English novels, a dangerous assumption. More recent scholarship has brought to light evidence that the texts were owned and read by the highly educated elite, not the 'bourgeoisie' (a class that anyway did not really exist in antiquity),[47] and in general assumed a male readership.[48] The matter is not closed, though. One scholar in particular argues that the novels display the ideals of an aspirational female readership in the empire.[49] We shall never know the answer for sure.

When we come to the texts themselves, we certainly encounter an intensive focus upon female subjectivity. There are numerous examples of women talking, even women thinking. In Longus' *Daphnis and Chloe*, a pastoral novel from the second century CE, Chloe experiences desire first and takes the initiative in the relationship; it is she who realizes that he is beautiful (1.13). As the narrative progresses, however, her role is increasingly muted, as Daphnis assumes an increasingly authoritative role. He loses his virginity to an oversexed neighbour (3.16–18), whereas she must – of course – wait for legitimately sanctioned marriage. And, indeed, her submissive role in that marriage is figured by images of violence that dapple the narrative: the myth of Pan's rape and butchery of Syrinx (2.34), the prediction that 'she will weep and wail and lie in a pool of blood as though slain' when deflowered (3.19), the 'harsh and raucous' wedding song that accompanies the marriage (4.40). This novel does not offer any straightforward promises of female empowerment.[50] (That, of course, does not itself rule out a female readership.)

Chariton's *Chaereas and Callirhoe* (first century CE) is sometimes presented as the primary candidate for a text 'inviting women readers' identification'.[51] And it is certainly true that Callirhoe monopolizes much of the action. But her primary role is to affect male viewers. Feminist criticism has made substantial use of the concept of 'the gaze', the deployment of filmic or narrative focalization of women as objects of and available to the male visual field.[52] Callirhoe is repeatedly presented as the object of the male gaze.[53] When, for example, the pirate Theron (who has abducted and enslaved her) is hawking her to a potential vendor, Leonas, he stages a show designed to stimulate its recipient's appetite:

> When he approached the villa, Theron devised the following plan. He unveiled Callirhoe and loosened her hair; then he opened the door and bade her enter first. Leonas and all those indoors were awestricken when she suddenly appeared, as if they had seen a goddess. Indeed, there was a rumour in the countryside of an epiphany of Aphrodite. (1.14.1)

Leonas' 'awestricken' reaction is carefully cued: Theron has created a fantasy glimpse of an interior woman's world. The 'unveiling' of Callirhoe reveals her to the public gaze; the loosening of the hair symbolizes the loosening of the constraints governing female sexuality. The dominated, enslaved woman is made to perform for the pleasure of her potential owner, flashing glimpses of a mystified interior at him. It is certainly the male who controls this presentation of female sexuality, and the male for whose benefit it is enacted.

Yet Callirhoe remains an inscrutable figure, one whose intentions are difficult to gauge. Why, in the grand trial scene at Babylon, does she seem unable to choose between her husbands? Why does she go behind the back of her first, legitimate husband, Chaereas, to send a letter to the second, Dionysius (8.4.5)? It is no coincidence that she is compared to Helen of Troy (5.2.8): both signify primarily in terms of their devastating effects upon men, both are emblems of what Freud calls 'the riddle of the nature of femininity'.[54] *Chaereas and Callirhoe*, as much as the *Iliad* and *Odyssey*, explores men's paranoia about the illegibility of women.

Later Greek texts place a much greater emphasis upon the representation of female subjectivity, and indeed commend female virtue to an extent that might have been problematic in classical Athens (with its emphasis upon the silencing and sequestering of women). But they do not reflect a greater 'liberation' of women. While it is true that women are represented out of the confined roles allotted them in the earlier period, there are also powerful counterforces that persist in normatively associating them with interior space. As we saw in the previous chapter, the literature of Roman Greece presents a more general turn away from public identities towards the private self; and it is because women are so closely identified with domestic interiors that they figure as emblems of that introspective turn.

Women throughout Greek literature are marginalized and repressed. A male-centred literary tradition seeks to master them by confining them to interiors. There are some important exceptions, but even the poetesses Sappho and Erinna seem most preoccupied by the theme of gender repression. There is evidence for increasing literacy and education among women of the elite, but also for equal and opposite forces that seek once again to confine women to the heart of the household. Yet paradoxically, it is women's association with the dark interiors of the house, the body and the mind that makes them fascinating and terrible to men. From Homer's Helen and Penelope to Chariton's Callirhoe and beyond, the most memorable women in Greek literature derive their power precisely from their inscrutability.

12

Sexing the Text

Where Does Desire Come From?

A young woman, Simaetha, cries to her servant, Thestylis, to bring her bay-leaves. Why? As her words (now lyrical, now angry) pour forth, readers of the second *Idyll* of the third-century Alexandrian poet Theocritus gradually piece together the plot. A young athlete has taken her virginity and abandoned her; the bay-leaves and other stuffs are the ingredients for a binding spell that will render her irresistible to him – or, if that fails, kill him. The speaker locates herself explicitly in a line with the powerful literary sorceresses Circe and Medea (2.15–16); she invokes the terrible forces of Hecate and Selene, goddess of the moon, to effect her dread spells.[1]

This awesome self-characterization, however, is undermined by the scene's implicit bathos. Although there is no explicit indication, ancient readers might well have taken her as a *hetaera*, or courtesan.[2] She has been jilted, we infer, by a playboy whose fancy has turned elsewhere (2.149–50); it is eleven days since she heard from him. His seductive words (2.114–38) seem to have been hollow flattery. Simaetha is powerless, crushed. It may be that magic is, by definition, the refuge of the resourceless, a practice that creates the illusion of influence over the world (Euripides' Medea turns to drugs at exactly the moment when she perceives herself abandoned and desperate, 384–5). Though she tries to present herself as a mighty witch, Simaetha is a realist. The overriding impression is of futility and resignation: 'I shall bear my passion as I have borne it so far', she concludes (2.164).

Theocritus' poems are full of forlorn love-sickness: of the thirty *Idylls* surviving under his name, twenty are on this theme. In the first, for example, a shepherd sings how Daphnis wasted away, 'cursed in his desire, and helpless' (1.85). In the third, a shepherd serenades his girlfriend, though she has no care for his sufferings (3.52). In *Idyll* 10, a reaper berates another for indulging his love, which interferes with his job: 'What desire can a labourer have for things outside his work?' (10.9). *Idyll* 13 transplants the hero Heracles into an erotic scenario, vainly searching for his boyfriend Hylas; an eroticized, Theocritean 'reading' of the scene that concludes the first book of Apollonius' recently published *Argonautica* (though the relative dating is not secure). *Idyll* 11, most famously, presents the Cyclops Polyphemus (a younger version of the monster who ate Odysseus' crew) lamenting that the sea-nymph Galateia does not want him (the theme is reprised in *Idyll* 6). That poem, with its framing address to the doctor Nicias, highlights particularly powerfully the central Theocritean image of desire as sickness: 'there is no other cure for desire, Nicias, neither unguent nor paste, it seems to me, than the Muses' (11.1–4). For Theocritus, one of poetry's central roles is to manage the pathology that is sexual desire – often an impossible task.

Simaetha's spell in *Idyll* 2 is built around two repeated refrains. The first is an authoritative imprecation invoking the coercive powers of the *iynx*, the magic wheel: '*iynx*, be sure to draw the man to my house'. Simaetha is confident, assertive, in control. At line 64, however, the tone changes; she is uncertain, full of doubt and questions. 'Now that I am alone, where shall I begin my lament over my desire? From what point shall I start? Who brought this bane upon me?' (64–5). Accompanying the new tone comes a new refrain: 'tell me, lady Selene, where did my desire come from?' Simaetha has ceased trying to control the desire of others; she turns now to the inscrutable puzzle of her own passions. In myth, magic can render women powerful and sexually dominant; in reality (the 'reality' manufactured by the poet, of course) it offers only the indulgent fantasy of escape from the unrelenting oppressiveness of desire. Sexuality is a *problem of power*. Partly the alluring power that others can exercise over the besotted subject; but also, and more urgently, the maddeningly unpredictable power that your own desires can exercise over you. Where *does* desire come from? Why does it make us act in this way? Why does it control us?[3]

Destructive Passions

Sexual desire in Greek literature is rarely a positive force; only occasionally do we find it linked (as in the Christian and romantic

traditions) to the concept of beneficent love. The Greek word *eros* –
usually better rendered 'desire' or 'lust' than 'love' – denotes a violent, disruptive possession. The body is in equilibrium only when in a state of self-control (*sophrosyne*), when the emotions are properly mastered. *Eros*, desire, is the enemy of calmness and order. As we saw in the previous chapter, sexual attraction can start wars. In tragedy, *eros* is one of those violent emotions, like anger and pride, that destroy households and society by flaying off the thin surface of civilized values and exposing the bestial urges that lie beneath (see chapter 5). Desire does not come from within the individual, but from without. When personified, Eros is an archer, a violent warrior who brings violent war. Even in the Hellenistic period, when he is reconceived as a cute and playful boy, his effects are nonetheless destructive. When he shoots Medea in book 3 of Apollonius' *Argonautica*, the effects are instant and excruciating: 'speechlessness seized her soul . . . the shaft burned deep beneath the maiden's heart, like a flame' (3.284–7). At night she cannot sleep, so raging is the sickness; Apollonius describes it (a characteristically Hellenistic touch) using the technical language of contemporary medicine (3.761–5).

Eros, in this particular guise (we shall explore others presently), is an entirely subject-centred phenomenon. It marks not the relationship binding two individuals, as the English word 'love' does, but the destructive psychological effects that ensue when a person realizes that she or he is emotionally bound to another. To be sure, not all genres represent the effects of desire as pernicious: tragedy and lyric do, but the 'new' comedy that appeared from the fourth century BCE and the Greek novels of the Roman period (chapter 9) present dynastic marriage within the state as an ideal conclusion.[4] Even here, though, *eros* is conceived of by characters as dangerous and threatening. 'I cannot bear the pain', cries one novelistic lover; 'Eros has attacked me in full force' (Achilles Tatius 1.9). Besotted lovers in the novel are frequently imaged as 'slaves'; like the servile class, they have lost the power of self-determination that defines the free.

This concern with subjectivity and self-reliance has implications for the imaginary construction of the body. If desire strikes from without, then the flesh is our only defence. The idealized male form represented in statuary (what Mikhail Bakhtin calls 'the classical body'[5]) is upright, lithe, and – crucially – *closed*; its self-sufficiency is figured by its impenetrability. The 'low' body, on the other hand, is open and porous. The female body – ever associated with base materiality in the Greek imagination – is sometimes imaged as a leaky or inverted jug.[6] In Plato's *Gorgias*, Socrates uses this very image of a leaky jug for the man who is incapable of controlling his appetites (493b). The masks of comedy present gaping mouths, orifices equally fit for emission and reception. The noble, dignified body is sealed; the debased, appetitive and desirous body is open.

But no body can be entirely sealed. The medical writers speak of *poroi*, of 'pores' that can allow infections to enter or emanations to be secreted. The *poros* of the illness that is desire, however, is particularly the eyes, which represent a threshold between the self's subjective interior and the world outside. Meeting the gaze of another is a dangerous communion. A fragment of the lyric poet Alcman (seventh century BCE) refers to the horrific effects of a sexy woman upon a beholder: 'her gaze is more liquefying than sleep or death' (fragments 3.61–2). 'Sight', says Plato's Socrates, 'is the sharpest of bodily senses' (*Phaedrus* 250d). By 'sharp', he does not simply mean 'perceptive'; the vision of the beautiful boy *punctures* your defences, you 'receive the effluence of beauty through your eyes' (251b). This famous passage was highly influential upon the Greek novelists' conception of desire, some half a millennium later: 'the effluence of beauty', Clinias tells the hero in Achilles Tatius' *Leucippe and Clitophon*, 'floods down through the eyes to the soul, and effects a kind of sex without contact' (1.9).[7] The eyes are the locus of an intense anxiety, as they are the self-enclosed subject's point of maximal vulnerability.

Where does desire come from? Throughout Greek literature, *eros* is associated with unknowability, the capitulation of the intellect, loss of control. In a culture predicated upon the close association between masculinity and self-sufficiency, desire compromises the subject. But as we shall see throughout the course of this chapter, the pleasures of desire sometimes outweigh the pains.

The Trials of Obscenity

For all its problematization of sexual impulses, however, Greek culture did not seek simply to suppress it, in the way that Victorian England is sometimes imagined to have done. 'Pornography' is a nineteenth-century concept; in this juridical sense, it is wholly irrelevant to the ancient world.[8] There were no legal prohibitions governing the representation of sexual acts. Obscene language in the comedies of Aristophanes (which were performed before the entire citizen population of Athens, at a religious festival in honour of Dionysus) is common enough to warrant one scholar's 250-page lexical analysis.[9]

The intriguing 'festival of the bridge' at Athens involved the use of legendarily filthy abuse. In the *Homeric Hymn to Demeter*, the bereaved goddess is cheered up by a string of dirty jokes (203).[10] Obscene jokes were also told at the various women's festivals of Demeter in Athens, and humorous genital icons were carried.[11] These manifestations of sexual and scatological explicitness occur in contexts that are culturally, indeed religiously, sanctioned; they have nothing to do with the sequestered timidity of modern pornography.

The symposium is another context in which the sexualized body might be displayed, as we saw in chapter 4. Sympotic poetry and pottery can include the sexually explicit. The culture of free-speaking openness can, moreover, even admit of jokey abuse of individuals. In third-century Alexandria, the poet Sotades seems to have got away with a very risqué verse on Ptolemy Philadelphus' marriage to his sister, Arsinoe: 'that is not a holy hole into which you coax your cock' (fragment 1). Philadelphus, otherwise rather intolerant of hostility, must surely have heard this remark at a symposium.[12]

On the other hand, there were of course (as in most cultures) widespread prohibitions on the display of sexuality. There were certainly things that should not normally be exposed or discussed in public, things governed by the code of *aidos* (often, and rather inadequately, translated 'shame' or 'reverence').[13] The standard word for 'genitals' is *aidoia*, the parts that should be kept to oneself. Diogenes, the founder of the Cynics (who liked to attack social conventions), made a name for himself by masturbating his in public. The point is, however, that the strict codes governing the display and representation of sexual acts were periodically lifted in *licensed* contexts, principally festivals and symposia. In these arenas, the regular protocols of sexual behaviour in everyday life were lifted, inverted even; these occasions functioned simultaneously as conservative corroborations of the 'normal' order of regular life and as exploratory experiments with alternatives.

Greeks dealt with the disruptive, violent force of *eros* not by suppressing the topic but by exploring it fully – in demarcated spaces at set times. The sexual body was not hidden away, but carefully *placed* within society.

Object Lessons

This chapter so far has suppressed the distinction between same-sex and different-sex desire. Ancient Greeks did not do so, any more than modern westerners. Greek 'pederasty' or boy-love (female–female relationships will be discussed in the following section) was an accepted practice with a widely acknowledged socially beneficial effect, namely the education and acculturation of young men.[14] Pederastic practice in no way excluded male–female relationships; Greek men were expected to marry, and most did. Only in the Roman period do we find men who have chosen a life of pederasty to the exclusion of marriage (this phenomenon will be discussed later in this chapter).

'Same-sex' and 'different-sex' relationships: I use these rather clumsy circumlocutions for a reason, because the terms 'homosexuality' and 'heterosexuality' are so crudely inappropriate to the ancient world. Studies of ancient sexuality in recent years have often concluded that such concepts are exclusively modern concepts, the product of a relatively recent and brief intellectual paradigm shift.[15] The English term 'homosexuality' only appeared in the late nineteenth century, in the context of a medical textbook; the term 'heterosexuality' appeared rather later. A 'cultural-constructionist' approach to sexuality would argue that the taxonomy of erotic relations a particular society adopts, for all that it may appear natural and universal to those within a given culture, in fact embodies that society's (and only that society's) particular ideological concerns.

For social constructionists, then, the homosexuality/heterosexuality divide has been 'constructed' in the modern era, an era that has striven to make sexuality the object of institutional control. According to Michel Foucault, the principal architect of the social-constructionist approach, the invention of homosexuality in the nineteenth century was part of a larger shift in society at the time towards the regulation of individual subjects by law, medicine, education and psychiatry. Prior to the modern period, he argues, sodomy was perceived as an act, and a sodomite merely one who practised the act; whereas '[t]he nineteenth-century homosexual became a personage, a past, a case history, and a childhood, in addition to being a type of life, a life form, and a morphology, with an indiscreet anatomy and possibly a mysterious physiology'.[16] According to this model, a homosexual is not simply someone with a *preference* for same-sex relationships, but one whose sexual identity is inscribed at the very core of her or his being. Hence the phenomenon that Eve Kosofsky Sedgwick describes as 'the epistemology of the closet', the belief that homosexual identity is a secret truth that will eventually be 'outed'.[17]

Greek pederasty, by way of contrast, was seen as a social institution, not as a psychological destiny (at least, not until the Roman

period).[18] A second fundamental difference from modern constructions of homosexuality is that it operated along an axis of asym-
metry: the older man was the active partner (in pursuit and congress),
the younger man the passive. Not all young men engaged in pederasty, but for those who did it served as a rite of passage; when the
man reached adulthood, he was expected to assume the active role in
sexual relations. This asymmetric model has been developed by some
scholars into a skeleton key to Greek sexual ethics, which is viewed
as a fundamentally phallocentric economy: to penetrate actively was,
they argue, coded as manly and empowered, to be penetrated pas-
sively weak and effeminate.[19] These same scholars argue that the
degenerate pederasts referred to as *kinaidoi* or *katapugones* were
guilty of desiring to play the sexually passive role though they were
now adult.

This 'constructionist' view that sexual desire is experienced according to the categories available in any society at a given time is
often opposed to the 'essentialist' view that it remains constant across
the ages.[20] Constructionism does have its problems. As one recent
critic has shown, the Greeks did, in fact, present inclination towards
boys or women as being dependent upon the nature of the individual
(whereas one of the orthodoxies of constructionism has been the
belief that the ancient world, unlike the modern West, did not view
sex-preferences as innate).[21] Another critic has objected that it im-
poses an overschematic – and indeed phallocentric – uniformity upon
a heterogeneous set of practices (and a diverse array of literary testimony).[22] The challenge is to analyse Greek representations of sexual
behaviour in a way that respects both their structural difference from
modern sexualities and their intrinsic variety, their irreducibility to
one single 'structure'.

Lesbians/lesbians

What of relationships between women? There is markedly less evidence for female–female eroticism in antiquity, because our sources
are predominantly male-centred, and – when it comes to sexuality
– 'phallocentric', or preoccupied with the role of the penis. This
phallocentrism, it must be said, has been replicated in modern scholarship: work in this field is still largely in its infancy.[23]

There is one figure, however, who has received a huge amount
of attention through the ages.[24] Sappho is antiquity's most famous
Lesbian. But of course the capital 'L' gives the game away: no one

denies that she lived on the island of Lesbos, but there is a vigorous debate as to whether she was a 'lesbian' in any sense that approximates to our own; and, conversely, what exactly it is that 'lesbian' means to us.

It is not in question that Sappho's poetry repeatedly indicates the narrator's desire for women. A number of women are named as objects of passion: among them Anactoria, Gongyla, Atthis. Poem 1 presents a prayer to Aphrodite, and Aphrodite's answer: 'though she flees now, she will soon pursue' (21). Sappho's poetry certainly focuses on eroticized desire between women. The difficulty is to decide whether or not it is helpful to think of history in terms of continuity in sexual experience between past and present – of, that is, lesbians in antiquity – or in terms of a rupture between the two. Does Sapphic desire work in the same way that lesbian desire does? An additional complication arises because of the particular role of Sappho in modern thought: how one interprets Sappho's role in antiquity has powerful implications for one's position vis-à-vis the sexual politics of the twenty-first century. There can be no reading of Sappho that is insulated from questions of political identity in the present.[25]

Many classicists have hesitated to use the term 'lesbian', on the grounds that categories that are so heavy with political significance in the present carry too many resonances that are inappropriate to a radically different culture.[26] We might also point out that Sappho's poems include positive references to what moderns would call 'heterosexual' sex: fragment 44, for example, a joyous celebration of the wedding of Homer's Trojans, Andromache and Hector (albeit the joy is overshadowed by the reader's awareness of their future tragedy). Again, fragment 112 hymns the 'fortunate bridegroom' on his wedding day.

To exemplify the complex issues that arise from these questions, let us take one of Sappho's most famous poems:[27]

> That man seems to me
> to be like the gods, who sits
> opposite to you, and listens to you
> speaking sweetly
>
> and laughing desirably.
> That certainly quickened the heart in my breast.
> For when I look on for a short while, then I can
> no longer speak,

but my tongue is broken,
and a slight fire has run under my skin,
and I see nothing with my eyes,
my ears hum,

sweat pours down me, fear
seizes all of me, I am paler
than grass, I seem to myself to be little
short of death. (Poem 31)

Is this a 'lesbian' poem? It clearly centres around the narrator's close emotional involvement with the person being addressed, but it is, in fact, very difficult to come to any secure conclusion about the dramatic situation being described here.[28] What are the girl and the male figure doing? Is this a wedding feast? Is the narrator's anxiety caused by desire for the woman or jealousy of the man? Is the male figure 'like the gods' because he is blessed with luck, or because he is strong enough to withstand the effects of the girl's beauty? What is quickening the narrator's heart, the sound of the girl's voice or the entire situation she beholds?

Perhaps we should not be expecting this poem to correspond to any real scenario we could imagine. Sappho's poetic strategy, here and elsewhere, is what we might call 'anti-narrative': rather than explaining cause and effect sequentially, rather than explaining the identities of the figures, she offers fragments of emotional experience. The structure of this very poem might be taken to embody this tactic: it moves progressively away from the public event being described and towards the inarticulate language, the 'broken tongue', of the inner self. On this interpretation, the incompleteness of the description is precisely part of Sappho's poetic strategy.

The exact relationships in this poem, then, are hard to determine. This should caution us against decoding the relationship between the three figures too hastily. The narrator articulates an intense passion focused on the woman – but to seek to turn poetics into literal biography, as though we could reconstruct the exact feelings and intentions of the narrator, is at best naive.

Some scholars, however, have taken a different tack, locating specifically woman-centred eroticism in her representation of desire itself. For these scholars, it is Sappho's emphasis upon private desires and upon erotic reciprocity, the lack of any sense of inequality between the subject and the object of desire, that marks out Sappho's erotics.[29] The line we have already quoted from poem 1 – 'though she flees now, she will soon pursue' (21) – is sometimes taken as evidence for the reversibility of subject positions.[30] The advantage of this approach is that it gets us away from the idea that erotic relationships should be defined in the narrow terms of the sexual act itself, a fixation of much modern thought on sexuality. Sappho's identity is, on this argument, to be considered in terms of social and ethical practice, not simply in terms of any particular range of genital acts with any particular class of person. Whether this is an argument for or against 'Sappho the lesbian' will depend on whether lesbianism is understood as a narrowly psychosexual identity, or as a wider stylistics of living – questions that are beyond the range of this book. But it is certainly helpful to take a broader view of Sapphic eroticism, one that encompasses much more than simply the sexual act (and desire for it).

Not that Greek literature lacks any concept of women who desire sex with women to the exclusion of men, however. Such women were known as *tribades*: the word presumably derives from *tribein*, 'to rub', a contemptuous allusion to the absence of the phallus. In Plato's *Symposium*, Aristophanes refers to 'women who have no interest in men, who focus their attention upon women' (191e; see also *Laws* 636c). In some cases, this tribadism is associated directly with Lesbos. The lyric poet Anacreon explains his rejection by a woman: 'she is from well-built Lesbos, and shows contempt for my mop of hair, white as it is; instead, she gawps at another' (fragment 358). The pronoun 'another' is feminine. The joke lies in the ambiguity. The syntax implies that the girl is gawping at another mop of hair (the noun is feminine), with the gender of its owner unspecified; but the reference to Lesbos suggests a different construal, that she is gawping at another *woman*. In Lucian's *Dialogues of the Courtesans*, three *hetaerae* are said to have gone to bed together, like the 'women in Lesbos . . . who sleep with women as if they themselves were men' (5.2).

All these cases, however, are male fantasies, scare-images of women who can subsist independently of men, like the Amazons of myth, the women who roam the hillsides of Thebes in Euripides' *Bacchae*, or the women who wrest political control in Aristophanes' *Lysistrata* and *Assembly Women*. There is no evidence here for lesbian subjectivity as such, except perhaps as dimly reflected through male anxieties. We do not have a single word authored by a self-identifying *tribas* (any more than we do of a self-identifying *kinaidos*: see the previous section).

My view is that on balance it is better to assume the 'cultural-constructionist' position, which allows us to locate more specifically the distinctive features of ancient (and by implication modern) experience; it also allows us to avoid the difficult, perhaps impossible, search for a definition of lesbianism broad enough to encompass ancient and modern female–female erotics (as well, presumably, as those found in other cultures too). Sappho's poetry, which provides our best evidence for the Greek world, represents female erotics as mutual, reciprocal and orientated towards the private sphere – in opposition to male erotics, which are hierarchical and orientated towards public identities. To understand Sappho's construction of desire, we need to consider the specific historical context of ancient Greek gender roles (discussed in the previous chapter), with their emphasis upon female confinement to private space. For this reason, it is preferable to find terms other than 'lesbian' to describe Lesbian Sappho.

As we saw in the previous section, however, constructionism is no more politically innocent than essentialism. For all that I believe it to be right from one perspective, the account I have given above makes me feel uneasy, particularly as a male writer. What I have done, in effect, is to deny the existence of lesbian sexuality in the ancient world, arguably perpetuating the silencing or suppression of female sexual expression. There were of course women who desired sex with women in the ancient world, and there can be little doubt that Sappho was among them. To deny them the name of 'lesbian' denies lesbianism the possibility of the prestigious, historically rooted identity that conventionally follows the adoption of classical precedents.

My justification would be that my ambition throughout this book has been to dismantle such grand metanarratives that link past to present, presenting instead a fragmentary, anti-teleological cultural history (chapter 1). It is precisely the easy assimilation of ancient Greek to modern western culture that we have challenged at every stage. But even anti-narratives are politically self-implicating; and it is in this section that that self-implication has, for me at least, *bitten hardest*; hence the intrusion of the personal voice into this self-consciously inadequate coda.

Sexual Agonistics

One final problem with the constructionist model is that it gives too much emphasis to the norms of sexual conducts. It focuses upon regulations and constraints, upon models of sexual order, without accounting for the diversity and experimentalism of erotic practice. '[T]exts', observes Matthew Fox, 'are not produced as records of positive norms, and to make that assumption is to succumb to our own desire for a normative and integrated picture of the past.'[31] An over-fixation with issues of similarity and difference – whether ancient sexualities were like 'ours' or not – runs the very strong risk of clumsy reifications. Who is to say that 'the Greeks' shared a common core of sexual norms? Who is to say that 'we' do? Certainly patterns can be identified, especially if we focus upon normative or conservative insitutions: say, the law courts in antiquity, or the tabloid press in the contemporary world. But why *should* we? Do such sources necessarily represent the best evidence for the sexuality in practice?

To consider these points, I want to turn now to consider a text we have met earlier (in chapter 4): Plato's *Symposium* (written in the fourth century, but set in the fifth). Does this dialogue, with its central focus on pederasty, present a coherent sexual ideology? Those in search of the 'meaning' of this text often focus exclusively upon the long speech of Socrates that concludes the praises of (pederastic) *eros* (199c–212c). Here Socrates reports the (supposed) words of a Mantinean prophetess called Diotima, who tells him that sexual attraction towards boys is the first stage in a process of philosophical enlightenment that leads from the contemplation of the particular (a beautiful boy) to the form (beauty itself). Sexual desire is thus integrated into the project of Platonic philosophy, namely the pursuit of abstract understanding. For Foucault, for example, this speech occupies a central place in his argument that Greek conceptions of sexuality were governed by a moralistic commitment to truth, understood as self-empowerment.[32]

It is true that the speech occupies a privileged position in the text: not only is it the last in the round, but also Socrates' performance has been carefully anticipated from the start of the text. 'Where is he?' asks Agathon when Aristodemus turns up unaccompanied (174e). But Diotima's Platonizing reading of desire as a step towards enlightenment is complicated and ironized by the larger framing of the dialogue, which – with delicious paradox – makes the ugly Socrates the object of desire by lascivious younger men. First of all, he is the object of some louche innuendo from Agathon (whom the comic poet Aristophanes – himself one of the guests at the party – had represented as an effeminate pederast in his play *Women at the Thesmophoria*). The reason for Socrates' delay has been, apparently, that he has stopped off in the neighbour's doorway, apparently to have a think (175a). When he enters, Agathon asks him to sit next to him, 'so that I can take a hold of and enjoy that "wisdom" that came upon you in that doorway' (175d). As befits the flirty joshing of a symposium, Agathon has greeted his distinguished guest with an accusation of masturbation and a come-on. Significantly, the regular protocols of the constructionist model of pederasty are flouted: the younger man, Agathon, pursues the older, Socrates.

At the conclusion of the text, we see more disruption of sexual protocol. The symposiasts, remember, have decided to drink only in moderation, as they are hungover; the flute-girls are banished, since the participants are betaking themselves to sober intellectualism. But immediately after Socrates' philosophical culmination, in bursts a drunken Alcibiades, with flute-girls in tow (212c). The philosophical exposition is hijacked by a hedonist. The literary Alcibiades comes inevitably laden with a number of associations attached to the historical figure: though a brilliant general, Alcibiades was a renowned voluptuary (the emblem of his shield was said to represent Eros), suspected of being involved in the mutilation of the herms (ithyphallic statues) in 415, and twice an exile.[33] A figure more antithetical to the high-minded philosophical ideals just espoused could not be imagined.

Alcibiades and Socrates then begin flirting with each other. On hearing that they have been praising *eros*, Alcibiades proceeds to praise Socrates. His speech, then, unwittingly travels in the opposite direction to that of Socrates, by moving from the abstraction of philosophical idealism to the particular desire for the material body (albeit the charms of the snub-nosed Socrates are of a paradoxical sort). The text closes as all the participants – apart from Socrates, who can take his drink – descend into drunkenness, the most telling indication that the earlier ideal of moderation has now been discarded.

The symposium is framed by the representation of Agathon and Alcibiades, two linked figures (both are younger men who flirt with Socrates; both call him an 'aggressor', *hybristes*: 175e; 215b) who represent unorthodox sexuality. Moreover, the high-minded abstemiousness of the philosophical symposium is undercut by the introduction at the conclusion of this figure of radical disorder. Why has Plato created such a jarring effect? A full answer would involve a searching analysis of Plato's strategies in his dialogues; it will be enough now to suggest that Plato's aim is not simply to inculcate moral messages, but to teach his readers to *think*. The unsettling dislocation between Socrates' speech and the outer frame shifts the burden of meaning-making onto the reader.

My central point here, however, is that regulation and constraint form only part of the picture of sexuality in Greek literature. What Plato's *Symposium* shows is that sexual ethics can coexist with subversive sexuality, with teasing flirtation and innuendo, with delicious irony.

The Pleasures of the Text

The interaction between moralism and subversive play that we identified in Plato's *Symposium* is, I want to argue in conclusion, canonic-
ally central to the Greek literary tradition. My final section in this
chapter returns to the earliest period of Greek literature, and to Homer
(see chapter 3). It also returns to different-sex relationships (there is
no explicit case of same-sex eroticism in Homer). This 'return' is not,
of course, intended to be sexually normative, as though a concluding 'heterosexual' section signified a familiar homecoming after the
exoticism of the previous sections. Greek literature in general does
not display any consistent prejudice against same-sex relationships,
between men at any rate, and could easily (as Plato's *Symposium*
shows) privilege them.

Erotic desire lies at the heart of the gripping, suspenseful narrative.
In Peter Brooks's classic work of literary criticism, *Reading for the
Plot*, Freud's theories of desire and the death-drive are brought to
bear on the experience of reading narrative.[34] For Brooks, '[n]arratives
portray the motors of desire that drive and consume their plots, and
they also lay bare the nature of narration as a form of human desire'.[35] In this analysis, the reading of narrative stimulates a desire for
the end of the plot. This ending yields both satisfaction and (given
that it marks the dissolution of the narrative) a sense of emptiness, so
that readerly desire impels both consummation and destruction (to use
Freud's terms from *Beyond the Pleasure Principle*, *eros* and *thanatos*).
For Brooks, the desire of characters *within* texts (for sex, marriage,
power, fulfilment, etc.) figures the desire of the reader (to reach the
end, to solve the mystery, to consummate the reading experience).

These 'motors of desire' drive many central Greek texts. Homer's
Iliad revolves around the contested desire of men for women:
Menelaus and Paris for Helen, Agamemnon for Chryseis, Agamemnon
and Achilles for Briseis. But I want to conclude with a discussion of
the *Odyssey*, which (as we shall see) balances a more normative map
of sexual ethics against a pleasurable sexual indulgence. This text
narrates the return home of Odysseus from the war at Troy to his
native Ithaca, and his gradual reclaiming of his position as head
of his household, which is being ravaged by suitors. There are two
primary narrative tensions. Will Odysseus successfully return home?
And will Penelope manage to repulse the advances of the suitors?
These are obviously intertwined: there is no point in Odysseus returning if Penelope has already remarried.

What is crucial, however, is that this is a narrative of *longing*. The principal decisions facing both protagonists concern the management of sexual relationships. Penelope wears away her soul weeping for her husband (19.263–4), but fears she must remarry for the sake of the household. For her, the options are different forms of sexual encounter: constancy to her husband or remarriage. Throughout the *Odyssey*, there are numerous references to the story of Clytaemnestra, who, in the absence of her husband Agamemnon, leader of the host at Troy, had an adulterous affair with a certain Aegisthus; the two of them killed Agamemnon on his return. Will Penelope follow Clytaemnestra's example? This is one of the text's teasing uncertainties. In book 11, for example, Odysseus meets the ghost of Agamemnon in the underworld. The latter's words are remarkably equivocal, praising Penelope for her trustworthiness and intelligence, before warning him to return in secret, since 'there is no longer any trust in women' (11.441–56). Is Penelope to be trusted? Which path will she choose?[36]

Odysseus, likewise, is faced by a series of desirous dilemmas. As the epic begins, he is imprisoned on the island of the goddess Calypso, who (in the words of Athena) 'charms him with soft, deceptive words, so that he might forget Ithaca; but he longs to see the smoke rising up from his land, and desires to die' (1.57–9). Whose desire will win out, Calypso's for Odysseus or Odysseus' for homeland or death? As he progresses through the narrative, he meets a series of alluring females, notably Circe and Nausicaa. Circe (book 10) is a magician who sleeps with Odysseus for a year, until the crew grow restless. Nausicaa (books 6–8, book 13) is a young girl who is offered to Odysseus by her father as a potential wife.

Odysseus' return to the centre of the household is also a return to a normative sexual economy, away from the magical world of goddesses and wizardry; and with the would-be adulterous suitors slain, the plot concludes with a restitution of the properly married couple to the house, and (hence) to Ithacan society. Above all, it is the famous bed of Odysseus and Penelope, built from a living tree and thus literally rooted to the house, that figures the durability and preferability of marriage.[37] The reader (I use the term broadly, to include listeners to an oral performance) thus receives an education in desire: 'reading for the plot', in this case, means learning to desire the protocols of proper sexual union.

But this is not the only way to read the *Odyssey*. If we read for the end of the plot, then we dutifully read the *Odyssey* as a normative guide to sexual ideology; but the *pleasures* of the text lie in its seemingly endless succession of episodes and subplots, its deferrals of closure. This is a narrative that constantly teases its readers with the possibility of a swift return, only to revoke that possibility. In book 10, Odysseus narrates how he comes within sight of Ithaca, only for him to fall asleep and his crew to open up his bag of winds; the ship is sent racing back into the unknown. Even in book 23, after the suitors have been slain and Odysseus has revealed himself, the reunion with Penelope is deferred; she famously tests him instead. The frustration of their son, Telemachus, figures that of the hasty reader: 'why do you keep apart from my father, why do you not sit by him . . . ?' (23.98–9).

Indeed, the *Odyssey*'s very narrative structure seems to indicate the possibility of two different forms of reading, the linear and the episodic. While the hardy, dutiful reader will read the entirety as a coherent plot orientated towards the return to the marriage bed, the more flittish will emphasize its ability to decompose into discrete episodes. These 'episodes' are figured geographically in the succession of islands visited by the sea-faring Odysseus: those of Calypso, the Cyclops, Nausicaa, and so forth. The episodic reader desires the thrill of illicit encounters, many of them sexual. When, for example, Odysseus meets the naive maiden Nausicaa on the shores of Scheria, the narrator compares him to 'a mountain-nurtured lion who . . . pursues cattle or sheep, or wild deer' (*Odyssey* 6.130–3); Nausicaa is imaged as a potential prey for the 'lion' Odysseus, and is thus offered up as a rape fantasy for the reader (shores were traditionally dangerous places for young girls).[38] The *Odyssey* presents two modes of reading, both sexualized: the dutiful, linear, narrative mode that leads to the family and the household, and the 'digressive', episodic, indulgent mode that gratifies and titillates.

How you read the *Odyssey*, then, depends in part upon what kind of values you bring to it, what kind of pleasures you seek. Tony Tanner's words on the eighteenth- and nineteenth-century novel hold true for Homer too: though the *Odyssey* 'may be said to move toward marriage and the securing of genealogical continuity, it often gains its particular narrative urgency from an energy that threatens to contravene that stability of the family on which society depends. It thus becomes a paradoxical object in society, by no means an inert adjunct to the family décor, but a text that may work to subvert what it seems to celebrate.'[39]

This chapter has explored the centrality of sexual desire in its various aspects to Greek literature. What we have seen is that Greek culture configured sexuality in radically different ways from those of the modern West, focusing upon *eros* as an ethical problem of self-mastery for the desiring subject. But counterbalancing this centripetal emphasis upon ethical propriety – the 'homecoming' reading of the *Odyssey*, if you like – stands a centrifugal pleasure in the indulgent, wandering play of sexuality. Despite the frequent recourse to normativity, Greek texts are rarely if ever *dull* when they confront eroticism. For all that it is important to identify historical differences in the way that desire is represented, we should beware any attempts to reduce ancient sexualities to single systems.

13

Status and Slavery

Further Voices in Archaic Epic

Greek literature, as we have seen repeatedly throughout this book, imagines a strong link between political power and the power to speak. Women, largely disenfranchised, were also systematically silenced, denied the right to self-representation (chapter 11). The same is true, as we shall see in this chapter, in most periods for the lower classes and slaves – although there are important exceptions. Literature, as a category of culturally privileged, specialist discourse, often preserves itself for society's dominant groups.

As so often with the Greek tradition, the Homeric poems provide the canonical models. The most significant manifestation of lower-class speech in the *Iliad* comes in the course of book 2. Inspired by Athena, Odysseus reviews the troops before battle, exhorting the men as he goes. The narrator draws a clear distinction between Odysseus' respectful treatment of the kings (2.188–97) and of the masses (2.198–206): whenever he finds any of the latter 'shouting' (2.198), he hits him with the sceptre and tells him that not everyone can be a king. This is a highly significant episode: the voice of the people is presented as mere shouting (which is to say inarticulate noise), and order is imposed on the rabble forcibly, by silence. Significantly, Odysseus hits the masses with the sceptre, the symbol of both kingship and the right to speak in public (see chapter 6). When the two armies engage at the beginning of book 3, the Trojans and their allies make a racket (*Iliad* 3.2–6); the Achaeans, by way of constrast, move in silence (3.8), having been 'put in order' by their leaders (3.1).

Odysseus' review of the troops is an exercise in military and verbal taxonomy: the ordering of the troops is symbolically linked to the quelling of their speech. As he proceeds, however, he encounters resistance in the figure of Thersites:

> Now the rest had sat down, and were restrained in their places,
> but one man, Thersites of the measureless speech, still scolded;
> he knew within his mind many words, but disorderly;
> vain, and without order, to insult the kings
> with anything he thought might be amusing to the Argives.
> (2.211–15)

Thersites will not sit down, will not shut up. His language, in implicit contrast with the ordering practised by Odysseus, is characterized by effusion and chaos ('measureless speech', 'many words, but disorderly'); his words are chosen not for their content (they are 'vain') but for their effect on the masses. His physical aspect further underlines his unruliness. In what follows, we learn that he is the 'ugliest' man to come to Troy, 'bandy-legged . . . lame of one foot, with shoulders stooped and drawn together over his chest, and above this his skull went up to a point with the wool grown sparsely upon it' (2.216–19). Homer is no Victor Hugo, Thersites no Quasimodo: physical appearance directly reflects moral worth (see chapter 3). (And indeed Thersites' extreme ugliness is matched at the lexical level, through the adoption of a series of obscure words unparalleled in Homer.)

Thersites' speech (2.225–42) accuses the leaders of self-interest and profiteering; why not, he suggests, go home now? In return for his abuse of his superiors, he receives a beating from Odysseus, who uses the sceptre to bring up the bloody weals on his flesh. Again the sceptre, symbolizing the interdependence of speaking and power, enforces the silence of the lower class, inscribing the very edict upon Thersites' flesh. The Iliadic narrator, it seems, grants the lower-class rebel a voice in the *Iliad* only so that we can observe that grant being rescinded.[1]

What of the masses? Do they treat Thersites as a champion? It would seem not. The masses 'laughed happily' at Odysseus' actions, we are told (2.270). The poem carefully neutralizes Thersites' challenge, isolating him from the wishes of the people. And yet there is more to this episode than simple promulgation of aristocratic ideology. Let us look more carefully at the entire sentence: '*Grieving though the men were*, they laughed over him happily' (2.270). Why are the rank-and-file soldiers said to be 'grieving'? The narrator gives no guidance. Are they sick of war and pining for their homes? Or perhaps manifesting a certain pity for Thersites? After all, his criticism of Agamemnon's military policy is not wholly unreasonable; and, indeed, Achilles (in the great speech in defiance of Agamemnon's proposals in book 9) will echo many of these concerns. Paradoxically, the best of the Achaeans finds moral support in the misshapen figure of the worst.

This ambiguous, unsettling reference to the grief of the people leaves the reader with troubling questions. Should we have reservations about the silencing of Thersites? Does the forcible imposition of order and silence on the troops have its costs? Do the leaders always get it right? The *Iliad* contains further voices, in addition to the dominant, repressive, silencing voice of the kings.[2] Indeed, for some readers of the *Iliad*, Thersites has been a privileged commentator on the action, one who (exceptionally) sees through the fog of aristocratic and martial ideology to the grim underlying truth: that it is only the leaders who benefit from war, at the expense of the troops' suffering. Shakespeare, in *Troilus and Cressida*, makes Thersites a knowing if vexatious cynic, blessed with insight. James Joyce privately identified the narrator of the Cyclops episode in *Ulysses* with Thersites.

Reclassifying Epic: The *Odyssey*

If the *Iliad* largely promotes the dominance of the ruling classes, though, the *Odyssey* presents a very different picture, and a very different paradigm of heroism. Iliadic values, including that text's heavy investment in aristocratic values, are repeatedly interrogated. In one particularly self-reflexive moment, Odysseus meets the ghost of Achilles (the central figure of the *Iliad*, of course) in the underworld. In response to Odysseus' admiration at the authority he wields, Achilles replies:

> Preeminent Odysseus, do not console me about death.
> I would rather be a farm labourer, in liege to another,
> to a man without wealth, lacking any great livelihood,
> than play the lord over all the corpses of the dead. (11.488–91)

In the *Iliad*, Achilles claimed that his fate was to choose between a short, glorious life, and a long but obscure one (9.412–15); by re-entering the battle, he implicitly chose the former. In this passage, he reneges on that choice: it is better to live ingloriously than not to live at all. Achilles is not turning his back on heroism per se, but reconceiving himself in terms of the different values of Odyssean heroism, where survival at any cost outweighs vainglory.[3]

It is particularly notable for our purposes, however, that the 'Odysseanized' Achilles imagines himself at the lower end of the social scale, as a serf. In pointed contrast to the *Iliad*'s repression of the sub-elite, the *Odyssey* presents a strikingly more positive appraisal.[4] In the course of the narrative, we meet the figures of Eumaeus the swineherd (who offers the disguised Odysseus hospitality in book 14, and later helps him in the battle with the suitors) and Philoetius, another herdsman (who also sides with Odysseus against the suitors). Both are slaves, albeit Eumaeus is of noble birth. Likewise, the nurse Eurycleia (who in book 19 recognizes him from his scarred thigh, but keeps quiet) is a sympathetic figure. There are, for sure, contrastingly malevolent figures from the sub-elite, particularly the abusive goatherd Melanthius (who kicks Odysseus on meeting him, 17.212–55) and the rival beggar Irus (at the beginning of book 18). In the *Iliad*, however, we find only negative portrayals of such figures; the fact that the *Odyssey* presents positive portrayals as well is a marker of how the latter poem redefines the social as well as the poetic boundaries of the former.

Indeed, even Odysseus himself, when disguised as a beggar, experiences life on the sharp end. In one moment of potential humiliation, one of the suitors (a certain Ctesippus) sarcastically offers to give the beggar a guest-gift: he picks up an ox-hoof, and hurls it at him (*Odyssey* 20.285–319). Odysseus, ducking the missile, smiles 'a sardonic smile, in his anger' (20.301–2). Like a real slave, he knows not to react to insults. This ability to suppress anger is a key difference between him and the Iliadic Achilles (who needs to be checked by divine intervention when he quarrels with Agamemnon), and is a lesson Odysseus has learned through experience. The previous night, seeing his maidservants going to sleep with the suitors, he had restrained himself from violence, reminding himself that he only escaped the Cyclops' cave by cunning (20.18–21). Trickery and deception are the tools of the disempowered.[5] When the odds are stacked against you, outright confrontation is inadvisable; and Odysseus repeatedly finds himself disempowered in critical situations.

Of course, Odysseus' status as a member of the sub-elite is only transitory: his stratagems rest upon implicit trust that the waiting game will pay off in the end, that he will be restored to the elite. The beggar narrative is driven by the contrast between the role he adopts and his identity underneath; and to reclaim his place in the house and in Ithacan society, his membership of the elite must be confirmed.

The narrative of the *Odyssey* is, perhaps, socially conservative, in that it concludes with the renewal and relegitimization of the elite order on the island of Ithaca. All the same, it significantly expands the demographic range of voices audible in epic, and (equally significantly) presents its central protagonist learning creatively from the ruses of the disempowered.

Similarly, the narrator of Hesiod's *Works and Days* assumes a different social persona from that of the *Theogony* (as we saw in chapter 3). The latter poem presents poetry as the servant of kingship; the *Works and Days*, on the other hand, presents a 'bottom-up' view of the world, replete with agricultural advice and griping at the immoral aristocrats who accept bribes in their judgements. Epic poetry certainly embodies aristocratic ideologies, but it also represents the reactions of communities to that power. It is not just propaganda: as public festival poetry, it is the site for a range of competing voices from a range of backgrounds.

Giving Voice

It is in democratic Athens, however, that we would expect to find the clearest signs of the corrosion of the elite monopoly on literary production. After all, one of the earliest tags for the political constitution of Athens was *isegoria*, 'equal opportunities for public speech' (see chapter 6). The entire topographical space of Athens was designed to ensure mass representation, from the theatre to (particularly) the assembly. 'Who wants to speak?' was the herald's cry as the assembly opened; debate was open to all classes of citizen, even if we may suspect that, in practice, the more educated predominated.

Unfortunately, however, all the texts surviving from this period are elite authored. Ordinary Athenian citizens, while technically enfranchised, had no access to the education and tools that would allow them to write, to memorialize their perspectives for posterity. Can we detect any traces of the voices of the masses in the literary texts we do have? There are certainly texts composed *for* the masses, particularly dramatic (see chapter 5) and oratorical (see chapter 6) texts, and such texts often reflect the values and aspirations of their audiences. For example, the prayer of the captive chorus in Euripides' *Trojan Women* that, of all places in Greece, they should be relocated to 'the famous and favoured land of Theseus' (208–9), also functions as a vote-winner for the Athenian public. Likewise, in the same poet's *Phoenician Women*, Polynices' comment that the most keenly felt suffering of the exile is the loss of freedom of speech (391). It is hardly plausible that a former monarch should lament the loss of this central democratic right: the sentiment is directed more towards the audience than towards the realistic portrayal of character.

But such obvious, direct cases of appealing to public ideology are only of minimal interest. It would be naive to assume that such texts in general straightforwardly reflect the values and aspirations of their audience. Granted, democratic institutions mean power to the masses, who could use their votes to express displeasure. But at the same time, the art of the orator or dramatist lay in the ability to guide, even to reorientate, established ideologies. The surviving public texts of democratic Athens do not simply depict the views of either the masses or the elite; rather, they are engaged in a constant, unresolved struggle between the fundamental expectations of a popular audience and the desire to manipulate those expectations.

Even when the faint echo of the Athenian masses is discernible in the transmitted texts, though, we need to bear in mind what a limited proportion of the Athenian population actually counted as citizens. This was not a democracy in the modern sense: women, free non-Athenians and slaves were all excluded from public representation. In particular, that a supposedly democratic state could tolerate slavery, the forcible subjection of other human beings, is a disturbing paradox. It is to this that I wish to turn now.

Conceptualizing the Slave

The *Odyssey*'s low-class figures, Eumaeus, Philoetius and Eurycleia, are conventionally referred to as 'slaves'.[6] What do we mean by this term? How does Homer conceptualize slavery? The word used in these cases is *dmos* (masculine)/*dmoe* (feminine); the word may suggest the root *damazein*, 'to subdue' or 'tame'.[7] Certainly, slaves are often imagined as part of the booty of conquest. In book 1 of the *Odyssey*, for example, Odysseus' son Telemachus refers to his intention to be 'lord of our house/and its slaves, whom godlike Odysseus plundered' (1.397–8). Homeric slaves seem to have been people who bear the traces of their former freedom, whether they themselves were born free or their descendants were. It is, clearly, consistent with the honour-based ideology of Homeric society and its 'zero-sum game' (see chapter 3) that the process of their subjection should be foregrounded: the forcible imposition of slavery on others is a sign of the master's power.

But the logical corollary is interesting: it implies that no individual is a slave by birth; she or he becomes only so through the intervention of others. By the classical period, however, slavery was imagined very differently. A different word was also used: *doulos* (masculine)/ *doule* (feminine) was by far the commonest term in this later period, and for the remainder of pagan antiquity. Unlike the Homeric *dmos*, the classical *doulos* certainly could be imagined as properly and naturally a slave, especially in Athens (where our literary evidence is based, and on which I shall concentrate in this section).[8] Only in exceptional circumstances (such as before the sea battle at Arginusae in 406 BCE) were any slaves freed; the contrast with Rome, where 'manumission' was a realistic ambition for many, is striking.

Slavery was now conceived of as not just a state in which one might find oneself, but as a nature, an essence. There were those (Aristotle tells us, *Politics* 1253b) who considered slavery the product of human violence rather than nature; but for the majority, it seems, slaves were slaves because they were naturally slavish. Dominion over those under your control, so the Athenians told the Melians before killing the menfolk and enslaving the women and children, is 'a general law of human nature' (Thucydides 5.105). And slaves were certainly imagined as weak. Certain kinds of impulse were considered inherently characteristic: appetitive desire, cowardliness, inconsistency, everything antithetical to the citizen ideal (particularly in Athens) of 'moderation' (*sophrosyne*). In Plato's *Republic*, the man whose reason is dominated by his appetites is presented as 'enslaved' to them (577c–e). The metaphor is deliberate and explicit: political domination is, Socrates (the principal speaker in the text) tells us directly, analogous to psychic domination, both indicating the natural weakness of the subject. It is right, then, that such creatures should be ruled by others.

Slaves invite subjection by their very nature; it is their destiny to be mastered. According to one cross-cultural account of slavery, this projection is a universal strategy of slaving ideology: 'The slaveholder ... define[s] the slave as dependent ... stereotyping the slave as a lying, cowardly, lazy buffoon devoid of courage and manliness.'[9] And because *douloi* were conceived of as inherently lacking in the primary requisites of civilized life, they could be thought of as (at best) minimally human. As Aristotle puts it in the *Nicomachean Ethics*, friendship cannot exist between a master and 'a slave qua slave, because the two parties have nothing in common; the slave is a living tool, just as a tool is an inanimate slave' (1161b).

This is the ideologically compelled justification of slavery in classical Athens, necessitated by the brutal conditions in which many slaves were kept (particularly in the notorious silver mines of Laurion). But let us not forget that slaves *were* human beings, and as such not in practice absolutely reducible to the state of functionality described above. Even Aristotle, not known for his sentiment, concedes (in the sentence following the passage cited above) that friendship can exist between a slave and a master, if not qua master and slave, then qua fellow human beings. Slaves are, for Aristotle (as they no doubt were for many Athenians), walking contradictions, living ambiguities; 'animate tools', as he puts it (the phrase reappears at *Politics* 1253b). Neither fully human nor yet inhuman, slaves occupied a disturbing – for those who paused to exercise themselves about the issue – position in between the two.

The Slave as Agent: Dramatic Paradigms

Aristotle's grudging admission of the common bond of humanity shared between masters and slaves concedes the possibility of a more positive view of the latter within free society. In Athenian drama, slaves are allowed to think, speak and act; in addition, they are not infrequently presented as sympathetic characters. Tragedy, to begin with that genre, focuses upon slaves with a particular closeness to the protagonists: tutors and nurses. Both tutors (in Sophocles' *Electra* and Euripides' *Medea*, for example) and nurses (in Aeschylus' *Libation-bearers*, for instance, or again in Euripides' *Medea*) can be presented as commendably loyal servants, endorsing the status quo without question. But I want to focus in this section on the nurse in Euripides' *Hippolytus*, whose role in the action is to be much more than a mere adjunct; her role in the narrative illustrates perfectly the ambiguities we have identified in the Athenian construction of slavery.

As we saw in chapter 5, the *Hippolytus* tells of the goddess Aphrodite's vengeance upon Hippolytus (who refuses to cultivate her): she causes his stepmother, Phaedra, to fall for him passionately. It is the nurse, Phaedra's confidante, who encourages her to express her feelings to Hippolytus; and the nurse who, when she refuses, tells him herself. This is the act that unleashes the catastrophic chain of events leading to the deaths of Phaedra and Hippolytus. The nurse's narrative role is closely tied to her status, since she would never have had access to such privileged knowledge had she been free. The ethical code of *aidos* ('shame', 'modesty') leads Phaedra to think that divulging her passion to another would be a sacrifice in social standing (see chapter 5); but she can tell the nurse, because (by implication) a slave has no authority over social arbitration. Divulging to a person without status is not divulging.

Indeed, slaves occupy an exceptional position within the economy of dramatic narrative. Because they have no social status themselves, slaves have a curious ability to make things *happen* within the narrative. Paradoxically, their social non-identity grants them a certain licence, licence at least to mediate between the free. In this respect, slaves occupy a different plane of existence in dramatic narratives: rather than being 'characters' (individuated subjects acting in accordance with their own individuated desires), they are closer to self-reflexive narrative devices. In the *Hippolytus*, Phaedra's desire needs to be communicated to Hippolytus, without implicating the virtuous Phaedra into the plot. (This last point was a priority: Euripides had offended Athenian audiences with his first attempt at a Phaedra, who had been considered too meretricious.) The nurse has no name, no real character (beyond a vague moralism), and certainly little sense of herself as an autonomous agent: her actions are directed (misguidedly, as it happens) towards benefiting her mistress. On the other hand, she cannot be said to be lacking in will: it is her independent choice to tell Hippolytus. In terms of the drama, she is as Aristotle would have us believe slaves are in general: ambiguously poised between (narrative) tool and human being.

Comic Plotters

Rather than in tragedy, however, it is in comedy that this uncertain middle ground is most brilliantly exploited. Not so much in the 'old comedy' of Aristophanes (which we met in chapter 5), however. Slaves do appear here, perhaps most memorably the cheeky Xanthias in Aristophanes' *Frogs*: the play begins with an elaborate series of role reversals between him and his master, the god Dionysus (in the opening scene, the god has to walk, while the slave gets the donkey).[10] In this context, the subversion of the expected hierarchy contributes to the utopian vision that lies at the heart of Aristophanic comedy. Xanthias' role in the narrative is principally to exemplify the fluidity of social boundaries. (Usually in Aristophanes, we would expect these boundaries to rematerialize at the end of the play, but by the end of *Frogs* the central preoccupation has shifted towards revivifying the poet Aeschylus.)

If it is slaves as narrative machinators that we are after, we need to turn to the 'new comedy' of Menander (fourth century), and to the 'new comedy' that survives principally in the Roman adaptations of Plautus and Terence.[11] The role of slaves in these texts is often to *plot*. The pun is eloquent: their elaborate conspiracies, against and on behalf of the free, determine the actions of the remaining characters and monopolize the narrative energy of the plays.

Plotting slaves are a ubiquitous feature of new comedy. I want to take here just one example, from Menander's *Girl with her Hair Cut*. The story is (as such dramas tend to be) complex, but the principal action revolves around the relationship between the soldier Polemo and his girlfriend Glycera. When Polemo sees her kissing Moschion – unaware that he is her brother – he flies into a rage and cuts off her hair. But it is Moschion's slave Davus who drives the plot. Davus is the most common name for the clever slave in Menander: arguably, like the nurse in the *Hippolytus*, he is more a type than an individuated character. But also like the nurse, he is a conduit for narrative plotting. When we first meet him (at least in the fragmentary text we have), he is directing fellow slaves to go to find their master, spotting a 'good opportunity' (266) for him to return. In the following scene, Moschion threatens Davus with a beating, but the slave responds by indicating how much he has achieved:

> I was the one who arranged all of this, Moschion,
> and (using countless words) persuaded Glycera to come
> here, and your mother to accept her, and do
> all you wanted. (272–5)

Davus clams to have arranged 'all' (the word is repeated) of the situation so far, and (as far as we can judge, with little of the earlier part of the play extant) this seems to be the case; he has more narrative control than any of the other characters. Moschion is appeased, but wants more machinations:

> Go inside, Davus, and spy on all
> the goings-on. What is she doing? Where is my mother?
>   How are they likely to welcome me? No need to
> spell out this role for you in detail; you're a savvy fellow. (295–8)

This time, it is knowledge that Davus is asked to assemble – 'all' (again the emphasis upon total control) the goings-on in the house. Once again, the slave is conceded a privileged but ambiguous position in the action. Davus' role oscillates between self-determination and dependence on others: Moschion gives the orders (and has been threatening severe violence); at the same time, though, he leaves Davus to make his own plans, acknowledging the slave's cunning. The slave occupies the grey area between a tool for others' use and a human being with his own agency and subjectivity. And indeed in this case it is precisely this ambiguity that will allow him to succeed in his task: as an insignificant presence, he can slip into company without notice; but as an intelligent human being, he can also cogitate and remember. As in the *Hippolytus*, it is at their peril that the free divulge to slaves, imagining them to be non-beings. Slaves can easily reactivate their repressed humanity.

In this sense, then, slaves are the architects of later comic narrative: it is thanks to their behind-the-scenes plotting and their eavesdropping that the intricate pleasures of the plot unfurl. At times, they can even represent the author himself, devising new complexities and steering the action. Plautus' *Pseudolus* is a play written in Latin, but based on a Greek original. To what extent Plautus' reflects the Greek play is impossible to judge, and speculation is no doubt idle. But the words adopted by the slave Pseudolus to characterize his role certainly draw out some of the ideas latent in the Greek comic tradition of plotting slaves:

> I suspect that you suspect
> that I'm promising all these great goings-on
> to gratify you while I act out this play,
> and that I won't do what I said I'd do.
> I won't go back on my word. Certainly, as far as I know,
> I don't yet know how I'll do it –
> only that I will do it! For anyone who steps out onstage
> should bring something newly invented by some new technique;
> if he can't do that, he should give over his space to one who can.
>   (562–70)

The slave here assumes the creative, inventive role of the author; and, indeed, steps outside the fiction (a feature sometimes called 'metatheatre') to represent himself as such. This slave's position is not just ambiguous in the sense described above (an inanimate human, an animate tool); he is also ambiguously poised in theatrical terms, both within the plot and without it, simultaneously dramatic character and dramatic creator.

Drama depends upon agents to make things happen; but agents, disturbers of the established order, are problematic figures. In Athenian tragedy, it is the fearsome but glamorously mythical individuals (in contrast to the docile choruses) who monopolize the narrative action. In post-classical comedy, however, it is often slaves who play this role. Slaves are figures of *displacement*: they rarely express their own desires (except for insignificant, 'slavish' commodities like food); rather, they design the consummations of, and indeed consummate, the desires of the free.[12] Comic slaves allow free characters – and, through identification, free spectators – to enact their desires, without debasing themselves through indulgence. Comic slaves liberate the repressed desires of the audience. It is a paradox that slaves should be agents of liberation, but not the first such paradox we have met in the ancient Greek conceptualization of slavery.

Playing the Other

The free man is the man who lives as he wants to.

These words open the third book of Arrian's *Discourses of Epictetus*. Epictetus was one of the dominant philosophers of the second century CE, a hardline Stoic who preached radical self-reliance and a wide-ranging rejection of the vanities of civil society. Arrian of Nicomedia (in Asia Minor), who claimed to record his words (as Xenophon and Plato claimed to record the words of Socrates), was an extraordinarily powerful figure: not only an influential and widely read author (of, among other things, the most accurate surviving account of Alexander the Great's expeditions, the *Anabasis*), but also a Roman senator, consul, military commander and governor (political and military) of the vital frontier province of Cappadocia. His *Circumnavigation of the Black Sea* is addressed to the emperor Hadrian, and there is no reason to suspect that he did not have the emperor's ear. An important man indeed.[13]

His teacher, Epictetus, occupied a very different social echelon, however.[14] He was a former slave (the name means 'purchased'). Roman conventions governing slavery were different from the ones we have met so far: a hardworking slave who saved his pay might expect to be able to purchase his freedom; other slaves might be freed as a reward. But although slaves were not debarred from Roman citizenship (if freed by a Roman citizen), freed slaves were considered low-level beings. To take just one example, Petronius' famous description of the dinner of Trimalchio, in his brilliant Roman novel *The Satyricon*, sneers malevolently at the class of freedmen. To compound his debasement, Epictetus had endured exile under Domitian, a status that involved loss of property and rights, and carried with it considerable social stigma. Epictetus should have been the lowest of the low (and indeed the satirist Lucian seems to be caricaturing him as a fugitive slave in his dialogue *The Runaways*). But Arrian clearly disagreed. What drew the *jeunesse dorée* of Asia Minor to the school of one of such low standing? What, indeed, induced the older Arrian to associate himself publicly with him?

In a word (and two inverted commas): 'authenticity'. The Greek world under the empire (see chapter 9) was dominated by numerous philosophers; and particularly Stoics, all preaching the importance of integrity and a virtuous life ahead of material profit and social status. It was easy to *say* 'the free man is the man who lives as he wants to'; doing so convincingly, however, was a different matter. This was a culture of relentless scrutiny, of hypocrisy-spotting (see also chapter 9). The works of the second-century satirist Lucian testify to this: in the *Symposium*, the philosophers get drunk and fight; in the *Fisherman*, they jettison their haughty pretences in return for the promise of some quick cash. For Lucian, a major part of the role of satire is to debunk the pretensions of philosophical pseuds.

In this competitive philosophical marketplace, real experience counts for much. In his third oration (supposedly addressed to the emperor Trajan), the orator Dio Chrysostom (first–second centuries CE) refers to his exile under Domitian (Trajan's predecessor-but-one and pet bogey) as 'the touchstone of my free-mindedness' (*Oration* 3.12). Unjust abasement could be viewed as a positive badge of honour. In a different speech, Dio expresses the fear that, if he narrates his exile, 'men will say that I am boasting' (*Oration* 45.1). Lucian even presents the unfortunate Proteus Peregrinus as *trying* to get himself exiled, a feat which he eventually achieves, with some difficulty (*Peregrinus* 18). This, Lucian tells us, associated him in the popular imagination with the other famous exiles, Musonius, Dio and Epictetus. And so Peregrinus won popular renown, as a result of his persistence if nothing else.[15]

Loss of social station, in other words, could be recouped as a marker of social station. But only – the point is obvious, but fundamental – if it was recognized within elite society. There was still no cachet attached to the general masses of slaves or abased people; only exceptions like Epictetus, or those who (like Dio) suffered transitory ill-treatment at the hands of those powerful figures whom later history condemned, could access that much-coveted philosophical authority. The allure of this paradigm of social abasement can be sensed in a variety of genres, from the Christian and pagan martyr acts to the novels (see chapter 9). In such texts, social abasement is glamorized, because appropriated for the loftier ends of religion or love; there is no corresponding evidence that the wretched of the earth were generally reappraised outside of such contexts.

Not for nothing is it that our primary source for Epictetus' words is Arrian.[16] For all this ex-slave's considerable achievements in the field of practical philosophy, it took a firmly established member of the elite to transform them into palatable discourse. Later Greek literature invokes, but also carefully regulates, the representation of the lower-class voice. The powerful moral authority of the dispossessed is carefully recontextualized within elite discourse. The sub-elite voice is imagined as *exotic*: powerful and alluring, but because of that requiring the neutralizing frame of elite acceptance.

The 'Invention of Literature'

What role does literature play in the management of class? Can literature be anything but an elitist institution? These are, as it happens, exactly the questions that we encountered at the start of chapter 1. I want to finish this chapter, and the discursive part of this book, by revisiting these issues. Over the course of this book, I have been chary in my approach to grand-scale narratives of historical change. There are a number of counter-examples that warn against crude, broad-brush approaches to historical narrative. The Victorian model of 'golden age' and subsequent decline, is (as we saw in chapter 1) obviously ideological – and, indeed, manifestly wrong. But (as we also saw in chapter 1) to discount historical narrative is to deny the possibility of history itself. And so it is that I conclude – hesitatingly, self-consciously – with a story: the invention of literature.

'Literature' in its modern sense is the product of a series of historical shifts that are specific to the present age (see chapter 1). The texts of antiquity were not lifestyle accessories, but central aspects of the identity of communities. Performing, reading and debating the consequences were definitive features of Greekness. But a significant change does occur over the course of the vast timespan (more than a millennium) we have tracked in the course of this book. One strong sign of this change is the development of literacy. The literary culture of early Greece was predominantly oral: it found its expression in festivals, symposia, theatres, public assemblies. Many of the texts produced in Alexandria and Roman Greece were book texts, composed for perusal in isolation or in small groups. It is important, of course, not to overstate the contrast: the Homeric texts *may* have been written down at an early stage (though I personally doubt that), and certainly many Alexandrian and Roman-Greek texts that we read in books will have had performance contexts. It is equally important not to invest increasing literacy with the clumsy and overschematic distinction between public and private. Oral performance can be private, book-reading can be public.

The crucial point is the invention of what we have called 'the archive'. In the final chapters of the middle section of this book, we explored the emergence (in fifth-century Athens), the building (in Ptolemaic Alexandria) and the manipulation (in Roman Greece) of an archival sensibility, an awareness that individual texts belong in a vast constellation of works – a library, whether real or virtual – that constituted the Greek tradition. By the Ptolemaic period, literature had become the principal means of expression of Greek identity – hence Ptolemy Philadelphus' enormous investment in the library, and the procurement of every book in the world.

With the archive came a different, more textualized approach to language: the invention, for example, of paratextual phenomena like dictionaries and commentaries on texts; but also a greater sense of the possibilities of embedding learning, through subtle allusion, self-referentiality, knowing metatextual polemic. The archive imagined *readers* of its texts, with the opportunity to linger, reread, to consult other texts. And, particularly, it imagined *learned* readers. To read an archival text required familiarity with and acceptance of the complex principles governing literary expression.

Composing and reading literary texts, then, increasingly became a central way of expressing Greek, elite and (usually) male identity. There was nothing new about the use of literature to promote the elite, male, Greek voice to the exclusion of others: as we have seen repeatedly, female and sub-elite voices are already being silenced in Homer's *Iliad*. What was new to the archival culture we have described was the strategy of distinction pursued within the texts themselves. Many of these texts demanded a level of education beyond the means of the vast majority in order to be read, even at a preliminary level. To read, then, was to aspire towards inclusion within a selective but large club, spanning not only much of the known world but also all of known history.

Did the Greeks, then, invent 'literature' as we know it today? An idle question, perhaps; too rhetorically flamboyant to merit an answer. But one thing is certain. The ancient Greeks' legacy to the later world was not simply a bewildering array of brilliant texts; it was also an entire system of comprehending and ordering these texts, of investing them with *value*. Aesthetic value, but also ideological value. A cultural history of ancient Greek literature is also an archaeology of the role of literature in our present society, a first step towards understanding how and why it occupies the privileged (if embattled) position it does.

Notes

1 Surveys of this kind can be found in *The Cambridge History of Classical Literature*; full details can be found in the bibliography under Easterling and Knox, eds (1989). Particularly recommended shorter surveys are Saïd and Trédé (1999) and, especially, Taplin, ed. (2001). The third edition of the *Oxford Classical Dictionary* (Hornblower and Spawforth, eds (1996)) contains a wealth of useful material.

CHAPTER 1   GREEK LITERATURE AND CULTURAL HISTORY

1 Williams (1958), (1961); Eagleton (1983): 17–53. See further Whitmarsh (2001): 3–4.
2 *The Training of the Orator* 2.1.4, 2.14.3. In the first passage, Quintilian states that he is translating the Greek word *grammatike*, or 'text-based training'.
3 See Easterling and Knox (1989).
4 For questions of orality and literacy in the Greek world, see esp. Thomas (1992); Bowman and Woolf, eds (1994).
5 Knox (1968).
6 Manguel (1996): 109–23.
7 A good introduction to the roots and diversity of cultural history can be found in Hunt, ed. (1989).
8 Forster (1974): 8.
9 Barthes (1977): 155–64 (also in Barthes (1986): 56–65).
10 Fowler (1996): 74 (also in Fowler (2000): 107).
11 Foucault (1979): 94.
12 Foucault (1986).

13 Especially Bloom (1988). Hanson and Heath (1998) approach these issues from a classical perspective; see Martindale (1993): 23–9 for a critical view.
14 Bloom (1995).
15 Ibid. 518.
16 Ibid. 531–2.
17 Ibid. 531.
18 In chapter 8 I use it more narrowly, of the period between the late fourth and late first centuries BCE.
19 For the general point, see White (1987): 1–25.
20 Golden and Toohey, eds (1997).
21 For a more detailed analysis than I can give here, see Turner (1981): esp. 15–76; Stray (1998); Whitmarsh (2002a); see also Jenkyns (1980). On classicism, see Porter, ed. (forthcoming).
22 For more on this, see Whitmarsh (2001): 41–5.
23 Hammond and Scullard, eds (1970): 44. The infinitely improved third edition is Hornblower and Spawforth, eds (1996).
24 Nietzsche (1993): 116.
25 See further Halperin (1990a): 1–4; Dowling (1994).
26 For a selective history of the various complex battles over the uses of Greek learning, see Goldhill (2002b).
27 Groningen (1965): 55–6.
28 Swain (1996); Goldhill, ed. (2001); Whitmarsh (2001). See also chapter 9.
29 Hallett (1993).
30 Holzberg (1988): see pp. 206–7 for the quotation from Geffcken; Goldhill (2002b): 93–106.

CHAPTER 2   THE PROBLEM OF TRADITION

1 Hobsbawm and Ranger, eds (1983).
2 Hall (1992): 292. See also Hall (1990); Hall and du Gay, eds (1996): 1–17.
3 Hall (1992): 310–11.
4 ~~Nonnus, *Adventures of Dionysus* 25.265.~~
5 For a brief but dazzling discussion, see Porter (2002).
6 On these ideas, see also chapter 7.
7 See Feeney (1991) on the response of later epic to these issues.
8 Plato, *Republic* 378c–e; Plutarch, *How a Young Man Should Listen to Poetry* 19e–f.
9 Lamberton (1989); Dawson (1992); Lamberton and Kearney (1992).
10 Conversely, Philo of Alexandria (first century CE) turns the allegorical toolbox onto the Jewish Torah, arguing for a substantial overlap with Greek thought.
11 On this tradition, see Graziosi (2002).

12 Reported by Aelian, *Miscellaneous History* 13.22. There is also a series of epigrams on the topic collected in the *Planudean Anthology* (292–302).
13 Bloom (1975): 33–4.
14 Griffin (1995): 1.
15 See especially West (1997); Haubold (2002).
16 Burkert (1992).
17 Hall (1989): 1–55.
18 Ibid.
19 See e.g. Turner (1981): 135–86.
20 See also Hardwick (2000): 97–111. Hardwick also discusses Seamus Heaney's *The Cure at Troy* (1990), a similarly post-colonial reading of Homer.
21 Bernal (1987), (1991). For vigorous responses, see Lefkowitz (1996); Lefkowitz and Rogers, eds (1996); and Bernal (2001).
22 See also Hall (1997): 4–16.
23 Bernal (1987): 2.
24 Said (1995).
25 Most, ed. (1998).
26 Reynolds and Wilson (1991) offer an excellent introduction.
27 Maas (1958); Reynolds and Wilson (1991).
28 Brink (1986): 175–6.
29 For an excellent account of these issues as they relate to classical texts, see Hardwick (2000); also Martindale (1993): 75–100.
30 I cite one more line of Rayor's translation, because she punctuates differently.
31 The clearest discussion is Derrida (1976), with Spivak's introduction. For a lucid discussion of these issues, see Culler (1975): 241–54.
32 Martindale (1993): 16–17.

CHAPTER 3   FESTIVAL

1 For a good general introduction to Homer (and orientation on the massive bibliography, from which I cite only relevant works in this chapter) see Morris and Powell, eds (1996).
2 On festival performance, see Stehle (1997): 170–212.
3 On rhapsodes, see Graziosi (2002): 21–40.
4 See Haubold (2000).
5 Nagy (1990).
6 This is the third of three songs that reflect upon Odysseus' persona, although the other two do so only at the metaliterary level (at the 'realist' level, the bard does not intend the resonances).
7 On Pindar and patronage, see Kurke (1991).
8 On the Hymns, see Clay (1989).

9 On choral performance, see Calame (1997); Stehle (1997). On elegy, see Bowie (1986).
10 See chapter 10.
11 Ford (1992).
12 Photius, *Library* codex 239.
13 For Hesiod, see especially Lamberton (1988).
14 See Lefkowitz (1981), and especially Graziosi (2002).
15 See Turner (1996) for a historical survey of the 'Homeric question'.
16 See especially the second edition of Lord's *The Singer of Tales* (2000), which comes with a CD of Yugoslav images and audio recordings.
17 This position has been best formulated by Greg Nagy: see Nagy (1990), (1996).
18 Vernant (1982): 33.
19 Scully (1981); Seaford (1994).
20 For the historical background, see in general Snodgrass (1980); Murray (1993).
21 On Typhoeus, see Too (1998): 20–2, with further references.
22 See Pucci (1977); Ferrari (1988): 45–7.
23 Or, at least, the most convincing of the four candidates for this title (the others being Agamemnon, Diomedes and Ajax): see Nagy (1979): 26–32.
24 Ibid. 174–210.
25 Ibid. 26–41. For more on Homeric boasting, see chapter 6.
26 Redfield (1994): 33–4.
27 Martin (1989); see also chapter 6.
28 On Achilles as an extremist, unassimilable into society, see Redfield (1994): 103–6.
29 Wees (1992).
30 Nagy (1979): 15–22; Goldhill (1991): 69–93; Vernant (1991): 50–74; Redfield (1994): 30–9.
31 Herzfeld (1985).
32 Vernant (1991): 50–91.
33 This passage should also be read in the context of king Priam's contrast between the 'beautiful death' of the young warrior and the ugly death that he envisages for himself (*Iliad* 22.71–3). See Vernant (1991): 84.
34 Halperin (1990a): 75–87.
35 Vernant (1991): 86.
36 As the escaping ship leaves, the Cyclops refers to a prophecy according to which he would be blinded at the hands of Odysseus; 'but I always expected some massive, fine person would come here, brimming with massive strength; as it is, a tiny, feeble, nobody of a man has deprived me of my sight' (*Odyssey* 9.511–16).
37 Murnaghan (1987); Goldhill (1991): 24–36.
38 Further discussion of class in the *Odyssey* can be found in chapter 13.
39 Further discussion in chapter 11.
40 For Hesiod's gender politics, see especially Zeitlin (1996): 53–86.

CHAPTER 4   SYMPOSIUM

1 For the Greek world, see Lissarrague (1990c); Slater, ed. (1991); Wilkins et al., eds (1996); Davidson (1997); Garnsey (1999); Wilkins (2000). There are many anthropological studies of habits of eating and drinking: particularly influential are Douglas (1982); Goody (1982).
2 Nagy (1979): 127–32.
3 Detienne (1989); on Greek sacrifice in general, see Burkert (1983).
4 Murray, ed. (1990); Murray (1993): 207–13; Lissarrague (1990c); Stehle (1997): 213–61; Davidson (1997): 43–52.
5 Excellent introductions to the political, historical and cultural changes of this period are in Murray (1993); Osborne (1996). For specifically cultural-historical issues, see Dougherty and Kurke, eds (1993).
6 Davidson (1997): 73–108.
7 Nevett (1999).
8 On pederasty, see also chapter 12.
9 Kilmer (1993) discusses many of these, though he has no interest in the sympotic context itself.
10 Keuls (1993): 160–5.
11 Whitmarsh (2002b): 182–4.
12 For some suggestions as to the range of possible sympotic genres (in the Hellenistic period, at least) see Cameron (1995): 71–103.
13 For the oral nature of this poetry, see Gentili (1988).
14 Most (1995): 31.
15 Kurke (1991) provides an excellent cultural-historical analysis of Pindar.
16 Bowie (1986).
17 See especially Figueira and Nagy, eds (1985).
18 Martin (1993).
19 Nagy (1985): 58–63.
20 Donlan (1985), quotation from p. 244.
21 Levine (1985).
22 Compare 77; 417–18; 449–53; 965.
23 Similar sentiments are expressed in tragedy: see Euripides, *Medea* 516–19, *Hippolytus* 925–31, *Mad Hercules* 659; also fragment 229 of the orator Hyperides.
24 Kurke (1999); Seaford (2004).
25 Prendergast (1985): 93.
26 See especially Loraux (1978); Osborne (2001).
27 Osborne (2001).
28 On these issues, see Rosenmeyer (1992). For an excellent discussion of Anacreon and masculinity, with many points of contact with my discussion, see Williamson (1998).
29 Homer, *Odyssey* 9.65; Theocritus 23.44.
30 As in the 'binding song' of Aeschylus' *Eumenides* 307–96, or in Theocritus 2 (see the beginning of chapter 12).

31 Though the only specifically *purple* ball in Homer is played with by male dancers at *Odyssey* 8.370–80.
32 Jeanneret (1991): 140–7; Relihan (1992).
33 On the strategies of Plato's *Symposium*, see especially Halperin (1992); Henderson (2000). For more bibliography, see chapter 12.
34 Braund and Wilkins, eds (2000). This text describes a series of meals and symposia; Plato's *Symposium* is explicitly invoked as a model (at least by the epitomator: see 2a).
35 Branham (1989): 104–23.

CHAPTER 5   THEATRE

1 Davies (1993) and Osborne (2000) offer excellent general introductions to classical Athens.
2 Beard (2002).
3 Ostwald (1992).
4 See especially Taplin (1999), a subtle analysis.
5 For the details, see Pickard-Cambridge (1988). Csapo and Slater (1994) translate and collect many of the central sources. Easterling, ed. (1997) provides much useful information in an accessible form. See also Green (1994); Rehm (1994); and especially Wilson (2000).
6 Henderson (1991b) – yes; Goldhill (1994), (1997) – no. On gender in tragedy, see chapter 11.
7 Goldhill (1987).
8 Wilson (2000).
9 For excellent interpretations of the codes underlying the format of the stage (focusing primarily on tragedy), see Padel (1990); Rehm (1994); Wiles (1997). Taplin (1977), (1978) shows the centrality of the exploitation of physical space to the meaning of the plays.
10 Vernant and Vidal-Naquet (1988): 23–48. See also Knox (1964), still an excellent analysis.
11 Loraux (1986).
12 Detienne (1996).
13 Lloyd (1987).
14 See Goldhill (1996) and Gould (1996) on the ambiguities of the chorus; see Griffith (1998) on the openness of strong, authoritative individual characters to audience identification.
15 Henrichs (1994/5) offers a powerful analysis of the chorus as mediators between the dramatic action and the collective cultic experience of the spectators.
16 The generally accepted view: see especially Foley (1985); Goldhill (1987), (2000); Vernant and Vidal-Naquet (1988); Winkler and Zeitlin, eds (1990); Loraux (1993); Scodel, ed. (1993); Croally (1994). Griffin (1998) attempts to reassert a more traditional view of tragedy as an emotive genre; see Seaford (2000) for a response.

17 For representations of non-Athenians in tragedy, see Goldhill (1986): 57–78; Zeitlin (1986); Hall (1997); Vidal-Naquet (1997).

18 For Dionysiac aspects of drama, see Foley (1981); Seaford (1981), (1994), (1996); Carpenter and Faraone, eds (1993); Sourvinou-Inwood (1994); Friedrich (1996); Easterling (1997a).

19 Easterling (1990).

20 Butler (1990).

21 On this play, see especially Knox (1977); Pucci (1980); Foley (1989); Rabinowitz (1993).

22 For 'autochthony', see p. 173.

23 On this heroic stance, see Knox (1977); and for the traditional code of helping friends and harming enemies, see Blundell (1989).

24 Boedeker (1991).

25 The question of gender in tragedy will be discussed in chapter 11.

26 See Poole (1990), though the conclusion that Euripides was a repressed homosexual is untenable. For pederasty, see chapter 12.

27 Zeitlin (1986), a crucial discussion for the ideas in this paragraph.

28 The Thebans claimed descent from the *Spartoi* or 'sown men'. For the central importance to Athenian identity of autochthony, see chapter 10.

29 See esp. Segal (1981a), (1997); also Vernant and Vidal-Naquet (1988).

30 On this play, see Conacher (1980).

31 Segal (1964); Crane (1989).

32 For sophists, see also chapter 6.

33 For the ambiguities of the *Antigone*, see Goldhill (1986): 88–106; Sourvinou-Inwood (1989). As Steiner (1984) shows, the play's meaning has been construed in numerous different ways through the ages.

34 On the central importance of personal conduct to political agency, see e.g. Winkler (1990b); Hunter (1994).

35 On the ideas in this section, see further Goldhill (1986), 168–98; Padel (1992), (1995).

36 On the *Hippolytus*, see especially Knox (1952); Segal (1965); Zeitlin (1985b).

37 See Cairns (1993); and on the *Hippolytus* passage, see Craik (1993).

38 Bourdieu (1977): 72–87.

39 Ibid. 90–5.

40 Ibid. 91.

41 On gender in tragedy, see also chapter 11.

42 See further Lada (1993), (1996).

43 Lissarrague (1990a).

44 Lissarrague (1990b), with the qualifications of Easterling (1997a): 41–2.

45 For cultural-historical approaches to Aristophanes, see especially Cartledge (1990); Henderson (1990); Redfield (1990); Goldhill (1991): 167–222; Konstan (1995). For more literary approaches, see Dover (1972); A. Bowie (1996), and especially Silk (2000). Russo (1997) discusses staging implications.

46 See Henderson (1991a) for sex; Wilkins (2000) for food.

47 See Allen (2000): 232–7 for this interpretation of the role of Athenian punishment.
48 Anderson (1991).

CHAPTER 6   THE POWER OF SPEECH

1 See esp. Martin (1989): 146–205.
2 See Martin (1989): 68–75 on flyting; Redfield (1994): 129–31 on boasting. Parks (1990) also discusses verbal aggression, though the ahistorical approach is less helpful.
3 See Wilson (1990), on 'face' in modern political contexts.
4 Geertz (1973).
5 A fuller history of political speaking in the Greek world would need to take into account late-archaic political poetry, especially the elegiac poet Solon (mentioned briefly in chapter 4).
6 On the development of Athenian oratory, see especially Cole (1991); Kennedy (1994); Worthington, ed. (1994). Biographical sketches of the orators can be found in Edwards (1994).
7 On Isocrates as a teacher, see Livingstone (1998).
8 For the links between assembly and theatre, see Ober and Strauss (1990); Wilson (1991): 174–80.
9 Ostwald (1969): 96–136.
10 Osborne (1985): 52–3. See further Hall (1995); Yunis (1996).
11 Hesk (2000): 202–41; also Ober (1989): 174–7.
12 Rhodes (1986): 141–2; Harding (1987); Ober (1989): 105–8.
13 On the circumstances, see Sealey (1993), and more briefly Kennedy (1994): 73–80. On the rhetorical strategies here, see further Hesk (2000): 209–15.
14 Wilson (1991); also Ober (1994).
15 For a recent, thorough discussion of the details of Athenian law, see Todd (1993).
16 Discussed primarily by historians of sexuality. See Dover (1978): 19–109; Winkler (1990a): 45–70; Davidson (1997; consult index under 'Timarchus').
17 Hunter (1994).
18 Carey (1994).
19 On the literary motifs, see Porter (1997). For the background of Athenian views of revenge, see Herman (1993).
20 Cohen (1991): 91–132; see also Omitowoju (2002).
21 Kraut (1984) discusses Socrates' philosophical vision for the city of Athens; Brickhouse and Smith (1989) read Plato's *Apology* as a philosophical programme.
22 Ancient rhetoricians also distinguish a third, 'epideictic' or display oratory. Examples would include fun, 'paradoxical' speeches like the *Defence of Palamedes* and the *Encomium of Helen* of the Sicilian orator Gorgias,

and the civilized, sophisticated pedagogy of Isocrates (see especially Too (1995); Livingstone (1998)). On the 'epideictic' genre of the funeral speech, see also chapters 7 and 10.

CHAPTER 7   INVENTING THE ARCHIVE: ATHENS

1   On Strabo, see especially Clarke (1999).
2   Lloyd (1987), and more specifically Goldhill (2002a); Whitmarsh (forthcoming).
3   For a later example, see Aelius Aristides, *Hymn to Sarapis* 8.
4   Thomas (1989).
5   Easterling (1997b).
6   Page, ed. (1981): 33–4.
7   Gould (1989); Lateiner (1989); Romm (1998); Bakker, Jong and Wees, eds (2002).
8   On this proem, see Rosenmeyer (1982); Nagy (1987).
9   Fragment F1 in F. Jacoby, *Die Fragmente der griechischen Historiker*, 14 vols (Leiden, 1961–8).
10   On Thucydides, see Gould (1989): 10; Hornblower (1987): 73–5. On the strategic role of Herodotean 'enquiry', see most recently Thomas (2000), especially 161–7.
11   Lateiner (1989); Thomas (2000): 214–48.
12   See further Romm (1998): 20–3; Boedeker (2002).
13   Nagy (1987); more generally on memory in Herodotus, see Gould (1989): 19–41.
14   Gould (1989): 64.
15   Barthes (1990): 84–6.
16   Gould (1989): 42–7.
17   Gray (2001).
18   Thomas (2000): 168–212; Lloyd (1987): 56–70 for the role of competitive self-presentation in contemporary Greek science.
19   Lloyd (1987): 70.
20   Especially concerning the role of Helen in the Trojan War: see Gorgias fragment 11 in H. Diels and W. Kranz, *Die Fragmente der Vorsokratiker* (Berlin: Weidmann, 1951–2); Euripides, *Trojan Women* 914–1032. Some have seen a parody of Herodotus' aetiology of warfare at Aristophanes, *Acharnians* 524–34.
21   Romm (1998): 142–7; and see Harrison (2000) for Herodotus' religious beliefs.
22   See in general Lloyd (1987): 1–49.
23   Lloyd (1979).
24   The best general account is Hornblower (1987). For detailed analysis, see also Hunter (1973); Connor (1984); Rood (1998).
25   Barthes (1986): 141–8. For a good treatment of Thucydidean realism, see Crane (1998).

26 On his treatment of sources, see Hornblower (1987): 73–109.
27 For the relationship between Thucydides and Hellanicus, see Smart (1986).
28 This is the strong conclusion of Hunter (1973); see also Rood (1998). Connor (1984) emphasizes ruptures and tensions in the narrative, but maintains a unitarian view of the text.
29 See Hornblower (1987): 45–72 for a sharp survey.
30 Loraux (1986).

CHAPTER 8   BUILDING THE ARCHIVE: HELLENISTIC ALEXANDRIA

1 For the historical background, see Walbank (1992); Shipley (2000); Erskine, ed. (2003). Bulloch et al., eds (1993), Green, ed. (1993) and Cartledge et al., eds (1997) offer useful collections of articles.
2 Hall (2001); Whitmarsh (2002b); see also chapter 10.
3 Pratt (1992).
4 On Jews in Alexandria, see Schäfer (1992): 136–60.
5 Pfeiffer (1968): 98–104; Fraser (1972): 1.312–35; Canfora (1989); El-Abbadi (1990); Blum (1991).
6 See Pfeiffer (1968): 100–1.
7 On translation and imperialism, see especially Cheyfitz (1991).
8 Andron, fragment 246 F1 in F. Jacoby, *Die Fragmente der griechischen Historiker*, 14 vols (Leiden, 1961–8).
9 On Alexandrian poetry in general, see Bing (1988); Hutchinson (1988); Hunter (2003). For Callimachus specifically, see especially Harder et al., eds (1993) and Lehnus (2002). Cameron (1995) is instructive but technical.
10 Pfeiffer (1968): 140–8.
11 Ibid. 152–70.
12 Foucault (1989): 44.
13 H. Lloyd-Jones and P. Parsons, eds, *Supplementum Hellenisticum* (Berlin, 1983): 786.
14 Athenaeus, *Sophists at Supper* 408f; see Callimachus, fragment 453.
15 Callimachus, fragments 443–8.
16 Pfeiffer (1968): 105–22, 171–209.
17 Rice (1983). For the Athenian Dionysia, see chapter 5.
18 Predominantly book-poetry: Bing (1988); performable: Cameron (1995). On these 'mimetic' hymns, see especially Depew (2000); Hunter and Fuhrer (2002).
19 Homer, *Odyssey* 6.162–3.
20 Cameron (1995) argues vigorously for a performance culture. See chapter 4 on symposia.
21 See especially Hunter (1992).
22 For Theocritus, see especially Segal (1981b); Halperin (1983); Hunter (1996); Hubbard (1998).

23 Bing (1998); Gutzwiller (1998); Thomas (1998).
24 On Hellenistic epigrams as riddles, see Cameron (1995): 71–103.
25 Schmitz (1999).
26 For recent discussion and guidance through the large bibliography, see Papanghelis and Rengakos, eds (2001); Harder et al., eds (2000). Hunter (1993) offers an excellent overview.
27 J. Powell, ed., *Collectanea Alexandrina* (Oxford, 1925): 4–8; see Krevans (2000).
28 Paskiewicz (1988); Goldhill (1991): 284–333.
29 See Hunter and Fuhrer (2002): 164–75.
30 For Callimachus' *Hymn to Zeus*, see Hopkinson (1984); for Theocritus 17, see Hunter (1996): 77–109.
31 Hunter (1996): 89, comparing a 'strikingly similar' contemporary hieroglyphic text. For Egyptian elements in Alexandrian poetry, see especially Selden (1998); Stephens (2003).
32 Hunter (1993): 162–9.
33 Ibid. 24–36.
34 Intriguingly, this phrase could also mean 'helpless thanks to his [i.e. Jason's] cowardice'.

CHAPTER 9   READING FROM THE ARCHIVE: ROMAN GREECE

1 On the transition of the Greek world to Roman dominion, see Gruen (1984); there is a convenient brief summary at Alcock (1993): 1–32.
2 For the ideas in this paragraph, see Whitmarsh (2001): especially 9–17; see also Swain (1996); Goldhill, ed. (2001).
3 Said (1978): 40.
4 Shear (1981).
5 Bourdieu (1986). Thomas Schmitz's excellent book applying such ideas to Roman Greece, *Bildung und Macht* (Munich, 1997), is unfortunately untranslated as yet.
6 Bowie (2002).
7 Pelling (1989); Swain (1990), (1996): 137–50; Duff (1999).
8 See Whitmarsh (forthcoming) on the politics of prose as a literary form; see Bowie (1989), (1990) on the poetry of the period.
9 Swain (1996): 43–64; Goldhill (2002b): 89–93.
10 See chapter 10 for autochthony.
11 More on these issues in Whitmarsh (2001). For the 'second sophistic', see also Bowersock (1969), focusing primarily upon political relationships; more attuned to literary content are Bowie (1974); Anderson (1993); the most thorough synopsis is Swain (1996).
12 See especially Gleason (1995).
13 Bowersock (1969).
14 Bowie (1974).

15 There are many excellent recent discussions of Pausanias: Jacob (1980); Habicht (1985); Elsner (1992), (1994), (1995); Arafat (1996); Bowie (1996); Swain (1996): 330–56; Alcock et al., eds (2001).
16 Goldhill, ed. (2001).
17 Whitmarsh (2001), 247–94. For important discussions of Lucian, see Jones (1986); Branham (1989); Swain (1996): 298–329; Goldhill (2002b): 60–107.
18 Foucault (1990).
19 Duff (1999).
20 Musurillo, ed. (1954).
21 Dodds (1965).
22 Perkins (1995).
23 For psychological debates in Homer and tragedy, see especially Gill (1995).
24 Goldhill (1994); Morgan and Stoneman, eds (1994); Tatum, ed. (1994); Schmeling, ed. (1996); Swain, ed. (1999).
25 Homer, *Odyssey* 9.298–305.
26 Hunter (1983); Zeitlin (1990).

CHAPTER 10   INVENTING THE GREEK: CULTURAL IDENTITY

1 Flinterman (1995); Anderson (1996); Swain (1996): 381–95; Elsner (1997); Hartog (2001): 199–209.
2 Whitmarsh (2001): 141–55.
3 Romm (1991): 116–20.
4 For general accounts of Greek cultural identity, see especially Hartog (1988); Hall (1989); J. Hall (1997), (2002); Malkin, ed. (2001); Whitmarsh (2001); Harrison, ed. (2001).
5 Hall (2001); Whitmarsh (2002b).
6 Isocrates, *To Philip* 32–4, 68, 76–7, 111–15; Demosthenes, *Oration* 1.17, 1.24, 3.31, 3.45. See also chapter 8.
7 Whitmarsh (2002b).
8 For the general point, see Pratt (1992).
9 Said (1995).
10 Hartog (2001): 15–39.
11 Malkin (1998); Dougherty (2001).
12 See further Vidal-Naquet (1986).
13 Cartledge (1993): 56–9; Vasunia (2001). Both are heavily indebted for their approach to Hartog (1988).
14 Thomas (2000): 28–134; this specific point is made on p. 112.
15 'Man is the measure of all things that are, that they are, and of those that are not, that they are not.' Quoted at Sextus Empiricus, *Against the Mathematicians* 7.60. See most recently Thomas (2000): 126–7; and Kerferd (1981): 83–110 for Protagoras.

16 Homer's language is a poetic amalgamation of Greek dialects, domin-
    ated by what we call 'Ionic'.
17 *Iliad* 2.683; 9.395, 447, 478; 16.595.
18 See Hall (1989): 14.
19 See most recently Fowler (1998): 10.
20 Archilochus fragment 102; Homer, *Iliad* 2.530; Hesiod, *Works and
    Days* 528; fragment 130.
21 Hall (1989).
22 Fowler (1998); also J. Hall (1997): especially 67–107; (2002): 23–9.
23 Fowler (1998): 9–16; Hall (2002): 27–9.
24 Fowler (1998): 11–12.
25 Detienne (1986).
26 Graham (1964).
27 See most recently Romeo (2002), with further references.
28 Whitmarsh (2001): 25–6, 35–6.
29 See especially Loraux (1993): 37–71.
30 Patterson (1981); Boegehold (1994).
31 Loraux (1986).
32 See further Hall (2002).
33 Usher (1993); Livingstone (1998).
34 E.g. Hall (2002); see Whitmarsh (2001) for a counter-argument.
35 Gleason (1995): 16–17; Whitmarsh (2001): 118–21; König (2001).

CHAPTER 11   A WOMAN'S PLACE

1 On the norms of ancient masculinity, see Winkler (1990b); Foxhall and
   Salmon, eds (1998a), (1998b).
2 Among the immense bibliography on Greek women, see particularly
   Pomeroy (1975); Foley, ed. (1981); Peradotto and O'Sullivan, eds (1984);
   Cameron and Kuhrt, eds (1993); Pomeroy, ed. (1991); Fantham et al.,
   eds (1995); Hawley and Levick, eds (1995).
3 Holst-Warhaft (1995); also Alexiou (1974).
4 I am thinking particularly of the work of Julia Kristeva; see most conveniently Moi (1985): 156–61.
5 Lévi-Strauss (1963): 61.
6 Vernant (1980): 23.
7 See Bergren (1980); Austin (1994); Doherty (1995); Worman (1997).
8 Worman (2001).
9 Homer, *Odyssey* 19.108; especially 24.196–8. See also Nagy (1979):
   36–41; Goldhill (1991): 97–9; Katz (1991): 77–113 ('what does
   Penelope want?'). Recent scholarship has particularly emphasized the
   narrative role of women in the *Odyssey*: Winkler (1990a): 129–61;
   Katz (1991); Felson (1994); Doherty (1995); Cohen, ed. (1995), in which
   see especially Zeitlin (1995).

10 Excellent collections of essays about Sappho in Greene, ed. (1996a); see also especially Winkler (1990a): 162–87; duBois (1995); Williamson (1995); Snyder (1997).
11 Greene, ed. (1996b).
12 Discussed by Parker (1993).
13 Stigers (1981); Winkler (1981).
14 duBois (1995): 115–26.
15 Rissman (1983).
16 See Kennedy (1993): 51–5 for analogous issues in Latin love poetry, and for the problems raised by the notion of erotic 'metaphor'.
17 For influential discussions of gender in Greek tragedy, see Zeitlin (1978), (1985a), (1996); Goldhill (1986): 107–37; Bouvrie (1990); Rabinowitz (1993); Wohl (1998); McClure (1999). Other relevant works are cited in notes below.
18 Nevett (1999). See also Lewis (2002): 130–71 on the women's quarters as represented in pottery.
19 Vernant (1980).
20 Cohen (1991): 70–97; Blok (2001).
21 See chapter 5.
22 Easterling (1987); Padel (1990); also Wiles (1997).
23 Williamson (1990). See also Rabinowitz (1993): 125–69. On transgressive women in Athenian drama, see also Shaw (1975); Foley (1981), (1982); for female speech, see McClure (1999).
24 Knox (1977).
25 Goldhill (1986): 79–137; Belfiore (2000).
26 Goldhill (1986): 151–4.
27 Zeitlin (1978).
28 Kristeva (1982), and Carson (1990) for the Greek world.
29 The title of Arthur (1983), an essay on Hesiod's (much earlier) *Theogony*.
30 Loraux (1986): especially 116–37.
31 Patterson (1986).
32 See Loraux (1978). On Hesiod's misogyny, see further (especially) Arthur (1983); Zeitlin (1996): 53–86; on Semonides, see Osborne (2001) and chapter 4.
33 Levine (1987) discusses the relationship between the *Lysistrata* and the tragic transgressive woman (focusing particularly on Euripides' *Bacchae*). On comic women, see further Shaw (1975); Foley (1982); Taaffe (1993); and Rosivach (1998) on new comedy.
34 On this play, see Henderson (1980); Loraux (1980–1); Foley (1982); Konstan (1993).
35 Schaps (1977).
36 Plutarch's conception of female education, however, is strongly normative and hardly emancipatory: see Whitmarsh (2001): 109–16.
37 See the careful and cautious survey at Pomeroy (1975): 120–230.
38 See further Burton (1995).
39 Hunter (1985): 83–95; Rosivach (1998).

40 Rosenmeyer (2001): 114–18.
41 On educated women in the Roman period, see Hemelrijk (1999).
42 Whitmarsh (2001): 109–16. Nussbaum (2002) compares and contrasts with Musonius' model, Plato (who includes a discussion of women's capacity for education at *Republic* 451b–57a). I am not fully convinced, however, that Musonius is simply adapting Plato's ideas to the 'reality' of Roman life. The idea that women should be educated so as to perform their household tasks better is also found in Xenophon's *Art of Household Management* 7.4–13: see Pomeroy (1994), 34, 267–8. Musonius Rufus is translated in Lutz (1947).
43 The dating of these poets is not certain. See in general Snyder (1989) and Rayor (1991) for translations. For a good recent discussion of Erinna, see Stehle (2001); of Nossis, Skinner (1989); Gutzwiller (1998): 74–88; of Anyte, Gutzwiller (1998): 54–75; Greene (2000).
44 Stehle (2001).
45 On gender in the novel, see especially Konstan (1994); Goldhill (1995); Cooper (1996); Haynes (2002).
46 Perry (1967): 177.
47 Bowie (1994); Stephens (1994).
48 Bowie (1994): 436–7.
49 Egger (1994a), (1994b).
50 Winkler (1990a): 101–26.
51 Egger (1994b): 43.
52 Mulvey (1975); Lauretis (1984); Kappeler (1986).
53 Elsom (1992).
54 Freud (1973): 146.

CHAPTER 12   SEXING THE TEXT

1 On ancient erotic magic, see Winkler (1990a): 71–98 and Faraone (1999); more generally on ancient magic, see Faraone and Obbink, eds (1991); Graf (1997); Dickie (2001).
2 Faraone (1999): 152–4; Dickie (2001): 99–104. For *hetaerae*, see chapter 4.
3 For discussions of Greek sexuality, see especially Halperin et al., eds (1990); Winkler (1990a); McClure, ed. (2002).
4 See Konstan (1994) for a slightly overstated account of 'sexual symmetry' as ideology.
5 Bakhtin (1984). For the body in antiquity, see Dean-Jones (1994); Wyke, ed. (1998); Porter, ed. (1999).
6 Carson (1990): 153–8; Hanson (1990): 314–20; also see Dean-Jones (1994).
7 On the theme of visuality in the novels, see Goldhill, ed. (2001).
8 Feminist criticism of pornography has been usefully applied to the ancient world, however: see Richlin, ed. (1992).

9 Henderson (1991a).
10 Olender (1990).
11 Winkler (1990a): 188–209.
12 Cameron (1995): 98–9.
13 Cairns (1993).
14 Dover (1978); Halperin (1990a); Percy (1996); Hubbard (2003).
15 See especially Halperin (1990a): 15–40, drawing on Foucault (1981); and against this interpretation, Richlin (1993).
16 Foucault (1981): 43.
17 Sedgwick (1991).
18 There is some evidence from this period for the view that pederastic and straight are exclusive categories: see the debates between adherents of women and boys in Plutarch's *Dialogue on Love*, Achilles Tatius 2.35–8 and Lucian's *Love Stories*.
19 Foucault (1985); Halperin (1990a); Winkler (1990a). Dover (1978) also collects much of the material on Greek homosexuality for the classical period, but without the overarching theory and narrative of his successors.
20 For 'constructionist' approaches, emphasizing discontinuity, see Halperin (1990a); Winkler (1990a); Halperin et al., eds (1990); Laqueur (1990). Halperin and Winkler are critiqued by Hexter (1991). For a broadly 'essentialist' approach, see Boswell (1996).
21 Hubbard (2003): 2–3.
22 Davidson (1997): 167–82; (2001).
23 See Dover (1978): 171–84 and especially Rabinowitz and Auanger, eds (2002) for important discussions of the available sources.
24 Full bibliography will be found in chapter 11, nn. 9–13.
25 Good discussion of these issues at Rabinowitz (2002): 15–18.
26 Lardinois (1991); Williamson (1995): 92–8.
27 Other translations of this poem were considered at the end of chapter 2.
28 See most recently Furley (2000), with full bibliography.
29 Associated with lesbian sexual identity by Snyder (1997) – though she in fact disavows the 'lesbian desire' of the title of her book – and especially Skinner (2002). Clearly, however, whether we choose to use the word 'lesbian' depends upon how we understand lesbian desire.
30 See especially Snyder (1997): 14–16; Greene (2002).
31 Fox (1998): 20–1. See also Goldhill (1995): 100–2.
32 Foucault (1985): 229–46. On Platonic *eros*, see further Penwill (1978); Halperin (1985), (1986). For interpretations of Diotima's speech in the light of gender politics, see duBois (1988); Halperin (1990b).
33 Gribble (1999).
34 Brooks (1984).
35 Ibid. 61.
36 Recent critics have emphasized the central role accorded to Penelope in determining the plot's outcome, as well as the artfully sustained

suspense as to the likelihood of her betraying her husband: see Winkler (1990a): 129–61; Katz (1991); Felson (1994); Zeitlin (1996): 19–52.
37 Zeitlin (1996): 19–32.
38 Wilde (2002).
39 Tanner (1979): 14.

CHAPTER 13   STATUS AND SLAVERY

1   Thalmann (1988); Rose (1992); Postlethwaite (1998).
2   For 'further voices' in Virgil's *Aeneid*, see Lyne (1987).
3   On Achilles' role in the *Odyssey*, see Edwards (1985), drawing different conclusions.
4   See in general Thalmann (1998).
5   A connection also drawn in the roughly contemporary Hesiod, in the story of how the Titan Prometheus tricks Zeus, king of the gods (*Theogony* 507–84; *Works and Days* 47–89).
6   For historical accounts of ancient slavery, see especially Finley (1980); Garlan (1988); Cartledge (1993): 118–51; Garnsey (1996). Patterson (1982) is a classic comparative account of slavery, offering numerous ancient examples and parallels.
7   See Thalmann (1998), 52–67 on Homeric words for slavery. He favours a different etymology for *dmoes*.
8   On theories of natural slavery, see de Ste Croix (1981): 416–18.
9   Patterson (1982): 337–8.
10 See also the figure of Carion in *Wealth*; also Dover (1972): 204–8.
11 See Wiles (1988) on Menander; on new comedy, see Fitzgerald (2000), especially 32–47, 81–6; Hunter (1985): 145–7.
12 Fitzgerald (2000): 41–2.
13 On Arrian, see Stadter (1980).
14 Bradley (1994): 173–82.
15 On exile in Roman Greece, see Whitmarsh (2001): 133–80.
16 Epictetus' *Manual* also survives, notionally in his words; but this too appears to be a compilation.

Chronology of Greek Literature

For simplicity, this chronology follows the traditional distinction of ancient Greek literature into four periods. On the various problems with these periodizations, see chapter 1. Most early dates are approximate, and the division by centuries is for ease of reference only: history is never, of course, neat. This is not a complete survey of either Greek history or Greek literature; it is merely designed to help readers navigate their way around this book.

Archaic Period

Eighth century BCE

History   Greece consists of a series of independent city-states (*poleis*; singular: *polis*), ruled by aristocrats. The first 'panhellenic' (all-Greek) festival, the Olympic games, is founded (traditionally in 776 BCE). The first signs of development of the collective-based culture of the later Greek *polis*, particularly in the appearance of 'hoplite' combat, involving heavily armed soldiers who fought in units rather than individually (as usually in the Homeric poems). The beginnings of Greek colonization in Italy, Sicily and the Near East.

Literature   The Greek alphabet (adapted from the Phoenician) makes its first appearance, but poetry is circulated almost entirely orally. The Homeric and Hesiodic traditions (see chapter 3) are taking shape, although they draw upon an older stock of poetry from the Mediterranean and the East.

Seventh century BCE

History   The first 'tyrant' (monarch who usurps sole power in a city-state) probably appears: Pheidon of Argos. Tyrants become an increasingly common feature in Greece, often seizing power with support from the people. Military expansion of Sparta. First Greek expeditions into Egypt. Developments in distinctively Greek architecture, including the earliest Doric temples (based on Egyptian models). The late seventh century sees the appearance of the earliest coinage, as well as 'black-figure' vase-painting.

Literature   Perhaps the formative period for the composition of the Homeric and Hesiodic poems. The earliest surviving lyric, elegiac and iambic poets, including Archilochus of Paros, Tyrtaeus and Alcman of Sparta, Semonides of Amorgos. At the turn of the following century, Sappho and Alcaeus of Lesbos begin composing.

Sixth century BCE

History   Solon introduces radical reforms to Athens' political and legal system, including the abolition of bondage for those who had fallen into debt (Solon is seen by later Athenians as a proto-democrat). Rise of the Persian empire, under Cyrus the Great: Persians gain control of the western coast of Asia Minor, including a number of key Greek cities.

Literature   Lyric and elegiac poets, including Solon of Athens, Anacreon of Teos, Simonides of Ceos and most parts of the Theognidean corpus (from Megara). The beginnings of the 'Ionian revolution', the flowering of rationalizing science in Asia Minor: Thales, Anaximander, Anaximenes.

Classical Period

Fifth century BCE

History   Cleisthenes' reforms in Athens (actually beginning in 508) inaugurate Athenian democracy. Failed Ionian revolt against Persian rule. First Persian invasion of Greece repelled by combined forces of an alliance of Greek states at battle of Marathon (490); second invasion repelled in 480–79. 'Delian league' (soon to become the Athenian empire) founded in 475, treasury later moved from Delos to the Athenian Parthenon. Pericles the central figure in Athenian politics from 461 to 429. 'Peloponnesian war' between allies of Athens and of Sparta from 431 to 404, ends in defeat for Athens.

Literature Athenian drama: tragedy (including Aeschylus, Sophocles and Euripides), satyr-plays (written by tragedians) and comedy (including Aristophanes). More rationalizing prose literature (particularly in later half of century), including the philosophers Protagoras and Democritus, the 'Hippocratic' medical texts, the histories of Herodotus and Thucydides. Socrates is active (executed in 399). The earliest orators and sophists, including Gorgias and (from the late fifth century) Lysias. Lyric and elegiac poetry still written copiously, especially by Pindar of Thebes, Bacchylides of Ceos; Simonides of Ceos writes epigram commemorating the dead at the battle of Thermopylae.

Fourth century BCE

History Spartan dominance broken by Thebans at the battle of Leuctra (371). Philip II becomes king of Macedon (359), subjugates Greece by defeating Athens and Thebes at the battle of Chaeroneia (338). Alexander accedes on death of Philip (336), and proceeds to conquer Middle East as far as the Punjab. Alexandria in Egypt founded in 331. Alexander dies in 323, his empire fragmenting into a series of kingdoms ruled by his generals.

Literature Athens the undisputed literary centre of Greece. Philosophy, especially Plato and Aristotle. Xenophon active as a philosopher, biographer, essayist and historian (and general); Isocrates as an orator, theorist, pamphleteer and letter-writer. Oratory, including Demosthenes and Aeschines. 'New' comedy pioneered by Menander.

Hellenistic Period

Third century BCE

History Complex struggles (military, diplomatic, cultural) between the various successor kingdoms, and increasingly with Rome too.

Literature Ptolemy I founds the Museum and Library at Alexandria (295). The Alexandrian poets: Philetas, Callimachus, Theocritus, Apollonius, Herodas (though his relationship to Alexandria is not secure). Criticism of the texts of Homer and others, particularly by Zenodotus, Apollonius, Aristarchus, Aristophanes. New comedy continues to be written. Philosophy, dominated by Epicureanism (founded by Epicurus in the late fourth century) and Stoicism (founded by Zeno, also late fourth century).

Second century BCE

History Increasing influence of Rome: Macedonia (149–8) and Pergamum (133) become Roman states; Roman general Mummius razes Corinth to the ground (146).

Literature Polybius writes his history of Rome. Some Greek poetry in the Hellenistic mode survives from this period, including a number of epigrams and the works of Moschus and (perhaps at the turn of the first century) Bion.

First century BCE

History Increasing Roman domination of the Mediterranean (despite political chaos at Rome). Battle of Actium in 31 sees final defeat of Cleopatra and Antony by Octavian; Egypt now in Roman hands. Octavian becomes 'Augustus' (27), and hence in effect the first Roman emperor.

Literature Grandiose historical and geographical prose, especially Strabo's geography and the world history of Diodorus of Sicily. The literary critic and historian Dionysius of Halicarnassus. A large number of epigrams, increasingly devoted to Roman patrons (Antipater, Crinagoras and others).

Imperial Period

First century CE

History Consolidation of imperial power at Rome, despite chaos and civil war in 69. Jewish revolts between 66 and 73 CE.

Literature   The earliest surviving novels, including Chariton and (perhaps) Xenophon of Ephesus. Jewish writers: the historian Josephus and the Platonist philosopher Philo. In the late first and early second centuries: the philosophical sophist Dio Chrysostom; the historian and philosopher Plutarch.

Second century CE

History   Peace across much of the empire. A succession of 'philhellenic' (or 'Greek-friendly') emperors: particularly Hadrian (117–38), Antoninus Pius (138–61) and Marcus Aurelius (161–80). Increasing numbers of Christians.

Literature   The philosopher Epictetus. The historians Arrian and Appian. The Greek novels of Longus and Achilles Tatius. The travel narrative of Pausanias. The satirist Lucian. A number of performing sophists, including Aelius Aristides, Favorinus and Polemo. The Christian authors Justin and Clement. The philosophical meditations of the emperor Marcus Aurelius. The medical writings of Galen.

Third century CE

History   Peaceable until the middle of the century, the so-called 'third-century crisis' which saw instability and a rapid succession of different emperors.

Literature   The polymath Philostratus; the historians Cassius Dio and Herodian. The *Sophists at Supper* of Athenaeus (possibly second century). Philosophers, including Sextus Empiricus and Plotinus. Christian authors, including Origen.

Fourth century CE

History   Constantine pronounces Christianity the state religion of Rome (312). Apart from a brief interlude under Julian the Apostate (360–3), Christianity is permanently established.

Literature   The novel of Heliodorus (probably). In the pagan sphere, the wide-ranging writings of Julian the 'apostate' emperor and Libanius of Antioch; in the Christian, the poetry and letters of Gregory of Nazianzus, and the letters and essays of Symmachus.

References

Alcock, S. (1993) *Graecia Capta: The Landscapes of Roman Greece* (Cambridge: Cambridge University Press).

Alcock, S., Cherry, J. and Elsner, J., eds (2001) *Pausanias: Travel and Memory in Roman Greece* (New York: Oxford University Press).

Alexiou, M. (1974) *The Ritual Lament in Greek Tradition* (Cambridge: Cambridge University Press).

Allen, D. (2000) *The World of Prometheus: The Politics of Punishing in Democratic Athens* (Princeton: Princeton University Press).

Anderson, B. (1991) *Imagined Communities: Reflections on the Origin and Spread of Nationalism*, 2nd edn (London: Verso).

Anderson, G. (1993) *The Second Sophistic: A Cultural Phenomenon in the Roman Empire* (London: Routledge).

Anderson, G. (1996) 'Philostratus on Apollonius of Tyana: The unpredictable on the unfathomable', in G. Schmeling, ed., *The Novel in the Ancient World* (Leiden: Brill), pp. 613–18.

Arafat, K. (1996) *Pausanias' Greece: Ancient Artists and Roman Rulers* (Cambridge: Cambridge University Press).

Arthur, M. (1983) 'The dream of a world without women: poetics and the circles of order in the *Theogony* prooemium', *Arethusa* 15: 97–114.

Austin, N. (1994) *Helen of Troy and her Shameless Phantom* (Ithaca: Cornell University Press).

Bakhtin, M. (1984) *Rabelais and his World*, trans. Hélène Iswolsky (Bloomington: Indiana University Press).

Bakker, E., Jong, I. de and Wees, H. van, eds (2002) *Brill's Companion to Herodotus* (Leiden: Brill).

Barthes, R. (1977) *Image Music Text*, trans. S. Heath (London: Fontana).

Barthes, R. (1986) *The Rustle of Language*, trans. R. Howard (Oxford: Blackwell).

Barthes, R. (1990) *S/Z*, trans. R. Miller (Oxford: Blackwell).

Beard, M. (2002) *The Parthenon* (London: Profile).

Belfiore, E. (2000) *Murder Among Friends: Violations of* philia *in Greek Tragedy* (New York: Oxford University Press).

Bergren, A. (1980) 'Helen's web: time and tableau in the *Iliad*', *Helios* 7: 19–34.

Bernal, M. (1987) *Black Athena: The Afroasiatic Roots of Classical Civilization*. Vol. I: *The Fabrication of Ancient Greece 1785–1985* (London: Free Association Books).

Bernal, M. (1991) *Black Athena: The Afroasiatic Roots of Classical Civilization*. Vol. 2: *The Archaeological and Documentary Evidence* (London: Free Association Books).

Bernal, M. (2001) *Black Athena Writes Back: Martin Bernal Responds to his Critics* (Durham, NC: Duke University Press).

Bing, P. (1988) *The Well-Read Muse: Present and Past in Callimachus and the Hellenistic Poets* (Göttingen: Vandenhoeck and Ruprecht).

Bing, P. (1998) 'Between literature and the monuments', in Harder et al., eds (1998), pp. 21–43.

Blok, J. (2001) 'Towards a choreography of women's speech in classical Athens', in Lardinois and McClure, eds (2001), pp. 95–116.

Bloom, A. (1988) *The Closing of the American Mind: How Higher Education has Failed Democracy and Impoverished the Souls of Today's Students* (London: Penguin).

Bloom, H. (1975) *A Map of Misreading* (New York: Oxford University Press).

Bloom, H. (1995) *The Western Canon: The Books and Schools of the Ages* (London: Macmillan).

Blum, R. (1991) *Kallimachos: The Alexandrian Library and the Origins of Bibliography*, trans. H. Wellisch (Madison: University of Wisconsin Press).

Blundell, M. (1989) *Helping Friends and Harming Enemies: A Study in Sophocles and Greek Ethics* (Cambridge: Cambridge University Press).

Boedeker, D. (1991) 'Euripides' *Medea* and the vanity of *logoi*', *Classical Philology* 86: 95–112.

Boedeker, D. (2002) 'Epic heritage and mythical patterns in Herodotus', in Bakker et al., eds (2002), pp. 97–116.

Boegehold, A. (1994) 'Perikles' citizenship law of 451/0 BC', in Boegehold and Scafuro, eds (1994), pp. 57–66.

Boegehold, A. and Scafuro, A., eds (1994) *Athenian Identity and Civic Ideology* (Baltimore: Johns Hopkins University Press).

Boswell, J. (1996) *The Marriage of Likeness: Same-Sex Unions in Premodern Europe* (London: Fontana).

Bourdieu, P. (1977) *Outline of a Theory of Practice*, trans. R. Nice (Cambridge: Cambridge University Press).

Bourdieu, P. (1986) *Distinction: A Social Critique of the Judgement of Taste*, trans. R. Nice (London: Routledge).

Bouvrie, S. des (1990) *Women in Greek Tragedy: An Anthropological Approach* (Oslo: Norwegian University Press).

Bowersock, G. (1969) *Greek Sophists in the Roman Empire* (Oxford: Oxford University Press).

Bowie, A. (1996) *Aristophanes: Myth, Ritual and Comedy* (Cambridge: Cambridge University Press).

Bowie, E. (1974) 'Greeks and their past in the Second Sophistic', in M. I. Finley, ed., *Studies in Ancient Society* (London: Routledge and Kegan Paul, 1974), pp. 166–209; minimally revised from *Past and Present* 46 (1970), pp. 3–41.

Bowie, E. (1986) 'Early Greek elegy, symposium, and public festival', *Journal of Hellenic Studies* 106: 13–35.

Bowie, E. (1989) 'Greek sophists and Greek poetry in the Second Sophistic', *Aufstieg und Niedergang der römischen Welt* 2.33.1: 209–58.

Bowie, E. (1990) 'Greek poetry in the Antonine age', in D. Russell, ed., *Antonine Literature* (Oxford: Oxford University Press), pp. 53–90.

Bowie, E. (1994) 'The readership of Greek novels in the ancient world', in Tatum, ed., pp. 435–59.

Bowie, E. (1996) 'Past and present in Pausanias', in *Entretiens de la Fondation Hardt* 41: 207–39.

Bowie, E. (2002) 'Hadrian and Greek poetry', in E. Ostenfeld, ed., *Greek Romans and Roman Greeks: Studies in Cultural Interaction* (Aarhus: Aarhus University Press, 2002), pp. 172–97.

Bowman, A. and Woolf, G., eds (1994) *Literacy and Power in the Ancient World* (Cambridge: Cambridge University Press).

Bradley, K. (1994) *Slavery and Society at Rome* (Cambridge: Cambridge University Press).

Branham, B. (1989) *Unruly Eloquence: Lucian and the Comedy of Traditions* (Cambridge, MA: Harvard University Press).

Braund, D. and Wilkins, J., eds (2000) *Athenaeus and his World: Reading Greek Culture in the Roman Empire* (Exeter: University of Exeter Press).

Brickhouse, T. and Smith, N. (1989) *Socrates on Trial* (Oxford: Oxford University Press).

Brink, C. (1986) *English Classical Scholarship: Historical Reflections on Bentley, Porson and Housman* (Cambridge: James Clarke and Co.).

Brooks, P. (1984) *Reading for the Plot: Design and Intention in Narrative* (Cambridge, MA: Harvard University Press).

Bulloch, A., Gruen, E. S., Long, A. A. and Stewart, A., eds (1993) *Images and Ideologies: Self-Definition in the Hellenistic World* (Berkeley: University of California Press).

Burkert, W. (1983) *Homo Necans: The Anthropology of Ancient Greek Sacrificial Ritual and Myth*, trans. Peter Bing (Berkeley: University of California Press).

Burkert, W. (1992) *The Orientalizing Revolution: Near-Eastern Influence on Greek Culture in the Early Archaic Age* (Cambridge, MA: Harvard University Press).

Burton, J. (1995) *Theocritus' Urban Mimes: Mobility, Gender and Patronage* (Berkeley: University of California Press).

Butler, J. (1990) *Gender Trouble: Feminism and the Subversion of Identity* (London: Routledge).

Cairns, D. (1993) *Aidos: The Psychology and Ethics of Honour and Shame in Ancient Greek Literature* (Oxford: Oxford University Press).

Calame, C. (1997) *Choruses of Young Women in Ancient Greece: Their Morphology, Religious Role, and Social Functions*, trans. D. Collins and J. Orion (Lanham, MD: Rowman and Littlefield).

Cameron, A. (1995) *Callimachus and his Critics* (Princeton: Princeton University Press).

Cameron, A. and Kuhrt, A., eds (1993) *Images of Women in Antiquity* (London: Routledge).

Canfora, L. (1989) *The Vanished Library: A Wonder of the Ancient World*, trans. M. Ryle (London: Vintage).

Carey, C. (1994) 'Rhetorical means of persuasion', in I. Worthington, ed., *Persuasion: Greek Rhetoric in Action* (London: Routledge), pp. 26–45.

Carpenter, T. and Faraone, A., eds (1993) *Masks of Dionysus* (Ithaca: Cornell University Press).

Carson, A. (1990) 'Putting her in her place: woman, dirt, and desire', in Halperin et al., eds (1990), pp. 135–69.

Cartledge, P. (1990) *Aristophanes and his Theatre of the Absurd* (Bristol: Bristol Classical Press; repr. 1999).

Cartledge, P. (1993) *The Greeks: A Portrait of Self and Others* (Oxford: Oxford University Press).

Cartledge, P., Garnsey, P. and Gruen, E., eds (1997) *Hellenistic Constructs: Essays in Culture, History, and Historiography* (Berkeley: University of California Press).

Cheyfitz, E. (1991) *The Poetics of Imperialism: Translation and Colonization from* The Tempest *to* Tarzan (New York: Oxford University Press).

Clarke, K. (1999) *Between Geography and History: Hellenistic Constructions of the Roman World* (Oxford: Oxford University Press).

Clay, J. S. (1989) *The Politics of Olympus: Form and Meaning in the Major Homeric Hymns* (Princeton: Princeton University Press).

Cohen, B., ed. (1995) *The Distaff Side: Representing the Female in Homer's* Odyssey (New York: Oxford University Press).

Cohen, D. (1991) *Law, Sexuality and Society: The Enforcement of Morals in Classical Athens* (Cambridge: Cambridge University Press).

Cole, T. (1991) *The Origins of Rhetoric in Ancient Greece* (Baltimore: Johns Hopkins University Press).

Conacher, D. (1980) *Aeschylus' Prometheus Bound: A Literary Commentary* (Toronto: University of Toronto Press).

Connor, W. R. (1984) *Thucydides* (Princeton: Princeton University Press; repr. Indianapolis: Hackett, 1992).

Connor, W. R. (1971) *The New Politicians of Fifth-Century Athens* (Princeton: Princeton University Press).

Cooper, K. (1996) *The Virgin and the Bride: Idealized Womanhood in Late Antiquity* (Cambridge, MA: Harvard University Press).

Craik, E. (1993) '*Aidos* in Euripides' *Hippolytus* 373–430: review and reinterpretation', *Journal of Hellenic Studies* 113: 45–59.

Crane, G. (1989) 'Creon and the ode to man in Sophocles' *Antigone*', *Harvard Studies in Classical Philology* 92: 103–16.

Crane, G. (1998) *Thucydides and the Ancient Simplicity: The Limits of Political Realism* (Berkeley: University of California Press).

Croally, N. (1994) *Euripidean Polemic: The* Trojan Women *and the Function of Tragedy* (Cambridge: Cambridge University Press).

Csapo, E. and Slater, W. (1994) *The Context of Ancient Drama* (Ann Arbor: University of Michigan Press).

Culler, J. (1975) *Structuralist Poetics: Structuralism, Linguistics and the Study of Literature* (London: Routledge and Kegan Paul).

Davidson, J. (1997) *Courtesans and Fishcakes: The Consuming Passions of Classical Athens* (London: HarperCollins).

Davidson, J. (2001) 'Dover, Foucault and Greek homosexuality: penetration and the truth of sex', *Past and Present* 170: 3–51.

Davies, J. (1993) *Democracy and Classical Greece*, 2nd edn (London: Fontana).

Dawson, D. (1992) *Allegorical Readers and Cultural Revision in Ancient Alexandria* (Berkeley: University of California Press).

de Ste Croix, G. (1981) *The Class Struggle in the Ancient Greek World* (Ithaca: Cornell University Press; repr. London: Duckworth, 1983).

Dean-Jones, L. (1994) *Women's Bodies in Classical Greek Science* (Oxford: Oxford University Press).

Depew, M. (2000) 'Enacted and represented dedications: genre and Greek hymns', in M. Depew and D. Obbink, eds, *Matrices of Genre: Authors, Canons, and Society* (Cambridge, MA: Harvard University Press), pp. 59–79.

Derrida, J. (1976) *Of Grammatology*, trans. G. Spivak (Baltimore: Johns Hopkins University Press).

Detienne, M. (1986) *The Creation of Mythology*, trans. M. Cook (Chicago: University of Chicago Press).

Detienne, M. (1989) 'Culinary practices and the spirit of sacrifice', in Detienne and Vernant, eds (1989), pp. 1–20.

Detienne, M. and Vernant, J.-P., eds (1989) *The Cuisine of Sacrifice Among the Greeks*, trans. Paula Wissing (Chicago: University of Chicago Press).

Dickie, M. (2001) *Magic and Magicians in the Greco-Roman World* (London: Routledge).

Dodds, E. R. (1965) *Pagan and Christian in an Age of Anxiety: Some Aspects of Religious Experience, from Marcus Aurelius to Constantine* (Cambridge: Cambridge University Press).

Doherty, L. (1995) *Siren Songs: Gender, Audiences, and Narrators in the* Odyssey (Ann Arbor: University of Michigan Press).

Donlan, W. (1985) '*Philos pistos hetairos*', in T. Figueira and G. Nagy, eds, *Theognis of Megara: Poetry and the Polis* (Baltimore: Johns Hopkins University Press), pp. 223–49.

Dougherty, C. (2001) *The Raft of Odysseus: The Ethnographic Imagination of Homer's* Odyssey (Oxford: Oxford University Press).

Dougherty, C. and Kurke, L., eds (1993) *Cultural Poetics in Archaic Greece: Cult, Performance, Politics* (Cambridge: Cambridge University Press).

Douglas, M. (1982) *In the Active Voice* (London: Routledge and Kegan Paul).

Dover, K. (1972) *Aristophanic Comedy* (Berkeley: University of California Press).

Dover, K. (1978) *Greek Homosexuality* (London: Duckworth).

Dowling, L. (1994) *Hellenism and Homosexuality in Victorian Oxford* (Ithaca: Cornell University Press).

duBois, P. (1988) *Sowing the Body: Psychoanalysis and Ancient Representations of Women* (Chicago: University of Chicago Press).

duBois, P. (1995) *Sappho is Burning* (University of Chicago Press).

Duff, T. (1999) *Plutarch's* Lives: *Exploring Virtue and Vice* (Oxford: Oxford University Press).

Eagleton, T. (1983) *Literary Theory: An Introduction* (Oxford: Blackwell).

Easterling, P. (1987) 'Women in tragic space', *Bulletin of the Institute of Classical Studies* 34: 15–26.

Easterling, P. (1990) 'Constructing character in Greek tragedy', in C. Pelling, ed., *Characterization and Individuality in Greek Literature* (Oxford: Oxford University Press), pp. 83–99.

Easterling, P. (1997a) 'A show for Dionysus', in Easterling, ed. (1997), pp. 36–53.

Easterling, P. (1997b) 'From repertoire to canon', in Easterling, ed. (1997), pp. 211–27.

Easterling, P., ed. (1997) *The Cambridge Companion to Greek Tragedy* (Cambridge: Cambridge University Press).

Easterling, P. and Knox, B., eds (1989) *The Cambridge History of Classical Literature*. Vol. I: *Greek Literature*, 4 parts (Cambridge: Cambridge University Press).

Easterling, P. and Knox, B. (1989) 'Books and readers in the Greek world', in Easterling and Knox, eds (1989), part 4: *The Hellenistic Period and the Empire*, pp. 154–97.

Edwards, M. (1985) *Achilles in the* Odyssey: *Ideologies of Heroism in the Homeric Epics* (Königsten: A. Hain).

Edwards, M. (1994) *The Attic Orators* (Bristol: Bristol Classical Press).

Egger, B. (1994a) 'Women and marriage in the Greek novels', in Tatum, ed. (1994), pp. 260–80.

Egger, B. (1994b) 'Looking at Chariton's Callirhoe', in J. Morgan and R. Stoneman, eds, *Greek Fiction: The Greek Novel in Context* (London: Routledge), pp. 31–48.

El-Abbadi, M. (1990) *The Life and Fate of the Ancient Library at Alexandria* (Paris: UNESCO).

Elsner, J. (1992) 'Pausanias: a Greek pilgrim in the Roman world', *Past and Present* 135: 3–29.

Elsner, J. (1994) 'From the pyramids to Pausanias and piglet: monuments, travel and writing', in S. Goldhill and R. Osborne, eds, *Art and Text in Ancient Greek Culture* (Cambridge: Cambridge University Press), pp. 224–54.

Elsner, J. (1995) *Art and the Roman Viewer: The Transformation of Art from Augustus to Justinian* (Cambridge: Cambridge University Press).

Elsner, J. (1997) 'Hagiographic geography: travel and allegory in the *Life of Apollonius of Tyana*', *Journal of Hellenic Studies* 117: 22–37.

Elsom, H. E. (1992) 'Callirhoe: displaying the phallic woman', in Richlin, ed. (1992), pp. 212–30.

Erskine, A., ed. (2003) *A Companion to the Hellenistic World* (Oxford: Blackwell).

Euben, P., ed. (1986) *Greek Tragedy and Political Theory* (Berkeley: University of California Press).

Fantham, E., Foley, H., Kampen, N. and Pomeroy, S., eds (1995) *Women in the Classical World: Image and Text* (New York: Oxford University Press).

Faraone, C. (1999) *Ancient Greek Love Magic* (Cambridge, MA: Harvard University Press).

Faraone, C. and Obbink, D., eds (1991) *Magika Hiera: Ancient Greek Magic and Religion* (New York: Oxford University Press).

Feeney, D. (1991) *The Gods in Epic: Poets and Critics of the Classical Tradition* (Oxford: Oxford University Press).

Felson, N. (1994) *Regarding Penelope: from Character to Poetics* (Norman: University of Oklahoma Press).

Ferrari, G. (1988) 'Hesiod's mimetic Muses and the strategies of deconstruction', in A. Benjamin, ed., *Post-Structuralist Classics* (London: Routledge), pp. 45–78.

Figueira, T. and Nagy, G., eds (1985) *Theognis of Megara: Poetry and the Polis* (Baltimore: Johns Hopkins University Press).

Finley, M. (1980) *Ancient Slavery and Modern Ideology* (London: Penguin; repr. and augmented Princeton: M. Wiener, 1998).

Fitzgerald, W. (2000) *Slavery and the Roman Literary Imagination* (Cambridge: Cambridge University Press).

Flinterman, J.-J. (1995) *Power, Paideia and Pythagoreanism: Greek Identity, Conceptions of the Relationship between Philosophers and Monarchs and Political Ideas in Philostratus*' Life of Apollonius (Amsterdam: Gieben).

Foley, H. (1980) 'The masque of Dionysus', *Transactions of the American Philological Society* 110: 107–33.

Foley, H. (1981) 'The conception of women in Attic drama', in Foley, ed., (1981), pp. 127–68.

Foley, H., ed. (1981) *Reflections of Women in Antiquity* (New York: Gordon and Breach).

Foley, H. (1982) 'The "female intruder" reconsidered: women in Aristophanes' *Lysistrata* and *Ecclesiazusae*', *Classical Philology* 77: 1–21.

Foley, H. (1985) *Ritual Irony: Poetry and Sacrifice in Euripides* (Ithaca: Cornell University Press).

Foley, H. (1989) 'Medea's divided self', *Classical Antiquity* 8: 61–85.

Ford, A. (1992) *Homer: the Poetry of the Past* (Ithaca: Cornell University Press).

Forster, E. M. (1974) *Aspects of the Novel* (London: Edward Arnold).

Foucault, M. (1981) *The History of Sexuality*. Vol. 1: *An Introduction*, trans. R. Hurley (Harmondsworth: Penguin).

Foucault, M. (1985) *The History of Sexuality*. Vol. 2: *The Use of Pleasure*, trans. Robert Hurley (Harmondsworth: Penguin).

Foucault, M. (1986) 'What is an author?', in P. Rabinow, ed., *The Foucault Reader* (Harmondsworth: Penguin), pp. 101–20.

Foucault, M. (1989) *The Order of Things: An Archaeology of the Human Sciences* (London: Routledge).

Foucault, M. (1990) *The History of Sexuality*. Vol. 3: *The Care of the Self*, trans. R. Hurley (Harmondsworth: Penguin).

Fowler, D. (1996) 'Even better than the real thing: a tale of two cities', in J. Elsner, ed., *Art and Text in Roman Culture* (Cambridge: Cambridge University Press), pp. 57–74; reprinted in Fowler (2000), pp. 86–107.

Fowler, D. (2000) *Roman Constructions: Readings in Postmodern Latin* (Oxford: Oxford University Press).

Fowler, R. (1998) 'Genealogical thinking, Hesiod's *Catalogue*, and the creation of the Hellenes', *PCPS* 44: 1–19.

Fox, M. (1998) 'The constrained man', in Foxhall and Salmon, eds (1998a), pp. 6–22.

Foxhall, L. and Salmon, J., eds (1998a) *Thinking Men: Masculinity and its Self-representation in the Classical Tradition* (London: Routledge).

Foxhall, L. and Salmon, J., eds (1998b) *When Men Were Men: Masculinity, Power and Identity in Classical Antiquity* (London: Routledge).

Fraser, P. (1972) *Ptolemaic Alexandria*, 3 vols (Oxford: Oxford University Press).

Freud, S. (1973) *New Introductory Lectures on Psychoanalysis* (Harmondsworth: Penguin).

Friedrich, R. (1996) 'Everything to do with Dionysus? Ritualism, the Dionysiac, and the tragic', in Silk, ed. (1996), pp. 257–83.

Furley, W. D. (2000) 'Fearless, bloodless . . . like the gods: Sappho 31 and the rhetoric of "godlike"', *Classical Quarterly* 50: 7–15.

Garlan, Y. (1988) *Slavery in Ancient Greece*, trans. J. Lloyd; revised and expanded edn (Ithaca: Cornell University Press).

Garnsey, P. (1996) *Ideas of Slavery from Aristotle to Augustine* (Cambridge: Cambridge University Press).

Garnsey, P. (1999) *Food and Society in Classical Antiquity* (Cambridge: Cambridge University Press).

Geertz, C. (1973) 'Deep play: notes on the Balinese cockfight', in *The Interpretation of Cultures* (New York: Basic Books), pp. 412–53.

Gentili, B. (1988) *Poetry and its Public in Ancient Greece: from Homer to the Fifth Century*, trans. A. T. Cole (Baltimore: Johns Hopkins University Press).

Gill, C. (1995) *Personality in Greek Epic, Tragedy, and Philosophy: The Self in Dialogue* (Oxford: Oxford University Press).

Gleason, M. W. (1995) *Making Men: Sophists and Self-presentation in Ancient Rome* (Princeton: Princeton University Press).

Golden, M. and Toohey, P., eds (1997) *Inventing Ancient Culture: Historicism, Periodization and the Ancient World* (London: Routledge).

Goldhill, S. (1986) *Reading Greek Tragedy* (Cambridge: Cambridge University Press).

Goldhill, S. (1987) 'The Great Dionysia and civic ideology', *Journal of Hellenic Studies* 107: 58–76; reprinted in Winkler and Zeitlin, eds (1990), pp. 97–129.

Goldhill, S. (1991) *The Poet's Voice: Essays on Poetics and Greek Literature* (Cambridge: Cambridge University Press).

Goldhill, S. (1994) 'Representing democracy: women at the Great Dionysia', in Osborne and Hornblower, eds (1994), pp. 347–69.

Goldhill, S. (1995) *Foucault's Virginity: Ancient Erotic Fiction and the History of Sexuality* (Cambridge: Cambridge University Press).

Goldhill, S. (1996) 'Collectivity and otherness: the authority of the tragic chorus. Response to Gould', in Silk ed. (1996), pp. 244–56.

Goldhill, S. (1997) 'The audience of Greek tragedy', in Easterling, ed. (1997), pp. 54–68

Goldhill, S. (2000) 'Civic ideology and the problem of difference: the politics of Aeschylean tragedy, once again', *Journal of Hellenic Studies* 120: 34–56.

Goldhill, S., ed. (2001) *Being Greek Under Rome: Cultural Identity, the Second Sophistic and the Development of Empire* (Cambridge: Cambridge University Press).

Goldhill, S. (2002a) *The Invention of Prose* (*Greece and Rome: New Surveys in the Classics*, no. 32; Oxford: Oxford University Press).

Goldhill, S. (2002b) *Who Needs Greek? Contests in the Cultural History of Hellenism* (Cambridge: Cambridge University Press).

Goldhill, S. and Osborne, R., eds (1999) *Performance Culture and Athenian Democracy* (Cambridge: Cambridge University Press).

Goody, J. (1982) *Cooking, Cuisine and Class* (Cambridge: Cambridge University Press).

Gould, J. (1989) *Herodotus* (London: Weidenfeld and Nicholson).

Gould, J. (1996) 'Tragedy and collective experience', in Silk, ed. (1996), pp. 217–43.

Graf, F. (1997) *Magic in the Ancient World*, trans. F. Philip (Cambridge, MA: Harvard University Press).

Graham, A. (1964) *Colony and Mother City in Ancient Greece* (Manchester: Manchester University Press).

Gray, V. (2001) 'Herodotus' literary and historical method: Arion's story (1.23–24)', *American Journal of Philology* 122: 11–28.

Graziosi, B. (2002) *Inventing Homer: The Early Reception of Epic* (Cambridge: Cambridge University Press).

Green, J. (1994) *Theatre in Ancient Greek Society* (London: Routledge).

Green, P., ed. (1993) *Hellenistic History and Culture* (Berkeley: University of California Press).

Greene, E., ed. (1996a) *Reading Sappho: Contemporary Approaches* (Berkeley: University of California Press).

Greene, E., ed. (1996b) *Rereading Sappho: Reception and Transmission* (Berkeley: University of California Press).

Greene, E. (2000) 'Playing with tradition: gender and innovation in the epigrams of Anyte', *Helios* 27: 15–32.

Greene, E. (2002) 'Subjects, objects and erotic symmetry in Sappho's fragments', in Rabinowitz and Auanger, eds (2002), pp. 82–105.

Gribble, D. (1999) *Alcibiades and Athens: A Study in Literary Presentation* (Oxford: Oxford University Press).

Griffin, J. (1995) *Homer*, Iliad *IX*, ed. with an Introduction and Commentary (Oxford: Oxford University Press).

Griffin, J. (1998) 'The social function of Attic tragedy', *Classical Quarterly* 48: 39–61.

Griffith, M. (1998) 'The king and eye: the rule of the father in Greek tragedy', *Proceedings of the Cambridge Philological Society* 44: 20–84.

Groningen, B. A. van (1965) 'General literary tendencies in the second century AD', *Mnemosyne* 18: 41–56.

Gruen, E. (1984) *The Hellenistic World and the Coming of Rome*, 2 vols (Berkeley: University of California Press).

Gutzwiller, K. (1998) *Poetic Garlands: Hellenistic Epigrams in Context* (Berkeley: University of California Press).

Habicht, C. (1985) *Pausanias' Guide to Ancient Greece* (Berkeley: University of California Press).

Hall, E. (1989) *Inventing the Barbarian: Greek Self-Definition through Tragedy* (Oxford: Oxford University Press).

Hall, E. (1995) 'Lawcourt dramas: the power of performance in Greek forensic oratory', *Bulletin of the Institute of Classical Studies* 40: 39–58.

Hall, E. (1997) 'The sociology of Athenian tragedy', in Easterling, ed. (1997), pp. 93–126.

Hall, J. (1997) *Ethnic Identity in Greek Antiquity* (Cambridge: Cambridge University Press).

Hall, J. (2001) 'Contested ethnicities: perceptions of Macedonia within evolving definitions of Greek identity', in Malkin, ed. (2001), pp. 159–86.

Hall, J. (2002) *Hellenicity: Between Ethnicity and Culture* (Chicago: University of Chicago Press).

Hall, S. (1990) 'Cultural identity and diaspora', in J. Rutherford, ed., *Identity: Community, Culture, Difference* (London: Lawrence and Wishart), pp. 222–37.

Hall, S. (1992) 'The question of cultural identity', in S. Hall, D. Held and A. McGrew, eds, *Modernity and its Futures* (Cambridge: Polity), pp. 273–316.

References

Hall, S. and du Gay, P., eds (1996) *Questions of Cultural Identity* (London: Thousand Oaks).

Hallett, J. (1993) 'Feminist theory, historical periods, literary canons, and the study of Greco-Roman antiquity', in Rabinowitz and Richlin, eds (1993), pp. 44–72.

Halperin, D. (1983) *Before Pastoral: Theocritus and the Ancient Tradition of Bucolic Poetry* (New Haven: Yale University Press).

Halperin, D. (1985) 'Platonic *eros* and what men call love', *Ancient Philosophy* 5: 161–204.

Halperin, D. (1986) 'Plato and erotic reciprocity', *Classical Antiquity* 5: 60–80.

Halperin, D. (1990a) *A Hundred Years of Homosexuality, and Other Essays on Greek Love* (New York: Routledge).

Halperin, D. (1990b) 'Why is Diotima a woman?', in Halperin et al., eds (1990), pp. 256–308; also in Halperin (1990a), pp. 113–51.

Halperin, D. (1992) 'Plato and the erotics of narrativity', in R. Hexter and D. Selden, eds, *Innovations of Antiquity* (New York: Routledge), pp. 95–126.

Halperin, D., Winkler, J. and Zeitlin, F., eds (1990) *Before Sexuality: The Construction of Erotic Experience in the Ancient Greek World* (Princeton: Princeton University Press).

Hammond, N. G. L. and Scullard, H. H., eds (1970) *The Oxford Classical Dictionary*, 2nd edn (Oxford: Oxford University Press).

Hanson, A. (1990) 'The medical writers' woman', in Halperin et al., eds (1990), pp. 209–337.

Hanson, V. and Heath, J. (1998) *Who Killed Homer? The Demise of Classical Education and the Recovery of Greek Wisdom* (New York: Free Press).

Harder, M. A., Regtuit, R. and Wakker, G., eds (1993) *Callimachus* (Groningen: Egbert Forsten).

Harder, M. A., Regtuit, R. and Wakker, G., eds (1998) *Genre in Hellenistic Poetry* (Groningen: Egbert Forsten).

Harder, M. A., Regtuit, R. and Wakker, G., eds (2000) *Apollonius Rhodius* (Leuven: Peeters).

Harding, P. (1987) 'Rhetoric and politics in fourth-century Athens', *Phoenix* 41: 25–39.

Hardwick, L. (2000) *Translating Words, Translating Cultures* (London: Duckworth).

Harrison, T. (2000) *Divinity and History: The Religion of Herodotus* (Oxford: Oxford University Press).

Harrison, T., ed. (2001) *Greeks and Barbarians* (Edinburgh: Edinburgh University Press).

Hartog, F. (1988) *The Mirror of Herodotus: The Representation of the Other in the Writing of History*, trans. J. Lloyd (Berkeley: University of California Press).

Hartog, F. (2001) *Memories of Odysseus: Frontier Tales from Ancient Greece*, trans. Janet Lloyd (Edinburgh: Edinburgh University Press).

Haubold, J. (2000) *Homer's People: Epic Poetry and Social Formation* (Cambridge: Cambridge University Press).

Haubold, J. (2002) 'Greek epic: a Near-Eastern genre?', *Proceedings of the Cambridge Philological Society* 48: 1–19.

Hawley, R. and Levick, B., eds (1995) *Women in Antiquity: New Assessments* (London: Routledge).

Haynes, K. (2002) *Fashioning the Feminine in the Greek Novel* (London: Routledge).

Hemelrijk, E. A. (1999) *Matrona Docta: Educated Women in the Roman Elite from Cornelia to Julia Domna* (London: Routledge).

Henderson, J. (1980) '*Lysistrata*: the play and its themes', *Yale Classical Studies* 26: 153–218.

Henderson, J. (1990) 'The *demos* and the comic competition', in Winkler and Zeitlin, eds (1990), pp. 271–313.

Henderson, J. (1991a) *The Maculate Muse: Obscene Language in Attic Comedy*, 2nd edn (New York: Oxford University Press).

Henderson, J. (1991b) 'Women and the Athenian dramatic festivals', *Transactions of the American Philological Society* 121: 133–47.

Henderson, J. G. W. (2000) 'The life and soul of the party: Plato's *Symposium*', in A. Sharrock and H. Morales, eds, *Intratextuality: Greek and Roman Textual Relations* (Oxford: Oxford University Press), pp. 287–324.

Henrichs, A. (1994/5) '"Why should I dance?": choral self-referentiality in Greek tragedy', *Arion* 3: 56–111.

Herman, G. (1993) 'Tribal and civic codes of behaviour in Lysias I', *Classical Quarterly* 43: 406–19.

Herzfeld, M. (1985) *The Poetics of Manhood: Contest and Identity in a Cretan Mountain Village* (Princeton: Princeton University Press).

Hesk, J. (2000) *Deception and Democracy in Classical Athens* (Cambridge: Cambridge University Press).

Hexter, R. (1991) 'Scholars and their pals', *Helios* 18: 147–59.

Hobsbawm, E. and Ranger, T., eds (1983) *The Invention of Tradition* (Cambridge: Cambridge University Press).

Holst-Warhaft, G. (1995) *Dangerous Voices: Women's Laments and Greek Literature* (London: Routledge).

Holzberg, N. (1988) 'Lucian and the Germans', in A. C. Dionisotti, A. Grafton and J. Kraye, eds, *The Uses of Greek and Latin: Historical Essays* (London: Warburg Institute), pp. 199–209.

Hopkinson, N. (1984) 'Callimachus' *Hymn to Zeus*', *Classical Quarterly* 34: 139–48.

Hornblower, S. (1987) *Thucydides* (London: Duckworth).

Hornblower, S. and Spawforth, A., eds (1996) *The Oxford Classical Dictionary*, 3rd edn (Oxford: Oxford University Press).

Hubbard, T. (1998) *The Pipes of Pan: Intertextuality and Literary Filiation in the Pastoral Tradition from Theocritus to Milton* (Ann Arbor: University of Michigan Press).

Hubbard, T. (2003) *Homosexuality in Greece and Rome: A Source-book* (Berkeley: University of California Press).

Hunt, L., ed. (1989) *The New Cultural History* (Berkeley: University of California Press).

Hunter, R. (1983) *A Study of* Daphnis and Chloe (Cambridge: Cambridge University Press).

Hunter, R. (1985) *The New Comedy of Greece and Rome* (Cambridge: Cambridge University Press).

Hunter, R. (1992) 'Writing the god: form and meaning in Callimachus, *Hymn to Athena*', *Materiali e discussioni per l'analisi dei testi classici* 29: 9–34.

Hunter, R. (1993) *The* Argonautica *of Apollonius: Literary Studies* (Cambridge: Cambridge University Press).

Hunter, R. (1996) *Theocritus and the Archaeology of Greek Poetry* (Cambridge: Cambridge University Press).

Hunter, R. (2003) 'Literature and its contexts', in Erskine, ed. (2003), 477–93.

Hunter, R. and Fuhrer, T. (2002) 'Imaginary gods? Poetic theology in the *Hymns* of Callimachus', in Lehnus, ed. (2002), pp. 143–75.

Hunter, V. (1973) *Thucydides the Artful Reporter* (Toronto: Hakkert).

Hunter, V. (1994) *Policing Athens: Social Control in the Attic Lawsuits, 420–320 BC* (Princeton: Princeton University Press).

Hutchinson, G. (1988) *Hellenistic Poetry* (Oxford: Oxford University Press).

Jacob, C. (1980) 'The Greek traveler's areas of knowledge: myths and other discourses in Pausanias' *Description of Greece*', *Yale French Studies* 59: 65–85.

Jeanneret, M. (1991) *A Feast of Words: Banquets and Table-talk in the Renaissance*, trans. J. Whiteley and E. Hughes (Chicago: University of Chicago Press).

Jenkyns, R. (1980) *The Victorians and Ancient Greece* (Oxford: Blackwell).

Jones, C. (1978) *The Roman World of Dio Chrysostom* (Cambridge, MA: Harvard University Press).

Jones, C. (1986) *Culture and Society in Lucian* (Cambridge, MA: Harvard University Press).

Kappeler, S. (1986) *The Pornography of Representation* (Cambridge: Polity Press).

Katz, A. (1991) *Penelope's Renown: Meaning and Indeterminacy in the* Odyssey (Princeton: Princeton University Press).

Kennedy, D. (1993) *The Arts of Love: Five Studies in the Discourse of Roman Love Elegy* (Cambridge: Cambridge University Press).

Kennedy, G. (1994) *A New History of Classical Rhetoric* (Princeton: Princeton University Press).

Kerferd, G. (1981) *The Sophistic Movement* (Cambridge: Cambridge University Press).

Keuls, E. (1993) *The Reign of the Phallus: Sexual Politics in Ancient Athens*, 2nd edn (Berkeley: University of California Press).

Kilmer, M. (1993) *Greek Erotica on Attic Red-figure Vases* (London: Duckworth).

Knox, B. (1952) 'The *Hippolytus* of Euripides', *Yale Classical Studies* 13: 3–31; reprinted in Knox (1979), pp. 205–30; also in Segal, ed. (1983), pp. 311–31.

Knox, B. (1964) *The Heroic Temper: Studies in Sophoclean Tragedy* (Berkeley: University of California Press).

Knox, B. (1968) 'Silent reading in antiquity', *Greek, Roman and Byzantine Studies* 9: 421–33.

Knox, B. (1977) 'The *Medea* of Euripides', *Yale Classical Studies* 25: 193–225; reprinted in Knox (1979), pp. 295–322; and in Segal, ed. (1983), pp. 272–93.

Knox, B. (1979) *Word and Action: Essays on the Ancient Theatre* (Baltimore: Johns Hopkins University Press).

König, J. P. (2001) 'Favorinus' *Corinthian Oration* in its Corinthian context', *Proceedings of the Cambridge Philological Society* 47: 141–71.

Konstan, D. (1993) 'Women and the body politic: the representation of women in Aristophanes' *Lysistrata*', in Sommerstein and Halliwell, eds (1993), pp. 431–44.

Konstan, D. (1994) *Sexual Symmetry: Love in the Ancient Novel and Related Genres* (Princeton: Princeton University Press).

Konstan, D. (1995) *Greek Comedy and Ideology* (New York: Oxford University Press).

Kraut, R. (1984) *Socrates and the State* (Princeton: Princeton University Press).

Krevans, N. (2000) 'On the margins of epic: the foundation poems of Apollonius', in Harder et al., eds (2000), pp. 69–84.

Kristeva, J. (1982) *Powers of Horror: An Essay on Abjection*, trans. L. Roudiez (New York: Columbia University Press).

Kurke, L. (1991) *The Traffic in Praise: Pindar and the Poetics of Social Economy* (Ithaca: Cornell University Press).

Kurke, L. (1999) *Coins, Bodies, Games, and Gold: The Politics of Meaning in Archaic Greece* (Princeton: Princeton University Press).

Lada, I. (1993) '"Empathetic understanding": emotion and cognition in classical dramatic audience response', *Proceedings of the Cambridge Philological Society* 39: 94–140.

Lada, I. (1996) 'Emotion and meaning in tragic drama', in Silk, ed. (1996), pp. 397–413.

Lamberton, R. (1988) *Hesiod* (New Haven: Yale University Press).

Lamberton, R. (1989) *Homer the Theologian: Neoplatonist Allegorical Reading and the Growth of the Epic Tradition* (Berkeley: University of California Press).

Lamberton, R. and Kearney, J. J. (1992) *Homer's Ancient Readers: The Hermeneutics of Greek Epic's Earliest Exegetes* (Princeton: Princeton University Press).

Laqueur, T. (1990) *Making Sex: Body and Gender from the Greeks to Freud* (Cambridge, MA: Harvard University Press).

Lardinois, A. (1991) 'Lesbian Sappho and Sappho of Lesbos', in J. Bremmer, ed., *From Sappho to de Sade: Moments in the History of Sexuality* (London: Routledge), pp. 15–35.

Lardinois, A. and McClure, L., eds (2001) *Making Silence Speak: Women's Voices in Greek Literature and Society* (Princeton: Princeton University Press).

Lateiner, D. (1989) *The Historical Method of Herodotus* (Toronto: University of Toronto Press).

Lauretis, T. de (1984) *Alice Doesn't: Feminism, Semiotics, Cinema* (London: Macmillan).

Lefkowitz, M. (1981) *The Lives of the Greek Poets* (London: Duckworth).

Lefkowitz, M. (1996) *Not Out of Africa: How Afrocentrism Became an Excuse to Teach Myth as History* (New York: Basic Books).

Lefkowitz, M. and Rogers, G., eds (1996) *Black Athena Revisited* (Chapel Hill: University of North Carolina Press).

Lehnus, L., ed. (2002) *Callimaque* (Geneva: Entretiens de la Fondation Hardt pour l'Étude de l'Antiquité Classique).

Lévi-Strauss, C. (1963) *Structural Anthropology*, trans. C. Jacobson and B. G. Schoepf (New York: Basic Books).

Levine, D. B. (1985) 'Symposium and the *polis*', in T. Figueira and G. Nagy, eds, *Theognis of Megara: Poetry and the Polis* (Baltimore: Johns Hopkins University Press), pp. 176–96.

Levine, D. (1987) '*Lysistrata* and *Bacchae*: structure, genre, and "women on top"', *Helios* 14: 29–38.

Lewis, S. (2002) *The Athenian Woman: An Iconographic Handbook* (London: Routledge).

Lissarrague, F. (1990a) 'The sexual life of satyrs', in Halperin et al., eds (1990), pp. 53–81.

Lissarrague, F. (1990b) 'Why satyrs are good to represent', in Winkler and Zeitlin, eds (1990), pp. 228–36.

Lissarrague, F. (1990c) *The Aesthetics of the Greek Banquet: Images of Wine and Ritual*, trans. Andrew Szegedy-Maszak (Princeton: Princeton University Press).

Livingstone, N. (1998) 'The voice of Isocrates and the dissemination of cultural power', in Y. L. Too and N. Livingstone, eds, *Pedagogy and Power: Rhetorics of Classical Learning* (Cambridge: Cambridge University Press), pp. 263–81.

Lloyd, G. (1979) *Magic, Reason and Experience* (Cambridge: Cambridge University Press).

Lloyd, G. (1987) *The Revolutions of Wisdom: Studies in the Claims and Practice of Ancient Greek Science* (Berkeley: University of California Press).

Lloyd-Jones, H. and Parsons, P., eds (1983) *Supplementum Hellenisticum* (Berlin).

Loraux, N. (1978) 'On the race of women and some of its tribes: Hesiod and Semonides', *Arethusa* 11: 43–87; reprinted in Loraux (1993), pp. 72–110.

Loraux, N. (1980–1) 'The comic acropolis: Aristophanes, *Lysistrata*', *Ancient Society* 11–12: 119–50; reprinted in Loraux (1993), pp. 147–83.

Loraux, N. (1986) *The Invention of Athens: The Funeral Oration in the Classical City*, trans. A. Sheridan (Cambridge, MA: Harvard University Press).

Loraux, N. (1993) *The Children of Athena: Athenian Ideas about Citizenship and the Division Between the Sexes*, trans. C. Levine (Princeton: Princeton University Press).

Lord, A. (2000) *The Singer of Tales*, 2nd edn (Cambridge, MA: Harvard University Press).

Lutz, C. E. (1947) 'Musonius Rufus, the Roman Socrates', *Yale Classical Studies* 10: 3–147.

Lyne, O. (1987) *Further Voices in Virgil's* Aeneid (Oxford: Oxford University Press).

Maas, P. (1958) *Textual Criticism* (Oxford: Oxford University Press).

Malkin, I. (1998) *The Returns of Odysseus: Colonization and Ethnicity* (Berkeley: University of California Press).

Malkin, I., ed. (2001) *Ancient Perceptions of Greek Ethnicity* (Cambridge, MA: Harvard University Press).

Manguel, A. (1996) *A History of Reading* (London: HarperCollins).

Martin, R. (1989) *The Language of Heroes: Speech and Performance in the* Iliad (Ithaca: Cornell University Press).

Martin, R. (1993) 'The seven sages as performers of wisdom', in Dougherty and Kurke, eds (1993), pp. 108–28.

Martindale, C. (1993) *Redeeming the Text: Latin Poetry and the Hermeneutics of Reception* (Cambridge: Cambridge University Press).

McClure, L. (1999) *Spoken like a Woman: Speech and Gender in Athenian Drama* (Princeton: Princeton University Press).

McClure, L., ed. (2002) *Sexuality and Gender in the Classical World: Readings and Sources* (Oxford: Oxford University Press).

Moi, T. (1985) *Sexual/Textual Politics* (London: Methuen).

Morgan, J. and Stoneman, R., eds (1994) *Greek Fiction: The Greek Novel in Context* (London: Routledge).

Morris, I. and Powell, B., eds (1996) *A New Companion to Homer* (Leiden: Brill).

Most, G. (1995) 'Reflecting Sappho', *Bulletin of the Institute of Classical Studies* 40: 15–38; reprinted in Greene, ed. (1996b), pp. 11–35.

Most, G., ed. (1998) *Editing Texts = Texte edieren* (Göttingen: Vandenhoeck and Ruprecht).

Mulvey, L. (1975) 'Visual pleasure and narrative cinema', *Screen* 16: 6–18.

Mulvey, L. (1989) *Visual and Other Pleasures* (Basingstoke: Macmillan).

Murnaghan, S. (1987) *Disguise and Recognition in the* Odyssey (Princeton: Princeton University Press).

Murray, O., ed. (1990) *Sympotica: A Symposium on the Symposium* (Oxford: Oxford University Press).

Murray, O. (1993) *Early Greece*, 2nd edn (London: Fontana).

Musurillo, H., ed. (1954) *Acts of the Pagan Martyrs* (Oxford: Oxford University Press).

Nagy, G. (1979) *The Best of the Achaeans: Concepts of the Hero in Archaic Greek Poetry* (Baltimore: Johns Hopkins University Press).

Nagy, G. (1985) 'Theognis and Megara: a poet's vision of his city', in Figueira and Nagy, eds (1985), pp. 22–81.

Nagy, G. (1987) 'Herodotus the *logios*', *Arethusa* 20: 175–84.

Nagy, G. (1990) *Greek Mythology and Poetics* (Ithaca: Cornell University Press).

Nagy, G. (1996) *Poetry as Performance: Homer and Beyond* (Cambridge: Cambridge University Press).

Nevett, L. (1999) *House and Society in the Ancient Greek World* (Cambridge: Cambridge University Press).

Nietzsche, F. (1993) *The Birth of Tragedy: Out of the Spirit of Music*, trans. S. Whiteside (Harmondsworth: Penguin).

Nussbaum, M. (2002) 'The incomplete feminism of Musonius Rufus – Platonist, Stoic, and Roman', in Nussbaum and Sihvola, eds (2002), pp. 283–326.

Nussbaum, M. and Sihvola, J., eds (2002) *The Sleep of Reason: Erotic Experience and Sexual Ethics in Ancient Greece and Rome* (Chicago: Chicago University Press).

Ober, J. (1989) *Mass and Elite in Democratic Athens: Rhetoric, Ideology and the Power of the People* (Princeton: Princeton University Press).

Ober, J. (1994) 'Power and oratory in democratic Athens: Demosthenes 21, *Against Meidias*', in Worthington, ed. (1994), pp. 85–108.

Ober, J. and Strauss, B. (1990) 'Drama, political rhetoric and the discourse of Athenian democracy', in Winkler and Zeitlin, eds (1990), pp. 237–70.

Olender, M. (1990) 'Aspects of Baubo: ancient texts and contexts', in Halperin et al., eds (1990), pp. 83–113.

Omitowoju, R. (2002) *Rape and the Politics of Consent in Classical Athens* (Cambridge: Cambridge University Press).

Osborne, R. (1985) 'Law and action in classical Athens', *Journal of Hellenic Studies* 105: 40–58.

Osborne, R. (1996) *Greece in the Making* (London: Routledge).

Osborne, R., ed. (2000) *Classical Greece* (Oxford: Oxford University Press).

Osborne, R. (2002) 'The use of abuse: Semonides 7', *Proceedings of the Cambridge Philological Society* 47: 47–64.

Osborne, R. and Hornblower, S. eds. (1994) *Ritual, Finance, Politics: Athenian Democratic Accounts Presented to David Lewis* (Oxford: Oxford University Press).

Ostwald, M. (1969) *Nomos and the Beginnings of Athenian Democracy* (Oxford: Oxford University Press).

Ostwald, M. (1992) 'Athens as a cultural centre', *The Cambridge Ancient History*, 2nd edn (Cambridge: Cambridge University Press), vol. 5, pp. 306–69.

Padel, R. (1990) 'Making space speak', in Winkler and Zeitlin, eds (1990), pp. 336–65.

Padel, R. (1992) *In and Out of the Mind: Greek Images of the Tragic Self* (Princeton: Princeton University Press).

Padel, R. (1995) *Whom Gods Destroy: Elements of Greek and Tragic Madness* (Princeton: Princeton University Press).

Page, D., ed. (1981) *Further Greek Epigrams* (Cambridge: Cambridge University Press).

Papanghelis, T. and Rengakos, A., eds (2001) *A Companion to Apollonius Rhodius* (Leiden: Brill).

Parker, H. (1993) 'Sappho schoolmistress', *Transactions of the American Philological Association* 123: 309–51; reprinted in Greene, ed. (1996b), pp. 146–83.

Parks, W. (1990) *Verbal Dueling in Heroic Narrative: The Homeric and Old English Traditions* (Princeton: Princeton University Press).

Paskiewicz, T. (1988) '*Aitia* in the second book of Apollonius' *Argonautica*', *Illinois Classical Studies* 13: 57–61.

Patterson, C. (1981) *Pericles' Citizenship Law of 451–450 BC* (New York: Arno Press).

Patterson, C. (1986) '*Hai Attikai*: the other Athenians', *Helios* 13: 49–67.

Patterson, O. (1982) *Slavery and Social Death: A Comparative Study* (Cambridge, MA: Harvard University Press).

Pelling, C. (1989) 'Plutarch: Roman heroes and Greek culture', in M. Griffin and J. Barnes, eds, *Philosophia Togata: Essays on Philosophy and Roman Society* (Oxford: Oxford University Press), pp. 199–232.

Pelling, C., ed. (1997) *Greek Tragedy and the Historian* (Oxford: Oxford University Press).

Penwill, J. (1978) 'Men in love: aspects of Plato's *Symposium*', *Ramus* 7: 143–75.

Peradotto, J. and O'Sullivan, J., eds (1984) *Women in the Ancient World* (Albany: State University of New York Press).

Percy, W. (1996) *Pederasty and Pedagogy in Archaic Greece* (Urbana: University of Ilinois Press).

Perkins, J. (1995) *The Suffering Self: Pain and Narrative Representation in Early Christianity* (London: Routledge).

Perry, B. (1967) *The Ancient Romances: A Literary-Historical Account of their Origins* (Berkeley: University of California Press).

Pfeiffer, R. (1968) *A History of Classical Scholarship from the Beginnings to the End of the Hellenistic Age* (Oxford: Oxford University Press).

Pickard-Cambridge, A. (1988) *The Dramatic Festivals of Athens*, revised by J. Gould and D. Lewis (Oxford: Oxford University Press).

Pomeroy, S. (1975) *Goddesses, Whores, Wives and Slaves: Women in Classical Antiquity* (New York: Schocken Books).

Pomeroy, S., ed. (1991) *Women's History and Ancient History* (Chapel Hill: University of North Carolina Press).

Pomeroy, S. (1994) *Xenophon, Oeconomicus: A Social and Historical Commentary* (Oxford: Oxford University Press).

Poole, W. (1990) 'Male Homosexuality in Euripides', in Powell, ed. (1990), pp. 108–50.

Porter, J. R. (1997) 'Adultery by the book: Lysias 1 (*On the Murder of Eratosthenes*) and comic *diegesis*', *Échos du monde classique* 41: 421–54.

Porter, J., ed. (1999) *Constructions of the Classical Body* (Ann Arbor: University of Michigan Press).

Porter, J. (2002) 'Homer: the very idea', *Arion* 10: 57–87.

Porter, J., ed. (forthcoming) *Classical Pasts: Classicism in Greco-Roman Antiquity* (Princeton: Princeton University Press).

Postlethwaite, N. (1998) 'Thersites in the *Iliad*', *G&R* 35: 123–36.

Powell, A., ed. (1990) *Euripides, Women and Sexuality* (London: Routledge).

Powell, J., ed. (1925) *Collectanea Alexandrina* (Oxford: Oxford University Press).

Pratt, M. L. (1992) *Imperial Eyes: Travel and Transculturation* (London: Routledge).

Prendergast, C. (1985) *The Order of Mimesis: Balzac, Stendhal, Nerval, Flaubert* (Cambridge: Cambridge University Press).

Prins, Y. (1999) *Victorian Sappho* (Princeton: Princeton University Press).

Pucci, P. (1977) *Hesiod and the Language of Poetry* (Baltimore: Johns Hopkins University Press).

Pucci, P. (1980) *The Violence of Pity in Euripides'* Medea (Ithaca: Cornell University Press).

Rabinowitz, N. (1993) *Anxiety Veiled: Euripides and the Traffic in Women* (Ithaca: Cornell University Press).

Rabinowitz, N. (2002) 'Introduction', in Rabinowitz and Auanger, eds (2002), pp. 1–33.

Rabinowitz, N. and Auanger, L., eds (2002) *Among Women: From the Homosocial to the Homoerotic in the Ancient World* (Austin: University of Texas Press).

Rabinowitz, N. and Richlin, A., eds (1993) *Feminist Theory and the Classics* (London: Routledge).

Rayor, D. (1991) *Sappho's Lyre: Archaic Lyric and Women Poets of Ancient Greece* (Berkeley: University of California Press).

Redfield, J. (1990) 'Drama and community: Aristophanes and some of his rivals', in Winkler and Zeitlin, eds (1990): 314–35.

Redfield, J. (1994) *Nature and Culture in the* Iliad: *The Tragedy of Hector*, expanded edn (Durham, NC: Duke University Press).

Rehm, R. (1994) *Greek Tragic Theatre* (London: Routledge).

Relihan, J. (1992) 'Rethinking the history of the literary symposium', *Ilinois Classical Studies* 17: 213–44.

Reynolds, L. and Wilson, N. (1991) *Scribes and Scholars: A Guide to the Transmission of Greek and Latin Literature*, 3rd edn (Oxford: Oxford University Press).

Rhodes, P. J. (1986) 'Political activity in classical Athens', *Journal of Hellenic Studies* 106: 132–44.

Rice, E. (1983) *The Grand Procession of Ptolemy Philadelphus* (Oxford: Oxford University Press).

Richlin, A., ed. (1992) *Pornography and Representation in Greece and Rome* (New York: Oxford University Press).

Richlin, A. (1993) 'Not before homosexuality: the materiality of the *cinaedus* and the Roman law against love between men', *Journal of the History of Sexuality* 3: 523–73.

Rissman, L. (1983) *Love as War: Homeric Allusion in the Poetry of Sappho* (Königstein: A. Hain).

Romeo, I. (2002) 'The Panhellenion and ethnic identity', *Classical Philology* 97: 21–40.

Romm, J. (1991) *The Edges of the Earth in Ancient Thought* (Princeton: Princeton University Press).

Romm, J. (1998) *Herodotus* (New Haven: Yale University Press).

Rood, T. (1998) *Thucydides: Narrative and Explanation* (Oxford: Oxford University Press).

Rose, P. (1992) 'Thersites and the plural voices of the *Iliad*', *Arethusa* 21: 5–25.

Rose, P. (1997) 'Ideology in the *Iliad*: *polis, basileus, theoi*', *Arethusa* 30: 151–99.

Rosenmeyer, P. (1992) *The Poetics of Imitation: Anacreon and the Anacreontic Tradition* (Cambridge: Cambridge University Press).

Rosenmeyer, P. (2001) *Ancient Epistolary Fictions: The Letter in Greek Literature* (Cambridge: Cambridge University Press).

Rosenmeyer, T. G. (1982) 'History or poetry? The example of Herodotus', *Clio* 11: 239–59.

Rosivach, V. (1998) *When a Young Man Falls in Love: The Sexual Exploitation of Women in New Comedy* (London: Routledge).

Russo, C. (1997) *Aristophanes: An Author for the Stage* (London: Routledge).

Rutherford, R. (1989) *The Meditations of Marcus Aurelius: A Study* (Oxford: Oxford University Press).

Said, E. (1978) *Orientalism: Western Conceptions of the Orient* (London: Routledge and Kegan Paul).

Said, E. (1995) *Orientalism: Western Conceptions of the Orient*, with a new afterword (London: Penguin).

Saïd, S. and Trédé, M. (1999) *A Short History of Greek Literature*, trans. T. Selous and others (London: Routledge).

Schäfer, P. (1992) *Judeophobia: Attitudes Towards Jews in the Ancient World* (Cambridge, MA: Harvard University Press).

Schaps, D. (1977) 'The woman least mentioned: etiquette and women's names', *Classical Quarterly* 27: 323–30.

Schein, S., ed. (1996) *Reading the* Odyssey: *Selected Interpretative Essays* (Princeton: Princeton University Press).

Schmeling, G., ed. (1996) *The Novel in the Ancient World* (Leiden: Brill).

Schmitz, T. (1999) ' "I hate all common things": the reader's role in Callimachus' *Aetia* prologue', *Harvard Studies in Classical Philology* 99: 151–78.

Scodel, R., ed. (1993) *Theater and Society in the Classical World* (Ann Arbor: University of Michigan Press).

Scully, S. (1981) 'The polis in Homer: a definition and interpretation', *Ramus* 10: 1–34.

Seaford, R. (1981) 'Dionysiac drama and the Dionysiac mysteries', *Classical Quarterly* 31: 252–75.

Seaford, R. (1994) *Reciprocity and Ritual: Homer and Tragedy in the Developing City-state* (Oxford: Oxford University Press).

Seaford, R. (1996) 'Something to do with Dionysus: tragedy and the Dionysiac. Response to Friedrich', in Silk, ed. (1996), pp. 284–94.

Seaford, R. (2000) 'The social function of Attic tragedy: a response to Jasper Griffin', *Classical Quarterly* 50: 30–44.

Seaford, R. (2004) *Money and the Early Greek Mind: Homer, Philosophy, Tragedy* (Cambridge: Cambridge University Press).

Sealey, R. (1993) *Demosthenes and his Time: A Study in Defeat* (New York: Oxford University Press).

Sedgwick, E. (1991) *The Epistemology of the Closet* (New York: Harvester Wheatsheaf).

Segal, C. (1964) 'Sophocles' praise of man and the conflicts of the *Antigone*', *Arion* 3: 46–66.

Segal, C. (1965) 'The tragedy of the *Hippolytus*: the waters of ocean and the untouched meadow', *Harvard Studies in Classical Philology* 70: 117–69; reprinted in Segal (1986), pp. 165–221.

Segal, C. (1981a) *Tragedy and Civilisation: An Interpretation of Sophocles* (Cambridge, MA: Harvard University Press).

Segal, C. (1981b) *Poetry and Myth in Ancient Pastoral* (Princeton: Princeton University Press).

Segal, C. (1986) *Pindar's Mythmaking: The Fourth Pythian Ode* (Princeton: Princeton University Press).

Segal, C. (1997) *Dionysiac Poetics and Euripides'* Bacchae, 2nd edn (Princeton: Princeton University Press).

Segal, E., ed. (1983) *Oxford Readings in Greek Tragedy* (Oxford: Oxford University Press).

Selden, D. (1998) 'Alibis', *Classical Antiquity* 17: 299–412.

Shaw, M. (1975) 'The female intruder: women in fifth-century drama', *Classical Philology* 90: 255–66.

Shear, L. (1981) 'Athens: from city-state to provincial town', *Hesperia* 50: 356–77.

Shipley, G. (2000) *The Greek World after Alexander* (London: Routledge).

Silk, M., ed. (1996) *Tragedy and the Tragic* (Oxford: Oxford University Press).

Silk, M. (2000) *Aristophanes and the Definition of Comedy* (Oxford: Oxford University Press).

Skinner, M. (1989) 'Sapphic Nossis', *Arethusa* 22: 5–18.

Skinner, M. (2002) 'Aphrodite garlanded: *Eros* and poetic creativity in Sappho and Nossis', in Rabinowitz and Auanger, eds (2002), pp. 60–81.

Slater, W., ed. (1991) *Dining in a Classical Context* (Ann Arbor: University of Michigan Press).

Smart, J. (1986) 'Thucydides and Hellanicus', in I. Moxon, J. Smart and A. Woodman, eds, *Past Perspectives: Studies in Greek and Roman Historical Writing* (Cambridge: Cambridge University Press), pp. 19–36.

Snodgrass, A. (1980) *Archaic Greece: The Age of Experiment* (London: Dent).

Snyder, J. (1989) *The Woman and the Lyre: Women Writers in Classical Greece and Rome* (Bristol: Bristol Classical Press).

Snyder, J. (1997) *Lesbian Desire in the Lyrics of Sappho* (New York: Columbia University Press).

Sommerstein, A. and Halliwell, S. eds. (1993) *Tragedy, Comedy and the Polis: Papers from the Greek Drama Conference, Nottingham 18–20 July 1990* (Bari: Levante).

Sourvinou-Inwood, C. (1989) 'Assumptions and the creation of meaning: reading Sophocles' *Antigone*', *Journal of Hellenic Studies* 109: 134–48.

Sourvinou-Inwood, C. (1994) 'Something to do with Athens: tragedy and ritual', in Osborne and Hornblower, eds (1994), pp. 269–89.

Stadter, P. A. (1980) *Arrian of Nicomedia* (Chapel Hill: University of North Carolina Press).

Stehle, E. (1997) *Performance and Gender in Ancient Greece: Nondramatic Poetry in its Setting* (Princeton: Princeton University Press).

Stehle, E. (2001) 'The good daughter: mothers' tutelage in Erinna's *Distaff* and fourth-century epitaphs', in Lardinois and McClure, eds (2001), pp. 179–200.

Steiner, G. (1984) *Antigones* (Oxford: Oxford University Press).

Stephens, S. (1994) 'Who read ancient novels?' in Tatum, ed. (1994), pp. 405–18.

Stephens, S. (2003) *Seeing Double: Intercultural Poetics in Ptolemaic Alexandria* (Berkeley: University of California Press).

Stigers, E. (1981) 'Sappho's private world', in Foley, ed. (1981), pp. 45–61.

Stray, C. (1998) *Classics Transformed: Schools, Universities, and Society in England, 1830–1960* (Oxford: Oxford University Press).

Swain, S. (1990) 'Hellenic culture and the Roman heroes of Plutarch', *Journal of Hellenic Studies* 110: 126–45; reprinted in B. Scardigli, ed., *Essays on Plutarch's Lives* (Oxford: Oxford University Press, 1995), pp. 229–64.

Swain, S. (1996) *Hellenism and Empire: Language, Classicism, and Power in the Greek World*, AD 50–250 (Oxford: Oxford University Press).

Swain, S., ed. (1999) *Oxford Readings in the Greek Novel* (Oxford: Oxford University Press).

Swain, S., ed. (2001) *Dio Chrysostom: Politics, Philosophy, Letters* (Oxford: Oxford University Press).

Taaffe, L. (1993) *Aristophanes and Women* (London: Routledge).

Tanner, T. (1979) *Adultery and the Novel: Contract and Transgression* (Baltimore: Johns Hopkins University Press).

Taplin, O. (1977) *The Stagecraft of Aeschylus* (Oxford: Oxford University Press).

Taplin, O. (1978) *Greek Tragedy in Action* (London: Methuen).

Taplin, O. (1993) *Comic Angels and Other Approaches to Greek Drama Through Vase-painting* (Oxford: Oxford University Press).

Taplin, O. (1999) 'Spreading the word through performance', in Goldhill and Osborne, eds (1999), pp. 33–57.

Taplin, O., ed. (2001) *Literature in the Greek World* (Oxford: Oxford University Press).

Tatum, J., ed. (1994) *The Search for the Ancient Novel* (Baltimore: Johns Hopkins University Press).

Thalmann, W. (1988) 'Thersites: comedy, scapegoats, and heroic ideology in the *Iliad*', *Transactions of the American Philological Association* 118: 1–28.

Thalmann, W. (1998) *The Swineherd and the Bow: Representations of Class in the* Odyssey (Ithaca: Cornell University Press).

Thomas, R. (1989) *Oral Tradition and Written Record in Classical Athens* (Cambridge: Cambridge University Press).

Thomas, R. (1992) *Literacy and Orality in Ancient Greece* (Cambridge: Cambridge University Press).

Thomas, R. (1998) 'Melodious tears: sepulchral epigram and generic mobility', in Harder et al., eds (1998), pp. 205–23.

Thomas, R. (2000) *Herodotus in Context: Ethnography, Science, and the Art of Persuasion* (Cambridge: Cambridge University Press).

Todd, S. (1993) *The Shape of Athenian Law* (Oxford: Oxford University Press).

Too, Y. L. (1995) *The Rhetoric of Identity in Isocrates: Text, Power, Pedagogy* (Cambridge: Cambridge University Press).

Too, Y. L. (1998) *The Idea of Ancient Literary Criticism* (Oxford: Oxford University Press).

Turner, F. (1981) *The Greek Heritage in Victorian Britain* (New Haven: Yale University Press).

Turner, F. (1996) 'The Homeric question', in Morris and Powell, eds (1996), pp. 123–45.

Usher, S. (1993) 'Isocrates: *paideia*, kingship and the barbarians', in H. A. Khan, ed., *The Birth of the European Identity: The Europe–Asia Contrast in Greek Thought* (Nottingham: University of Nottingham), pp. 131–45.

Vasunia, P. (2001) *The Gift of the Nile: Hellenizing Egypt from Aeschylus to Alexander* (Berkeley: University of California Press).

Vernant, J.-P. (1980) *Myth and Society in Ancient Greece*, trans. J. Lloyd (Brighton: Harvester Press).

Vernant, J.-P. (1982) *The Origins of Greek Thought* (London: Methuen).

Vernant, J.-P. (1991) *Mortals and Immortals: Collected Essays*, trans. various (Princeton: Princeton University Press).

Vernant, J.-P. and Vidal-Naquet, P. (1988) *Myth and Tragedy in Ancient Greece*, trans. J. Lloyd (New York: Zone Books).

Vidal-Naquet, P. (1986) 'Land and sacrifice in the *Odyssey*: a study of religious and mythical meanings', in *The Black Hunter: Forms of Thought and Forms of Society in the Greek World*, trans. A. Szegedy-Maszak (Baltimore: Johns Hopkins University Press), pp. 15–38; reprinted in Schein, ed. (1996), pp. 33–53.

Vidal-Naquet, P. (1997) 'The place and status of foreigners in Athenian tragedy', in Pelling, ed. (1997), pp. 109–19.

Walbank, F. (1992) *The Hellenistic World*, third impression with amendments (London: Fontana).

Walcott, D. (1990) *Omeros* (London: Faber and Faber).

Wees, H. van (1992) *Status Warriors: War, Violence and Society in Homer and History* (Amsterdam: Gieben).

West, M. (1997) *The East Face of Helicon: West Asiatic Elements in Greek Poetry and Myth* (Oxford: Oxford University Press).

White, H. (1987) *The Content of the Form: Narrative Discourse and Historical Representation* (Baltimore: Johns Hopkins University Press).

Whitmarsh, T. (2001) *Greek Literature and the Roman Empire: The Politics of Imitation* (Oxford: Oxford University Press).

Whitmarsh, T. (2002a) 'What Samuel Butler saw: classics, authorship and cultural authority in late Victorian England', *Proceedings of the Cambridge Philological Society* 48: 66–86.

Whitmarsh, T. (2002b) 'Alexander's Hellenism and Plutarch's textualism', *Classical Quarterly* 52: 174–92.

Whitmarsh, T. (forthcoming) 'Quickening the classics: the politics of prose in Roman Greece', in J. Porter ed. (forthcoming).

Wilde, O. (2002) 'Nausicaa, authoress of the *Odyssey*', *Omnibus* 45: 31–3.

Wiles, D. (1988) 'Greek theater and the legitimation of slavery', in L. Archer, ed., *Slavery and Other Forms of Unfree Labor* (London: Routledge), pp. 53–67.

Wiles, D. (1997) *Tragedy in Athens: Performance Space and Theatrical Meaning* (Cambridge: Cambridge University Press).

Wilkins, J. (2000) *The Boastful Chef: The Discourse of Food in Ancient Greek Comedy* (Oxford: Oxford University Press).

Wilkins, J., Harvey, D. and Dobson, M., eds (1996) *Food in Antiquity* (Exeter: University of Exeter Press).

Williams, R. (1958) *Culture and Society, 1780–1950* (London: Chatto and Windus).

Williams, R. (1961) *The Long Revolution* (London: Chatto and Windus).

Williamson, M. (1990) 'A woman's place in Euripides' *Medea*', in Powell, ed. (1990), pp. 16–31.

Williamson, M. (1995) *Sappho's Immortal Daughters* (Cambridge, MA: Harvard University Press).

Williamson, M. (1998) 'Eros the blacksmith: performing masculinity in Anakreon's love lyrics', in Foxhall and Salmon, eds (1998a), pp. 71–82.

Wilson, J. (1990) *Politically Speaking: The Pragmatic Analysis of Political Language* (Oxford: Oxford University Press).

Wilson, P. (1991) 'Demosthenes 21 (*Against Meidias*): democratic abuse', *PCPS* 37: 164–95.

Wilson, P. (2000) *The Athenian Institution of the Khoregia: The Chorus, the City, and the Stage* (Cambridge: Cambridge University Press).

Winkler, J. (1981) 'Gardens of the nymphs: public and private in Sappho's lyrics', in Foley, ed. (1981), pp. 63–90; reprinted in Greene, ed. (1996a), pp. 89–109.

Winkler, J. (1990a) *The Constraints of Desire: The Anthropology of Sex and Gender in the Ancient World* (New York: Routledge).

Winkler, J. (1990b) 'Laying down the law: the oversight of men's sexual behaviour in classical Athens', in Halperin et al., eds (1990), pp. 171–209; reprinted in Winkler (1990a), pp. 45–70.

Winkler, J. and Zeitlin, F., eds (1990) *Nothing to Do with Dionysus? Athenian Tragedy in its Social Context* (Princeton: Princeton University Press).

Wohl, V. J. (1998) *Intimate Commerce: Exchange, Gender and Subjectivity in Greek Tragedy* (Austin: University of Texas Press).

Worman, N. (1997) 'The body as argument: Helen in four Greek texts', *Classical Antiquity* 16: 151–203.

Worman, N. (2001) 'This voice which is not one: Helen's verbal guises in Homeric epic', in Lardinois and McClure, eds (2001), pp. 19–37.

Worthington, I., ed. (1994) *Persuasion: Greek Rhetoric in Action* (London: Routledge).

Wyke, M., ed. (1998) *Gender and the Body in the Ancient Mediterranean* (Oxford: Oxford University Press).

Yunis, H. (1996) *Taming Democracy: Models of Political Rhetoric in Classical Athens* (Ithaca: Cornell University Press).

Zeitlin, F. (1978) 'The dynamics of misogyny: myth and mythmaking in the *Oresteia* of Aeschylus', *Arethusa* 11: 149–84; reprinted in Peradotto and Sullivan, eds (1984), pp. 159–94, and in Zeitlin (1996), pp. 87–119.

Zeitlin, F. (1985a) 'Playing the other: theater, theatricality and the feminine in Greek drama', *Representations* 11: 63–94; reprinted and revised in Winkler and Zeitlin, eds (1990), pp. 63–96; and (again revised) in Zeitlin (1996), pp. 341–74.

Zeitlin, F. (1985b) 'The power of Aphrodite: *Eros* and the boundaries of the self in Euripides' *Hippolytus*', in P. Burian, ed., *Directions in Euripidean Criticism* (Durham, NC: Duke University Press), pp. 52–111; reprinted in Zeitlin (1996), pp. 219–84.

Zeitlin, F. (1986) 'Thebes: theater of self and other in Athenian drama', in Euben, ed. (1986), pp. 101–41; reprinted in Winkler and Zeitlin, eds (1990), pp. 130–67.

Zeitlin, F. (1990) 'The poetics of *eros*: nature, art and imitation in Longus' *Daphnis and Chloe*', in Halperin et al., eds (1990), pp. 417–64.

Zeitlin, F. (1995) 'Figuring fidelity in Homer's *Odyssey*', in Cohen, ed. (1995), pp. 117–52; reprinted in Zeitlin (1996), pp. 19–52.

Zeitlin, F. (1996) *Playing the Other: Gender and Society in Classical Greek Literature* (Chicago: University of Chicago Press).

Index of Greek Authors

General Index

Foucault, M. 7, 8, 127, 132, 153, 201, 207
Fowler, D. 6
Fox, M. 206–7
freedom of speech *see parrhesia*
Freud, S. 47, 180, 194, 209
friendship 54–5
funeral speeches 72, 118–20, 174–5

gaze, the 194
Geertz, C. 89
gender 7–8, 15, 61–6, 177–95
genealogy 38–9, 43, 170–2
Genesis 50
glory *see kleos*
Griffin, J. 23–4
Groningen, B. van 14–15

Hadrian 143, 146, 153–4, 175–6
Hall, S. 19–20
Hanson, V. 23
Harrison, Tony 187
Heath, J. 23
Hector 46–7, 149, 178–9, 189, 203
Helen 47, 179–82, 194
Hellenistic period, 10–13, 122–38, 190–3
Helm, R. 12
Hesk, J. 93
hetaera (prostitute/courtesan) 53, 61–2, 64–5, 196
heterosexuality 155, 201, 203
hieros gamos (holy marriage) 137
Hipparchia 191
Hippolytus 81–3
history, writing of 110–21
Hitler, A. 13
Hobsbawm, E. 19
'Homeric question' 39–40
Homeric texts: authorship of 39–40; textual criticism of 127–8

homosexuality 47–8, 201; *see also* pederasty
honour *see time*
Horace 143
houses, fifth-century 183
Hugo, V. 214

imagined communities 85–6
imperialism 140–1
incest 137
India, Indians 115, 122, 161–2, 166–7
Indo-European 35
infanticide 184–5
inscriptions 27, 109, 172
irony 65–6
isegoria (equal right to public speech) 90, 217

Jason 170
Jewish literature 16, 126, 154
jokes 54–5, 190
Joyce, J. 215
Julia Domna 191
Julius Caesar *see* Caesar, G. Julius
Juvenal 143

kings *see basileus*
kleos (glory) 44, 71, 111
knowledge 61–3, 66–7

Lacan, J. 47
law courts 91–2, 95–6, 97–104
lesbianism 202–6; *see also tribades*
Lesbos 202, 205
Lévi-Strauss, C. 178
lexicography 128–9, 144
Library (of Alexandria) 124–6
literature, definitions of 3–5
liturgy 70
Livius Andronicus 141
logographer (speech-writer) 99
Loraux, N. 186

Printed in Great Britain
by Amazon